Theatre for Women's Participation in Sustainable Development

Though development researchers have proven that the participation of women is necessary for effective sustainable development, development practitioners still largely lack culturally appropriate, gender-sensitive tools for including women, especially women living in poverty. Current tools used in the development approach often favor the skill set of the development practitioner and are a mismatch with the traditional, gendered knowledge and skills many women who are living in poverty do have. This study explores three case studies from India, Ethiopia, and the Guatemala that have successfully used applied theatre for women's participation in sustainable development.

This interdisciplinary book has the opportunity to be the first to bring together the theory, scholarship, and practice of theatre for women's participation in sustainable development in an international context. This work will be of great interest to scholars and practitioners in a wide variety of fields who are looking for creative solutions for utilizing the contributions of women for solving our global goals to live in a sustainable way on this one planet in a just and equitable manner.

Beth Osnes, Ph.D., is an assistant professor of theatre at the University of Colorado.

Routledge Studies in Sustainable Development

Theatre for Women's Participation in Sustainable Development

Beth Osnes

Routledge
Taylor & Francis Group

NEW YORK AND LONDON

First published 2014
by Routledge
2 Park Square, Milton Park, Abingdon, Oxon OX14 4RN

Simultaneously published in the USA and Canada
by Routledge
711 Third Avenue, New York, NY 10017

*Routledge is an imprint of the Taylor & Francis Group,
an informa business*

© 2014 Beth Osnes

British Library Cataloguing-in-Publication Data

A catalogue record for this book is available from the British Library

Library of Congress Cataloging-in-Publication Data

Osnes, Beth.
Theatre for women's participation in sustainable development / Beth
    Osnes.
        pages cm. — (Routledge studies in sustainable development)
    Includes bibliographical references and index.
    1. Theater and society—Developing countries.   2. Women in
sustainable development.   3. Sustainable development.   4. Drama
in education—Developing countries.   5. Non-formal education—
Developing countries.   I. Title.   II. Series: Routledge studies in
sustainable development.
    PN3032.O86 2014
    792.091724—dc23
    2013016565

ISBN13: 978-0-415-82049-3 (hbk)
ISBN13: 978-0-203-47129-6 (ebk)

Typeset in Times
by Apex CoVantage, LLC

MIX
Paper from
responsible sources
FSC
www.fsc.org   FSC® C013056

Printed and bound in Great Britain by
TJ International Ltd, Padstow, Cornwall

Contents

Photos

Acknowledgments

My first acknowledgment is to my family—my husband, J.P., and our kids, Peter, Melisande, and Lerato—who gave me loving support and encouragement while writing this book. I thank them for using every possible vacation in the past eight years to travel to places where I can do applied theatre work with women in sustainable development. Their involvement and help has truly enriched what I know and what I have to offer. They have been fantastic traveling companions on this life journey. I especially thank J.P. for continuing to believe in the worth of the work I am doing, invigorating the way I think about everything, and sharing the load of parenting so beautifully.

My thanks also go out to my extended family, from whom I gain such strength, courage, and happiness. Juliana Forbes, my dear friend and the editor for this manuscript, has my extreme gratitude for her astute advice, thoughtful insights, and embodied intelligence. Enormous thanks go out to the women with whom I cofounded and worked at Mothers Acting Up, 2002–2011: Joellen Raderstorf, Erica Shafroth, Juliana Forbes, Anjali Kochar, Sarah Kraft, and Tina Garforth. With them I discovered my passion for acting up with women on behalf of our global family. Together we learned many fundamental lessons that are inextricably woven into the fabric of this book.

I thank my wonderful colleagues at the Department of Theatre and Dance at the University of Colorado (CU). Professor Bud Coleman lent his guidance generously to the formation of this project at many stages of its development. I am also grateful for the support of Michelle Ellsworth, Amma Ghartey-Tagoe Kootin, Cecilia Pang, Oliver Gerland, Wendy Franz, Cass Marshall, Stacy Witt, and Onye Ozuzu. I also offer my thanks to my students who continually advance my understanding of my own work.

Several University of Colorado students provided valuable research assistance for various sections of this book. Angela Hunt served as research assistant for the Indian applied theatre group, Jana Sanskriti. Rebecca Holly provided research assistance on the Jamaican women's group Sistren Song. Jason Bisping contributed research assistance on applied theatre in general. Genevieve Smith provided research assistant on gender issues, especially in regard to clean energy development. Lindsay Wietkamp was a research assistant for theatre and gender issues in India. Daniel Oxenhandler conducted interviews in Pune, India, with several members of the staff at the Appropriate Rural Technology Institute. I am extremely grateful for their excellent work that significantly enriched this book.

For the chapter on Guatemala, I thank the Philanthropiece Foundation for their support of the *MOTHER tour* that allowed me to do my work with Starfish One by One. Specifically at Philanthropiece, I thank Katie Doyle-Myers, Libby Cook, Joanie Knudson, Colleen King, and Lee Lazar. I extend my gratitude to everyone at Starfish One by One, including Connie Ning, Vilma Saloj, Norma Bajan, and Travis Ning. I also acknowledge my collaborators for the workshops, Chelsea Hackett and Kelly Gibson—both CU Theatre students at the time—who traveled with me.

For the chapter on India, I am grateful for the research support from the University of Colorado Outreach. I thank the amazing staff at the Appropriate Rural Technology Institute (ARTI) including: Dr. Priyadarshini Karve, Dr. A. D. Karve, Arun Patwardhan, and R. D. Deshmukh. I also extend warm thanks to Meena Karve for participating in the applied theatre work I did for ARTI and offering her sage guidance. Rebekah Anderson traveled with me to India and captured the experience of the applied theatre work there through her beautiful photographs.

For the chapter on Ethiopia, I would like to acknowledge the generous support from the Compton Foundation towards the film project that we were shooting while I was in Ethiopia, *Mother: Caring for 7 Billion*. I acknowledge the hospitality and assistance from the Population Media Center (PMC), especially William Ryerson, PMC's founder. I learned so much from him while in Ethiopia and am very grateful for his generous support of my research through interviews and the sharing of internal reports and sources. Kriss Barker, Vice President for PMC's International Programs, was also extremely helpful answering questions as they arose. At the PMC-Ethiopia office, I thank Dr. Negussie Teffera for whom I have the upmost respect. I also extend my sincere thanks to the entire staff of PMC-Ethiopia. I am extremely grateful for all I learned from Katie Elmore, former Communication Director for PMC, and my traveling companion while in Ethiopia. I extend warm thanks to Christoph Fauchere and Joyce Johnson, the director and producer of the film *Mother,* for choosing me to be the "human thread" in their film. My research was deeply enriched by traveling with Christoph through Ethiopia while making the film. I also extend sincere thanks to Professor Jane Plastow at the University of Leeds for her guidance through email communications and a phone interview on theatre forms in Ethiopia.

Referenced many times through this book is the work I am currently doing in the Navajo Nation with Eagle Energy for the newly formed Navajo Women's Energy Project. In this work I acknowledge the contributions of: Doug Vilsak, founder of Elephant and Eagle Energy; Katie Murphy, Executive Director of Elephant and Eagle Energy; Melton and Theresa Martinez, staff with Eagle Energy in the Eastern Agency of the Navajo Nation; Adrian Manygoats and Julaire Scott, Navajo student interns; and Mike Dow and Lindsay Weitkamp, CU volunteers. I also acknowledge my collaborators in this CU Outreach sponsored project, Francy Milner, Associate Director for the Center for Education on Social Responsibility at CU's Leeds Business School, and Sarah Krakoff, Professor of Law at CU's Law School.

Several other interviews conducted as research for this book greatly enhanced my understanding of gender, applied theatre, and sustainable development. At the Global Alliance for Clean Cookstoves (GACC), I thank Corinne Hart, Program Manager of Gender and Markets for GACC, for her interview about clean cookstoves and gender issues surrounding sustainable development. At CARE International, I thank Doris Bartel, Director of the Gender Unit in the Program Partnerships Learning and Advocacy division, for her interview about applied theatre for women's participation. At Oxfam International I thank Dr. Ines Smyth, Senior Gender Advisor, for inviting me to interview her in Oxford, UK.

There are several other people who have provided precious guidance for me at key points in my own development. Dr. David Silver is both a dear friend and has served as an incredible advisor for me in sustainable development, empowerment issues, and in the use of popular theatre. I extend extreme gratitude to Dr. Tom Barton for his generous research assistance in locating a veritable gold mine of resources for the study of applied theatre for sustainable development. I am grateful for the mentorship and friendship of Dr. Barbara Farhar, former Senior Policy Analyst at National Renewable Energy Laboratory and now a Senior Researcher with the Renewable and Sustainable Energy Institute at CU. Lakshman Guruswamy, Professor of Law at CU and Founder and Director of the Center for Energy and Environmental Security (CEES), has had an enormous influence on my development. He first introduced me to the serious impact of indoor air pollution on women's health from cooking on three-stone fires. Now as a board member of CEES, I have worked with him on numerous international Energy Justice conferences. Dr. Larry Frey, a Communication professor at CU, has my gratitude for his guidance in writing. I thank my collaborators in our newly formed Inside the Greenhouse—engaging CU students in creative climate communication—Dr. Max Boykoff of Environmental Studies and Dr. Rebecca Safron of Ecology and Evolutionary Biology. Lastly I acknowledge what I refer to as my "sustainability buddies" on the CU campus: David Newport, Director of the Environmental Center; Dr. James White, Director of Institute of Artic and Alpine Research; Dr. Kevin Krizek, Professor of Environmental Design; and Moe Tabrizi, Campus Director of Sustainability. Working with them on training CU educators to include issues of sustainability in their courses has significantly advanced my own understanding of sustainability.

Finally I extend my sincere gratitude to everyone at Routledge, especially Khanam Virjee, Associate Editor of the Environment and Sustainability/Development Studies, Helen Bell, and Charlotte Russell. I am very proud to have this book disseminated throughout the world by a publisher that has done so much to support applied theatre work, women's studies, and sustainable development. I also thank Tim Riggs at the University of Colorado with helping me to prepare the final manuscript for publication.

I dedicate this book to my sister, Patricia Hackett, who died while I was writing this book. She had a deep love for her family, life, Guatemala, and making a positive difference. Throughout her life she continually did wildly big things to help those who largely were living in the margins of acceptance, outsiders, those forgotten, rejected, or dismissed by society. *And* she didn't wave a righteous flag while doing any of it and seemed to be having a really good time. To my mind she unlocked the trick for sustainable goodness: turn down the self-congratulatory earnestness and turn up the joy. Make it fun. As my big sister, she inspires my moral compass, and I hope this book captures a part of her spirit.

Photo Acknow-1 Pat Hackett on a trip to Guatemala providing dental care to families without medical access.

Preface

On June 19, 2012, at Rio+20—the Earth Summit, UN Conference on Sustainable Development—Anita Nayar, Executive Committee Member of Development Alternatives with Women for a New Era (DAWN), referred to the official deliberations occurring as an "absurd piece of theatre." Noting that these are very uncertain times for our world, especially for women in the Global South, she stated that the greatest danger of this "performance" is that people believe we can continue with business as usual. This is not true with such pressing issues as climate change upon us. We are beginning to face dramatic, irreversible changes that will especially impact the poorest women—who are the most vulnerable and did the least to cause it. So how do we change the narrative, and articulate a new narrative that exposes our current contradictions, such as espousing dedication to protecting the Amazon forests while relaxing restrictions on mining?

Though Nayar was referring to theatre metaphorically, this book proposes that theatre—beyond serving as a useful metaphor for reality—can literally be used as a powerful tool for advancing women's participation in sustainable development. Harkening back to Nayar's call for a "new script," the solution that this book puts forward is for women to become authors of the scripts of their own lives, and to actively participate in the creation of our future. Applied theatre can effectively support this aim for women's participation in sustainable development. Beyond existing as a form of entertainment, theatre can serve as a powerful tool for destabilizing realities and currently held truths that support our current unsustainable global development practices.

Participation in theatre-based methods helps women living in poverty to (a) strengthen their voices, (b) declare their most passionate concerns, (c) gain confidence for using their voices in the public arena, and (d) rehearse using their voices to act on their self-identified concerns. It allows women to encounter likely obstacles to their actions in a safe and supportive environment, and to devise and rehearse various solutions to those obstacles. It allows women to identify possible unintended negative consequences to their actions and—due to the collaborative nature of interactive theatre—provides a forum in which to consider the likely benefits and costs of new behavior. Additionally, interactive applied theatre methods allow multiple stakeholders in a development project to rehearse various approaches before investing resources. Ultimately theatre can be an expression that unsettles our current ways of life and helps citizens imagine new social realities that are more just and equitable. In short, theatre can be a powerful tool for transforming our world.

Theatre involves representation. To represent something assumes choices are being made according to a specific system of values, and for an intended aim. When we passively receive a theatrical representation, we can become inured to the values and aims of the theatrical creator—simply through immersion in that reality. In our silent acceptance as members of an audience, we become complicit in perpetuating those values and aims. Conversely, when we *actively* participate in theatrical representation, we can become aware of choices, question values, interrogate aims, and recognize that—like theatre—social reality is a *malleable* thing formed by an author, or authors, to advance their values and aims. If women are currently not prominent authors of this reality, it stands to reason that their commonly held values and aims are not being adequately represented. Add to this that women have generally not been authors of our historical accounts—the body of literature from which we draw lessons and store our accrued knowledge as a society.

My own use of applied theatre in response to all of this began in 2004 when I developed an applied theatre workshop for mothers through an organization that I cofounded, Mothers Acting Up (MAU, 2002–2011)—dedicated to mobilizing mothers to speak out and act up on behalf of the world's children. Given that historically mothers have been silenced and kept in the private realm, I recognized that some deliberate support was needed before mothers would step into new public leadership roles. As a theatre artist and teacher, I knew the power of vocal exercises and began to design a workshop for mothers that could give them a transformational, physical experience of their voices as strong. Then I led them in using their strong voices to declare their most passionate concerns. I also began to apply the simple idea of rehearsing, or practicing, using their strong voices to act on these concerns. I have been giving and refining this workshop for mothers and others in diverse communities around the world with a special focus on my home state of Colorado.

Through a partnership between the Philanthropiece Foundation and MAU, from 2008 to 2010 I was able to make the workshop part of a program called the *MOTHER tour*, which traveled to communities in Colorado, North America, and many other parts of the world. This tour used theatre as a tool for mothers to inspire, educate, and empower themselves to act on behalf of their most passionate concerns facing the world. It began with a one-woman show, *M-other*, that I wrote and performed at most locations. This performance explored what it might just take for the mothers of one country to authentically care about the mothers and children of another country. The show was based on a fictional program, called "Baby Swapping," created by the United Nations to generate care for the world's children. In a small, limited pilot program, seven mothers from seven nations were required by their governments to swap their six-month-old babies with another mother from another nation for one month. It follows the life of one American woman who at first whole-heartedly resists having to give up her baby, then falls in love with the baby she receives from Ethiopia, and ultimately becomes an advocate for the community in Indonesia where her child has been sent. The fiction that the "other" is not part of the "mother" is washed away. What remains is a powerful affirmation of our interconnectedness in both our challenges and our solutions as a global community. The last line of the show states, "*I think the hardest part about going back to my old life will be facing my old self that believed I was separate from you, facing the part of myself that believed you were 'other.' Everything has changed. Before I had asked, Why me? Why now? Now I ask, if not me, who? If not now, when?*" A recorded version of the performance and the workshop is available for downloading or a DVD copy can be requested through the website, www.mothertour.org.

Since the closing of MAU in 2011, I have continued developing this workshop for a variety of different host organizations locally and around the world that have invited me to facilitate my workshop and to present applied theatre programs for a variety of purposes. As a full-time professor at the University of Colorado since 2008, I have moved towards a focus on women's participation in sustainable development, with an emphasis on women in clean energy development (Farhar et al. 2012; Osnes 2012a, b). Concurrently, in 2011 I launched *Striking the Match: Performance to Ignite Positive Social Change,* a Web-performance site hosting many brief solo performances (www.strikingthematch.org). Each of the performances uses humor or quirkiness to illuminate a fresh perspective on social issues related to sustainability. Many are less than two minutes in length. Viewers of each video can connect to websites of several nonprofit organizations working on the video's issue, via links below the video (Osnes & Gammon 2013).

Both in my own creative work and in the applied theatre work that I facilitate, I base my practice on the revolutionary potential of art and performance to evolve the underlying attitudes and beliefs upon which our personal and political behaviors are rooted. I understand that the multiple crises we face as a global family require broad and immediate actions to avoid crossing irrevocable thresholds environmentally, politically, culturally, and socially.

By nature of the fields I am including in this book, it is likely that some readers will not feel completely represented by the views put forth. The three fields—applied theatre, women's studies, and sustainable development—are all relatively young and still developing. Terminology and parameters in each field are hotly contested. My hope is to learn and grow in my own understanding of this work through my academic writing and the responses it evokes. My desire is to encourage further debate and interest in the whole range of women's activity in applied theatre for participation in sustainable development.

It is also written from a feminist perspective, with a goal towards highlighting positive and creative solutions. I position myself—as the researcher and author of this book—as a practitioner of applied theatre for women's participation in sustainable development. I write as a woman, an activist, a performer, a scholar, a mother, and a teacher, because those experiences inform what I have to offer this conversation. Much of this is derived from embodied personal experience in the world—working with women to use theatre as a tool for them to participate in the public aspects of their own lives.

My inspiration for writing this book is to get to the point that author Domnica Radulescu got to when she wrote, "I understand intellectually now what I instinctively understood then" (2007, p. 35). In order to disseminate this knowledge of theatre-based methods for women's participation, I need to make that translation from experience to knowledge making. This book is my attempt to bring my personal knowledge into conversation with the larger discourse and literature on this subject, to generate new knowledge. Since one of the fundamental aims of this book is to acknowledge multiple knowledges, I don't see this book as *claiming* something so much as *offering* something. My goal is to make available the stories of how a wide variety of organizations are using applied theatre to engage women's participation. My hope is that these stories will deepen our collective understanding of how theatre can be used to support women's participation in sustainable development.

I acknowledge that all three case studies in this book are from countries other than my own home of residence. Although I began my work with using theatre to support women's voices within my own community and nation through Mothers Acting Up, my subsequent work on other continents has taught me the most about the challenges of bridging cultural differences. It also raised my awareness about the shared international challenges we face as a global community regarding sustainable development. As is evident from examples shared in the conclusion to this book, I am now engaged in a long-term project on the Navajo Nation here in the United States, only hours from my home, working with women on the Navajo Women's Energy Project. Here with my local Navajo partners, we are using applied theatre to facilitate women in deeply considering how they want to approach acting on the clean energy future they envision for their nation. Currently we are focusing on outreach and awareness raising of energy issues in the Navajo Nation and are creating a women's radio show in partnership with the local chapter of National Public Radio to make public women's views on energy.

One of the challenges in beginning applied theatre work is how to form the relationships that will lead to useful collaborations. Interdisciplinary collaborations at academic institutions can certainly foster these relationships across the arts and sciences. At the University of Colorado (CU), I am involved in several activities that are actively building relationships of this nature: I am a cofounder of Inside the Greenhouse: Creative Climate Communication (Inside the Greenhouse 2013); a participant in Peak to Peak: Teaching Sustainability at CU (Peak to Peak 2013); and a board member for the Center for Energy and Environmental Security (CEES) through the CU Law School (CEES 2013). Many other universities are likewise moving towards these kinds of collaborations. Some are even establishing colleges of sustainability with programs that support these collaborations or degree programs in development.

Curriculum in higher education can also support and encourage collaborations. The Association for the Advancement of Sustainability in Higher Education is an organization that has a comprehensive list of courses being offered on issues of sustainability on campuses across the United States (AASHE 2013). In a graduate course I teach at CU—Applied Performance for Justice and Development—I have theatre and dance graduate students as well as students from the Information, Technology, and Communication for Development program, and even an engineering graduate student who is the president of CU's Engineers Without Borders. Having such a diverse group of students all working together in a course involving both the theory and practice for applied theatre paves the way for rich collaborations in the future.

I also highly recommend that more applied theatre practitioners present on their work at scientific and development conferences. I first met Dr. Priyadarshini Karve (with whom I collaborated with ARTI) at a scientific conference, the World Renewable Energy Congress (WREC). I was invited to present at WREC by a social scientist, Dr. Barbara Farhar, who was working with the National Renewable Energy Laboratory after we met at an Energy Justice conference through CEES, and who has a long-time commitment to exploring the nexus of women, poverty, and energy. From the relationships formed at WREC, I was able to present on my applied theatre work at Rio+20—United Nations Conference on Sustainable Development (the Earth Summit), at the "Partnerships for Advancing Gender Equity and Sustainability." Applied theatre practitioners could also be publishing more in development related journals to disseminate more awareness, understanding, and appreciation for applied theatre in sustainable development.

The fact that the official negotiations at Rio+20 produced a disappointingly weak document doesn't negate—as UN Secretary General Ban Ki-moon expressed—"the further evolution of an undeniable global movement of change" (United Nations News Service 2012) . Returning from the conference, I was sobered yet affirmed in my understanding that it is *not* going to be yet another unfulfilled international environmental sustainability goal that is going to solve our global problems. Nor do I suspect that the governments of the world alone are going to solve the challenges we face. Indeed, many of their policies, practices, investments, and laws seem to enforce the structures that perpetuate the social injustice and environmental loss we are witnessing. The solutions will come from the ingenuity, commitment, and work of citizens at every level of society, utilizing their talents and skills to move from concern to *action*. For nearly a decade I've been using theatre to engage women's participation in development and social justice aims. I have been steadily moved, surprised, encouraged, and astounded at the resilience and creativity of participants and the capacity of women for change. In that spirit, I feel newly inspired to articulate how theatre can be an effective tool for increasing the necessary participation of women in achieving global sustainability.

1 Introduction

Vocal empowerment workshop in Guatemala

One rainy afternoon in a cloud-forest village in Guatemala, indigenous Mayan women began streaming into our applied theatre workshop until nearly 70 mothers were present. Speaking only their native Ixil language, they giggled at the strangeness of our vocal warm-up exercises but gamely raised their arms and called out with a strong "ah" sound (see Photo 1.1). When it came time for each woman to declare her most passionate concern, many women voiced concerns about poverty as it related to their lives and the lives of their children. When rehearsing ways they could use their voices to act on these concerns, the group decided to focus on a concern common to the majority of these mothers: their children's education.

I was conducting this workshop for Limitless Horizons Ixil (LHI), whose mission was, and is, to create opportunities for the indigenous youth, women, and families of Chajul to develop academic and professional skills (Limitless Horizons Ixil 2013). As a part of LHI's ongoing efforts, this workshop was specifically designed for women to help increase their vocal confidence in advocating for

Photo 1.1 Beth Osnes facilitating a Vocal Empowerment Workshop in Chajul, Guatemala.

themselves and their children's and families' well-being. Throughout the workshop, the Program Director for LHI, Veronica Yat Tiu, translated as we collectively explored ways these mothers could use their voices to act on their concerns.

Though illiterate themselves, these mothers knew that their children all needed to do well in school to earn a scholarship to continue their schooling. So how could they help their students do well? They all acknowledged that they couldn't understand their children's homework, so were unable to help or even guide them. When asked what could help with this, one woman suggested that mothers could talk to their student's teachers. Together we created a skit to rehearse this solution. We asked for volunteers who had never spoken with their children's teacher to act as mothers in the skit. It became obvious that very few of the women ever had. Three brave women stepped forward to portray the mothers in the scene and another woman volunteered to portray the teacher, since she was actually a teacher in this community.

The scene enacted between them—witnessed by the entire community of mothers present—demystified approaching a teacher to ask for assistance. The teacher assured them that educators were glad to talk with parents about how to support their children and gave the mothers tips for making sure their students were doing their homework, even if they couldn't read the work themselves. She told them to set aside a certain amount of time each night for the student to study in a supervised place in the home, and to check that the entire homework sheet had been written on. In a lively discussion following the skit, it was clear that many of the women felt they could now imagine talking with their children's teachers and discussed how they could implement the teacher's advice in practical terms. They also noted how the intimidating power of an authority figure, such as a teacher, had been somewhat diminished since an actual teacher had just demonstrated how she could be approached, and was willing to give useful advice. More importantly, the women themselves demonstrated to each other how they could effectively begin to act on their concerns.

I want to underscore certain aspects of this applied theatre workshop: one, it provided an opportunity for these women to practice participating in their own sustainable development in a safe, supportive, and creative environment; two, the participants identified their own challenges *and*, most importantly, potential solutions; and finally, participants witnessed and supported each other's empowerment.

Women's participation in sustainable development

Before continuing to explore the use of theatre for women's participation in sustainable development, it is useful to compare what it looks like when women do and do not participate in their own sustainable development.

Without women's participation

Pictured in Photo 1.2 is Isabella who lives in Chajul, Guatemala. In preparation for a visit by applied theatre researcher Jason Bisping to discuss her energy concerns, she proudly lit a fire in the fuel-efficient, clean-burning cookstove that had been

Photo 1.2 A Guatemalan woman named Isabella cooking on a three-stone fire with a gifted clean-burning cookstove burning in the background.

gifted to her by a government program, Proyecto Ixil, in an effort to reduce indoor air pollution. This *plancha,* or griddle-style cookstove, is warmly burning in the background (located in the center of the photo), mounted on a stone table with a chimney taking the smoke out above the roofline.

Note where and how Maria is *actually* cooking though: on an open fire on the ground that emits high amounts of indoor air pollution. When asked why, she said that she does not actually use the gifted clean-burning cook stove because it is too high for her to stir the food in the pot on the burner. She often cooks in big pots since 12 members of her family live in this home. However, she can't reach into even a small pot on this stove. She can't see into the pots, and if she needs to add anything or take anything out of the pots, she has to stand on a stool. Since that is dangerous and awkward, she prefers to use an open fire.

Clearly she—and the other women in her village who are mostly of a comparable height—were not consulted in even the most primary design elements of this stove, or likely in the planning of this project. This photo shows what it literally can look like when women do not participate in development. It illustrates how sustainable development projects that do not authentically partner with women can miss the opportunity to be successful in making real change. Unfortunately this project wasted precious resources and the cookstove is taking up valuable space in her small home.

Photo 1.3 A Guatemalan woman named Rosa tending her clean-burning cookstove.

With women's participation

Pictured in Photo 1.3 is a woman named Rosa, also from Chajul, Guatemala, who is inserting wood into the clean-burning cookstove that she received in partnership with a local nongovernmental organization (NGO), Limitless Horizons Ixil (LHI). When asked about the stove, she said that she likes her stove because it uses the same amount of wood in a month that an open fire uses in 20 days. Because her family purchases wood, the efficiency of the stove meant substantial savings. Notice the appropriate height of the stove so Maria can easily see into it and reach the pots in which she cooks.

LHI has utilized applied theatre in its programming to actively engage women and men in discussing what clean energy solutions are appropriate for their lives and values. In 2010, the Philanthropiece Foundation sponsored Jason Bisping's use of applied theatre to assist LHI in collecting the input from families in the area about what problems they experienced with open fires and what they liked about clean-burning cookstoves (Bisping 2012). At the time, LHI had sold a few cook-stoves to local families, but wanted to discover how they could get more families to adopt them. Bisping visited families that had cookstoves (both gifted ones and ones purchased from LHI), and families that did not yet own a cookstove but were interested in the technology.

To gather this input, Bisping developed a form of applied theatre to actively engage family members in identifying their energy challenges and how the clean-burning cookstoves improved their lives. Bisping adapted a popular form of applied theatre originated by Augusto Boal, known as *image theatre* (Boal 1985), into a new form of *digital image theatre*. Interestingly, he conducted this directly in the homes of the people he was visiting. This allowed people to interact with their own energy situation while enacting scenes of their energy use, and to critique their energy situation in context. After participants had self-identified a problem associated with using an open fire, he asked them, "Can you show me what that looks like?" Once family members created the scene that dramatized the problem, Bisping took a digital photo of what they enacted. Leaving that pose, they all gathered together and looked at the image displayed on the camera's LCD screen. Together they discussed the problem, using the photograph as a point of reference.

In Photo 1.4, this woman is dramatizing how she has to prevent her children from playing near the fire so they do not get burned.

Photo 1.4 A Guatemalan woman dramatizes how she has to prevent her children from playing near the fire so they do not get burned.

Photo 1.5 A Guatemalan woman dramatizes how she repeatedly burns herself in the same spot on her arm because her open fire is placed in the corner.

In Photo 1.5 this woman is dramatizing how she repeatedly burns herself in the same spot on her arm because her open fire is placed in the corner, and she is forced to reach across pots.

The woman in Photo 1.6 is dramatizing how she has a constant headache from the smoke from her open fire. Her daughter (pictured) approached her during the digital image theatre performance and seemed to console her mother.

Family members were also asked to dramatize scenes of what they identified as benefits of owning and using a clean-burning cookstove.

To dramatize how a cookstove emits less smoke into the house than an open fire, this man in Photo 1.7 is enacting how he can sleep in the same room as his clean-burning cookstove without smoke waking him.

Digital image theatre captured an image of this woman in Photo 1.8 pantomiming making a tortilla near her clean-burning cookstove, affirming she liked that the chimney removed most of the smoke from the house.

Bisping reported that no participant refused or claimed to be unable or uncomfortable with creating an image. To the contrary, many participants enjoyed performing, and they needed very little instruction. Because community members had physically and mentally invested in expressing their concerns through this theatrical method, the resulting discussions were most likely more richly detailed than they would have been had the community members simply been asked their views. The photos resulting from this unique process demonstrate what women's participation in sustainable development through applied theatre can look like. It

Photo 1.6 This Guatemalan woman is dramatizing how she has a constant headache from the smoke from her open fire.

Photo 1.7 A Guatemalan man (right) dramatizes how he can sleep in the same room as his clean-burning cookstove without smoke waking him.

Photo 1.8 A Guatemalan woman pantomiming making a tortilla near her clean-burning cookstove.

stands as a testimony to the untapped potential of people to express for themselves their preferences and values surrounding their own sustainable development

Introduction

Development researchers have learned that the participation of women is essential for effective sustainable development. However, many development professionals who want to support women's participation still lack culturally appropriate, gender-sensitive tools for including them, especially women living in poverty. Many current tools used in development favor the skill set of the development practitioner and are a mismatch with the traditional, gendered knowledge and skills that many women who are living in poverty bring to development. Applied theatre is an effective and appropriate tool for women to participate in their own sustainable development. Theatre can serve as a dynamic tool for women to imagine, discuss, and rehearse solutions to the obstacles that constrain their participation in sustainable development. Applied theatre can provide a safe forum in which ideas can be rehearsed and tested by women in the context of their community before actual resources are invested and without fear of negative consequences. Theatre also serves as an informal tool to promote acceptance of women in public, decision-making roles and for dissemination of new social arrangements at the community, national, and global level.

The concept of applied theatre used throughout this book is inspired and informed by the "pedagogy of the oppressed" developed by Paulo Freire (Freire 2000), the "theatre of the oppressed" by Augusto Boal (Boal 1985), and by feminist theatre methodologies for embodied work towards equity and social justice (Armstrong & Juhl 2007). Applied theatre generally refers to theatre that involves a given community in exploring its own concerns, often in a process-oriented way, and usually in a nontraditional performance space. Applied theatre may or may not result in a performance. The performance may not be as important as the resulting empowerment of the participant/performers. The Forum Theatre techniques established by Augusto Boal have been adopted and used by theatre practitioners in various forms. These have proven effective in actively involving women. Because applied theatre necessitates that participants take an *active* rather than a *passive* role, it promotes critical engagement and growth in consciousness of one's oppression and potential. As supported by the theoretical foundation for this study, this book establishes that this active engagement is necessary for any kind of sustained social change.

Sustainable development, a term that has come into popular usage in the last few decades, is a concept that most people grasp but that many would be hard-pressed to define. The 1987 publication *Our Common Future* by the World Commission on Environment and Development puts it quite simply. It states that sustainable development is development that "meets the needs of the present without compromising the ability of future generations to meet their own needs" (1987, p. 8). The idea of sustainable development evolved along with the collective understanding that environmental preservation and poverty alleviation are interconnected. Ecofeminist scholar Vandana Shiva further developed this idea specifically as a women's issue through her work with women in India. She writes that, "Indian women have been in the forefront of ecological struggles to conserve forests, land and water. They have challenged the western concept of nature as an object of exploitation and have protected her as Prakrati, the living force that supports life" (1989, p. xvii). She rallies against the commodification of the earth's resources for the maximization for profit, and advocates for a balanced existence with nature that recognizes and honors it as the source that sustains all life.

Sustainable development and the fight against poverty may thus be viewed as two sides of the same coin (Johnsson-Latham & Miljövårdsberedningen 2007, p. 16). Clarification of how poverty is understood is important for building support and the political will to relieve the effects of poverty. The United Nation report *Rethinking Poverty* includes the following insights:

> Extreme poverty does not entail just having unsatisfied material needs or being undernourished. It is often accompanied by a degraded state of powerlessness. Even in democratic and relatively well-governed countries, poor people have to accept daily humiliations without protest. Often they cannot provide for their children and have a strong sense of shame and failure. When they are trapped in poverty, the poor lose hope of ever escaping from their hard work for which they often have nothing to show beyond bare survival. (United Nations Dept. of Economic and Social Affairs 2010, p. 2)

The implied social justice aim permeating this book is positive social change for those living in poverty. Bethany Barratt in *Human Rights and Foreign Aid* eloquently articulates this when she writes, "By positive change I mean making the poorest people less poor and more empowered, making people who cannot express themselves free to do so, and making governments that would abuse the people to whom they are responsible unable to do so" (2008, p. 2).

The term *participation* denotes taking part in an endeavor and having a share in the outcome. Achieving authentic participation, though highly desirable, is difficult in practice. Applied theatre practitioner Sheila Preston writes that "to achieve genuine participation is in itself complex and difficult amidst the myriad of agendas, power relations and competing ideological interests rife in most projects and settings" (2008, p. 127). Participatory development emerged out of an acknowledgment of the failure of much of the top-down development. According to Robert Chambers, "outsiders," those who are concerned about rural poverty but are neither poor nor rural, "underperceive rural poverty" (1995, p. 2). He therefore advocated for a type of development that puts the people first in the development planning process over which they previously had little or no influence. Participatory development seeks to recognize local people's knowledge, perspectives, and priorities, hopefully rendering this development more sustainable, relevant, and empowering. Participation can happen at many levels, from information giving, to deciding or acting together. Though participatory development has been largely recognized as a necessity in sustainable development, methods for actualizing authentic participation—especially among women living in rural areas who are marginalized—are still urgently needed.

In the article "Popular Theatre, Development and Communication," Mrinalini Thyagarajan links the importance of dynamic communication forms to participation in sustainable development.

> Communication is the strongest tool by which participation occurs. Without effective communication, participation is compromised, and without an acceptable degree and level of participation, development becomes a process imposed upon a population rather than designed and implemented by the population. . . . If participation is essential to development, then communication is as essential to participation. (2002, p. 4)

Theatre can serve as a dynamic and inclusive form of communication and, thereby, substantially contribute to participation in development.

This book draws upon case studies from three continents to discover useful approaches, strategies, and tools for women to participate in their own sustainable development through applied theatre. Through an intimate exploration of each organization's work, the stories and rich details will put flesh on the idea of women using theatre for participation. The first case study is an exploration of the Guatemalan organization Starfish One by One that mentors and supports education for young Mayan women to help break the cycle of poverty and equip young leaders with education, skills, and confidence. This organization is at the beginning phases of experimenting with applied theatre to realize their program objectives; it does not yet have a core staff trained or proficient in using theatre as a tool and has primarily relied on outside facilitators. The second case study, the Appropriate Rural Technology Institute in India, has used both outside facilitators and their own staff to apply theatrical methods to promote clean energy cooking solutions to rural women. Two staff members are experienced enthusiasts in the theatre, one of whom, interestingly, is also a scientist. The third case study, Population Media Center (PMC) in Ethiopia, bases nearly all of its programming on theatre-based methods and has had remarkable success in realizing its objectives through the use of entertainment-education. PMC staff guide these projects based on the Sabido methodology, training talent in whatever country in which they are working to serve as scriptwriters and actors. These three programs were chosen to provide insight into how various organizations use applied theatre. The goal is to demonstrate the range of ways in which it is used, from those who are interested but whose staff doesn't have the expertise within their organization, to those who have their own trained staff who in turn train local writers and actors using the organization's methodology.

Since this book is interdisciplinary—including the scholarship of applied theatre, women's studies, and sustainable development—the intended audience for this book is also diverse. For development professionals, NGOs, and governments, this book can provide an in-depth understanding of how theatre can be utilized as a tool to authentically support women's participation. Those coming from a women's studies or gender equity approach can more deeply understand this active and participatory method for realizing their objectives in the field of sustainable development. Those in theatre can understand the power of their art as a tool for making substantial contributions towards women's ability to participate in the formation of their own lives and communities. The objective of this book is to richly describe—and thus make more accessible—how theatre-based tools can help women who are living in poverty participate in their own sustainable development. Beyond that, the goal is to demonstrate why these tools are uniquely effective and culturally appropriate for the inclusion of women.

Current unsustainability

Applied theatre has the potential to help solve multiple societal problems. Naming these problems is necessary for comprehension of the argument and to illuminate obstacles to women's full participation. The first problem is that our current way of life is unsustainable. While attending the 2012 Earth Summit conference in Rio, I attended multiple panels on a wide array of issues, such as clean water access, clean energy access, reproductive rights for women, population growth, the rights of nature, food security, the state of our oceans, disaster relief, and protection for the environment. Each session examined the unsustainable practices that have resulted in inequity, hardship, environmental destruction, and scarcity of resources for vulnerable populations. The declaration from the Peoples Sustainability Manifesto—released just days after the completion of the conference—eloquently describes the ideological position from which this book is being written.

> Humankind faces multiple and daunting crises that are more than likely to confront and impact billions of people in the decades to come. In addition, research is showing us that our actions are very likely to cause us to transgress multiple planetary thresholds and boundaries. Despite this, governments at Rio+20 are missing yet another opportunity to formulate an effective response to these crises. Indeed, since 1992, there has been a retrogression in the consensus that was reached at the Earth Summit—and reflected in such principles as burden sharing, articulation of rights, mobilization of support, and protection of the vulnerable. Repeated attempts to revive this consensus— at Johannesburg in 2002, Bali in 2007, Copenhagen in 2009, and now Rio de Janeiro in 2012—have come up empty handed, thus thwarting efforts to build upon it. Despite unprecedented growth in the global economy since 1992, governments are trapped in making insatiable demands for still more unsustainable growth and rising inequity to remedy problems that economic globalization itself has caused. (People's Sustainability Treaties 2012)

Though it seems an obvious point to make—that our current way of life is unsustainable—most of our societal structures persist in operating under the assumption that business as usual can and will continue in the decades to come with only small adjustments. We continue our economy based on constant growth, even though the ecosystems that sustain our economies are collapsing under the impact of rising consumerism (Jackson 2009). Though we receive continual warnings from the scientific community that irreversible climate change is upon us, most do little to authentically change their lives. The primary conclusions of the Intergovernmental Panel on Climate Change (IPCC) state that "anthropogenic greenhouse gases have been responsible for most of the unequivocal warming of the Earth's average global temperature over the second half of the 20th century" (Anderegg et al. 2010, p. 12107) and that 97–98% of top climate scientists agree with this claim (Anderegg et al. 2010, p. 12107). The impacts of climate change pose the most risk for those living in poverty because people with the fewest assets are most vulnerable to adverse impacts (Smith 2006, p. xvi). From the book *Climate Change and Global Poverty*, authors Lael Brainard, Abigail Jones, Vinca LaFleur, and Nigel Purvis state that in our age we face two defining challenges: lifting the lives of the global poor and stabilizing the Earth's climate. They go on to state that "our success or failure in meeting these challenges will shape the future for our children and successive generations, and many choices we make today will drive consequences for years to come" (2009, p. 10). Global security and sustainability are linked with the solving of global poverty, given that "human suffering anywhere poses risks to stability everywhere" (Brainard, Jones, & Purvis 2009, p. 10).

Another pressing challenge is for our world to establish means for valuing and preserving environmental assets such as standing forests, unspoiled rivers, biodiversity, and ecosystems on which humankind's well-being depends (Brainard et al. 2009, p. 16). My suspicion is that many of us have become so inured to these types of facts and warnings that we become somewhat numb to the human dimension of many sustainability issues such as climate change, poverty, and environmental destruction. Perhaps we lack the imagination to visualize how our way of life could be other than how it is now. It is also often difficult to make the connections between an issue like climate change—which can seem distant and coldly scientific—and more human threats, such as population stabilization, or violence against women. Therefore, in the spirit of this book to explicitly value the inclusion of women's participation in sustainable development, I include a story told by Constance Okollet, Chairperson for the Osukuru United Women's Network from Uganda, to elucidate our current reality. At an event entitled Rio+20 and Women's Lives: A Cross-generational Dialogue that took place on June 20, 2012, Ms. Okollet conveyed the unsustainability of our current reality through a gender-sensitive medium appropriate to her culture—oral transmission in a community gathering—and brought to life the humanity of climate and poverty issues, both central to sustainable development. The inclusion of her story in this book furthers the goal to incorporate a gender perspective in all policies and initiatives working to solve the climate crisis and to include indigenous knowledge upon which our path to sustainability relies (Wildcat 2009).

We used to have all types of food in my community, but these days there is nothing. There is nothing on the ground, but there are floods. People lost many things due to floods: property, chickens, lives. We thought it was God trying to do family planning, until we were called to a meeting in my village by Oxfam. They told us it was climate change and that pollution brought the floods. It was man-made. I went back and told my village it is not God. We need to ask people to pollute less. We need to talk about how we can conserve our lives. Our group came up and said, "let us do conserving." We talk about this a lot; we talk for the voiceless. We approach governments through our local councils. In the past we used to have two growing seasons. No more. Now we gamble with agriculture every time we put our seed in the ground. Now with climate change we don't get the proper yields.

Let me talk about the floods in 2007 and 2008 and 2009 . . . I don't know when they will end. The floodwater gets contaminated. It brings sickness like malaria, cholera. It brings disease and poverty and hunger. When there is no food and the body is weak with sickness, we get crime. A boy of 15 years violated and then murdered a girl of 12 years. They think that's the solution, but that is not. We need to change our lifestyles. What will you do to help the vulnerable? They want to plant trees and grow food. They want to make their lives better. I have much more to my story, but I think I should stop. Thank you for listening. I have stories. Come to me; I will tell you them. (Okollet 2012)

Women are not adequately participating

Another problem this book seeks to address is that women, especially women living in poverty, are not adequately participating in sustainable development due largely to gender inequity. An adequate level of participation would be a level of participation sufficient to meet women's basic needs in such areas as access to food, health, clean water, energy, and freedom from violence. An ideal level of participation would be equal to that of men of their same social/economic status. This would result in women having some agency and ownership over what they produce and the land they cultivate. It would allow women to have access to family planning and decide for themselves how many children they can adequately provide for.

Though not exhaustive, what follows is support for the claim that women are currently not adequately participating due to gender inequity:

- Women have a higher incidence of poverty than men, and women's poverty is more severe than that of men (Budlender & United Nations Development Fund for Women 2004). The United Nations report, *Rethinking Poverty*, states that, "Women are overrepresented among people living in poverty and suffer from exclusion from basic education, landownership and employment" (2010, p. 74).
- Women are disadvantaged in agricultural systems, producing up to 80% of food worldwide, but owning little land upon which this food is grown (University of Essex, Centre for Environment and Society 1999).
- Women tend to concentrate on economic activities with low earnings that are irregular and insecure, with little protection from labor laws (Winniefridah 2011, p. 319).
- In many countries, women face continuing legal discrimination. They are not treated as equal to men, whether regarding property rights, rights of inheritance, laws related to marriage and divorce, or the rights to acquire nationality, manage property, or seek employment (Latifee 2003, p. 4).
- The fact that young women spend much more time working at home and in unpaid work than do boys of the same age, keeps women—especially those living in poverty—from access to education (King & Hill 1998).

These inequities conspire to keep many women from being able to participate in the sustainable development occurring within their communities, their nations, and the world. Women's lack of access, education, time, empowerment, personal agency, rights, and mobility have effectively blocked their engagement in sustainable development.

The necessity of women's participation

Women's participation—beyond being more just—is actually a prerequisite for sustainability. In her opening remarks on June 19, 2012, for *The Future Women Want*, at Rio+20, Michelle Bachelet, head of UN Women, stated that the full and equal participation of women strengthens democracy, peace, and sustainable development. Later at that same event, Gro Harlem Brundhand, former prime minister of Norway and now a special envoy on climate change for the United Nations, stated that women are essential to sustainable development and that gender equity is central to all sustainable development goals. A press release from UN Women on June 14, 2012, outlined policy actions needed to usher in gender equity, noting how at Rio's first Earth Summit in 1992, there was unanimous agreement that sustainable development cannot be realized without gender equity. The press release states that:

> Advancing equal rights and opportunities is critical for a sustainable future. Addressing climate change and other challenges requires women's full participation and the world's collective wisdom and intelligence available today. Women are key actors for sustainable development, and sustainable development solutions can greatly improve women's lives by reducing poverty, freeing up women's time and protecting them from violence and other adverse health and environmental impacts. (UN Women 2012)

The consideration of achieving sustainable development in relationship with women's participation and gender equity has certainly increased in prominence in recent decades. The marriage of gender with global initiatives—such as the Millennium Development Goals—highlight the importance of gender equity in achieving sustainable development and the reduction of poverty (United Nations Millennium Development Goals 2000). UNICEF's report, *The State of the World's Children 2007: Women and Children, The Double Dividend of Gender Equity*, states that "Gender equality will not only empower women to overcome poverty, but also their children, families, communities and countries. When seen in this light, gender equality is not only morally right, it is pivotal to human progress and sustainable development. Moreover, gender equality produces a double dividend: It benefits both women and children" (UNICEF & UNICEF 2006, p. viii). In establishing the necessity of participation by women from the global South, author Rashmi Luthra writes, "Because of their location at the intersection of multiple oppressions, their subsistence perspective, and their marginality, women of the South are strategically situated to offer radically alternative visions that hold out the possibility of creating more sustainable and equitable futures" (Luthra 2003, p. 54).

The popular book, *Half the Sky: Turning Oppression into Opportunity for Women Worldwide*, puts forth an argument that helping women to participate can be a successful poverty-fighting strategy and the key to economic progress. From a very commonsense economic perspective it states, "Consider the costs of allowing half a country's human resources to go untapped. Women and girls cloistered in huts, uneducated, unemployed, and unable to contribute significantly to the world represent a vast seam of human gold that is never mined" (Kristof & WuDunn 2009, p. 239).

However, caution should be considered in making women the focus of extensive development attention from a merely economic perspective and not a more holistic perspective, as the result can be the piling of more work on an already oppressed and impoverished population because "earning money may extend women's options, but may also intensify their workload and responsibilities without necessarily increasing their autonomy" (Pearson 2007, p. 207). In one study it was noted how most of the working women had little or no access to the income they generated (Abbi et al. 1991, p. 23). It is also possible that even a slightly increased income can result in decreased contributions from a husband who resents being displaced as the family provider, increasing domestic violence and other unintended negative consequences.

Ideally, plans to increase women's participation in the economy are best designed in a holistic manner with women's participation so that program decisions are based on the actual realities of women's lives—which often include substantial amounts of unpaid caregiving and numerous other household and community related duties upon which her family, community, and nation's economy all depend, and for which she is not compensated. Efforts to humanly vitalize women's presence in the economy can work to transform and improve upon currently used models for women's employment options. Women's employment often tends to be low-wage-earning, unskilled labor, which tends to be exploitative, include hazardous working conditions, no health benefits, long hours, little sick leave, and no childcare—all of which are not sustainable for women or society in general.

Obstacles to women's participation

There are numerous obstacles that constrain women, especially women living in poverty, from participating in their own sustainable development. Primary to these obstacles are the entrenched patriarchal values and norms in many communities throughout the world that restrict women's participation and diminish their worth (Rashid & Alim 2005, p. 30). These are often perpetuated through culture, religion, traditional practices, and economic systems. Related to this is the rampant amount of domestic abuse and other forms of violence against women. This violence keeps women from participating in changing mores, for fear their actions might cause a backlash of increased violence or other negative consequences. The violence women face during times of war (Integrated Regional Information Networks & United Nations. Office for the Coordination of Humanitarian Affairs 2007) and the violence of being involved in sex trafficking (Farr 2005) are other significant obstacles. Another major obstacle is the amount of unpaid care work that is expected of women, especially women who are living in poverty (Budlender 2008) and the "time poverty" that results from the many jobs they perform in addition to this care work.

Women who are living in poverty and have had limited access to education sometimes lack fluency or even basic skills in the dominant, often colonial, language in which most development negotiations take place. They may also lack skills of reasoning, abstraction, and critical thinking, and the confidence necessary for participation. Accompanying this lack of skills and education is often a lack of awareness or consciousness of their own oppression. Due to the historic silencing of women in public matters, many women lack the skills and confidence to participate in public discussions.

Internalized oppression is another obstacle to women's participation and is a complex force that often keeps women from even self-identifying as possible agents of change and development. Indeed, they may not consider that they *should* have a public voice. Women may have an idea of their role in society that does not include participation. In addition, many mothers of small children suffer the double bind of being the primary caretakers for the children and of being unable to participate in decision making due to the fact that children are not tolerated in some public forums in which participation would often take place.

Paramount among women's obstacles is the inability to control their own reproductive bodies. As long as women do not have the right or ability to choose how many children they have, they cannot live in a sustainable way. As long as women cannot live in a sustainable way, the world cannot be sustainable. In *Of Woman Born,* author Adrienne Rich wrote, "women are controlled by lashing us to our bodies" (1976, p. 13). Women's poverty is greatly impacted by the number of children their bodies have, the impact of those births on their health, the amount of unpaid care required for each child, and their ability to provide for those children. Author Matsa Winniefridah states that "Global poverty and dependency are socially constructed by those who benefit from such arrangements, so is women's poverty and dependency. . . . Both capitalism and patriarchy benefit from poverty of women just as they benefit from that of Third world countries" (2011, p. 314). Societal structures that are largely informed by capitalism and patriarchal values are forces that keep women from having rights and control over their own reproductive bodies. To ensure that women have sexual reproductive rights and health, societal structures need to be radically changed. This change is a critical precursor for our world to be sustainable.

Another obstacle for women is that any knowledge women have gained over the centuries from their connection to the earth, reproduction, and nurturing—that is not the result of scholarly studies, scientific method, or intellectual pursuits—tends to be undervalued in our society. For women to be included in every stage and level of sustainable development, the gendered knowledge that women hold needs to be acknowledged, disseminated, and used. The book *Harvesting Feminist Knowledge for Public Policy* (Devaki & Elson 2012) explores the flaws in the current patterns of development, especially in regard to the use of gendered knowledge to inform policies, theories, and practice. The contributors in this collection call upon all involved in development to draw upon the experiences and knowledge of women. They argue that this could rejuvenate the very approach being taken to understand and measure progress and to plan for and evaluate development. On this subject, feminist researchers Gwendolyn Beetham and Justina Demetriades add that, "From a gender perspective, researchers have noted that traditional methodologies, epistemologies, and methods are not scientifically 'objective' but the opposite: they generally ignore women's knowledge by showing bias towards the male perspective" (2007, p. 199). Indeed, to meet the challenges associated with sustainable development, our world needs all forms of knowledge to guide and inform efforts being made.

I do not intend to paint an overly simplistic picture of women living in poverty. Of course, some do overcome the obstacles they face and rise up to become community organizers, attend university, or transgress other societal norms within their communities. And many do this without the support of applied theatre. What I am asserting is that for a number of entrenched reasons, women are largely *not* participating in sustainable development, that they are *essential* to the success of any sustainable development efforts, and that applied theatre can be a tool to engage women in sustainable development. Applied theatre can serve as an invitation to those women who have not even conceived of imagining another way their lives could be, and it can contribute to a woman's process of empowering herself and overcoming internalized oppression.

Proposing a solution

Since our current way of life—which does not adequately allow for women's participation—is unsustainable, we need to imagine new societal structures and ways of being together in community that support women's participation. Applied theatre can serve as an effective and culturally appropriate method for supporting women's participation. First, it can be used to raise awareness among women of the fact that they are not adequately participating and that sustainable development goals are unreachable as a result. Also, applied theatre can be used to promote understanding of ideas, concepts, and issues that are important to understand for effective participation. Through applied theatre, participants can subvert the dominant narrative, make up a new story, recast the parts, and rehearse a new reality that is more equitable and just. Creating significant cultural change is likely to meet with resistance and possibly pose risks for those involved. Rehearsing these changes—which applied theatre allows for in a semipublic yet safe environment—allows likely benefits, costs, and risks to be identified, considered, and weighed by the participants themselves, according to their knowledge of their own communities. The fact that this all occurs *before* actual resources are invested into a given development project makes applied theatre cost-effective as well.

In practice, this process need not be limited to women, but, rather, can engage both men and women of various ages. In my own experience, I consistently have asked men to participate from within the community who understand the worth of and need for women's participation. For an entire community to accept new structures, gender roles, and behaviors, it is ideal that various stakeholders from a community be involved in authoring this new reality. This process is complex and benefits from creative ways of framing the change, so as to appeal to various parties impacted by the change. Through applied theatre, participants can devise ways to present new arrangements that highlight shared benefits and model unlikely partnering around shared values and objectives.

Awareness

"Scales off our eyes" is a phrase that was often repeated by women involved in a social drama project in Cameroon (Samba 2005, p. 190). This phrase demonstrates the transformation the women perceived in themselves as having been blind but now seeing, due to their increased awareness of their lives and their situation. Some women are not aware of the structures and causes that either allow or restrict their participation in making decisions regarding their reproductive bodies, their life trajectory, or their family's, community's, and nation's development. They may not even be aware of the need for change, or see that another way of life is possible, let alone that they could be an agent of change working towards a different—and better—way of life.

Some women's lack of basic awareness could be seen as a factor in their inability to participate. Indeed, one of the features that makes us human is an awareness of one's self within the larger structures of society. Author Mrinalini Thyagarajan wrote, "Dehumanization is the basis of oppression. It is the depravation of dignity, of respect, of equity and equality, of value, of choice, of freedom and, importantly of power" (2002, pp. 16–17). Participation in applied theatre can be humanizing for women who want to overcome oppression. Women can increase their feeling of value by being the subject of the theatrical process and the author of it. Women can gain a sense of dignity, exercise freedom in the act of creating and making choices, and experience power. To further this point, author Osa Egonwa writes that theatre, "when properly harnessed, can help to stimulate the consciousness of a people and mobilize them towards an understanding of their problems. The awareness created may become a tonic for positive actions that may replace an existing social order" (2011, p. 221).

On a larger community level, theatre can influence thought and opinions about issues related to women's participation by creating awareness that can stimulate thought and perception while transforming them into actual communicable forms that will help a community reimage its way of life (Egonwa 2011, p. 220). Since many of the issues influencing women's participation are taboo or at least highly sensitive—such as patriarchal values or sexual mores—applied theatre can be an appropriate way to explore these key issues in a community. Development scholar Robert Chambers wrote that theatre can "open up a wonderful scope across the whole range of learning, analysis and exploring realities and implications. In roleplay and theatre there is special license: the unsayable can be said; the hidden can be revealed; power can be mocked and made to laugh at itself. By acting out situations, people can uncover and discover aspects otherwise overlooked and unknown" (2002, p. 138).

Before women can participate in changing our unsustainable way of life, they need to have at least some awareness from multiple perspectives. This presupposes at least a beginning understanding of the ideas, concepts, and influences that have brought about our current way of life. Applied theatre can communicate ideas, concepts, and influences in a direct and tangible manner that is easy to identify with and understand. It conveys these ideas and concepts within social situations from participant's lives and can "subtly convey a sense of injustice, inequality and oppression that can be identified and mirrored into lived reality" (Thyagarajan 2002, p. 19). What is key is that no formal education—which many women living in poverty have not had access to—is necessary for participation in applied theatre. Skills in reading and writing are not necessary, since the means of communication is action, a medium in which women living in poverty are fluent. Through the applied theatre process, women can engage with these ideas, concepts, and influences so as to reflect on them, react to them, and begin to imagine how they could act on them in their own lives.

Imagining change

Before a new future can be created, it has to be imagined. With some base level of awareness, women can begin to participate in using applied theatre to imagine changes to the dominant story that could usher in a more sustainable future. Theatre not only supplies the opportunity for a community to come together and reflect on itself, it also "helps to shape the perception of that culture through the power of its imagining" (Wilkerson 1991, p. 239). In applied theatre this imagining is often spurred on through various methods that involve improvisation. A facilitator can guide participants in setting up a scene that represents an aspect of their lives that they would like to change, guide them in assigning roles, help identify an objective, and set the scene in action with participants improvising the action.

For example, when facilitating a "Training of the Trainers" for my Vocal Empowerment Workshop in Nicaragua, the women participating wanted to explore ways of prosecuting domestic violence. They explained that many women in their community were afraid to speak up for themselves—or try to work towards a better life—because their husband's abuse kept them in a subservient position in the marriage. Through an extended improvisation—including many attempts of various ideas to be able to make a husband accountable for his abuse—participants finally came up with the idea of using a cell phone to photograph bruises and wounds from the abuse as proof in court. It was the engagement in improvisation that led them to the idea to utilize a technology that most women in their community possess—a cell phone—for their own protection. As theatre educator Amy Seham wrote, "Social justice activists use improv as a way to enable spectators to imagine alternatives and even rehearse resistance to oppression" (2007, p. 135).

There is a liberation that occurs from participating in simply *imagining* change. It assumes a certain amount of freedom from internalized oppressive forces that restrict a woman's participation in even imagining an alternative. It can be a step towards undoing internalized oppression that may restrict a woman's ability to participate. Done in a public and supportive setting, it can improve a group of women's opinion of their gender in terms of creative ability, agency, worth, and intelligence. Done in a community that includes all genders, it can assist an entire community in questioning and reassessing any gender biases and prejudices that exist. Imagining is an indispensible first step for the telling of any new story. It allows established roles, such as the role of mother or husband, to be reimagined. It allows new goals, values, and perspectives to be introduced and considered.

Improvisation is a dynamic tool for undermining the power and authority of oppressive forces because participants in improvisation are, by definition, departing from a predetermined script and are making up a new story that might just give power to people not currently in positions of power. As Carolyn Heilbrun writes in her book *Writing a Woman's Life,* "Power consists to a large extent in deciding what stories will be told" (2008, p. 43). Improvisation is a tool for exploring and thereby exposing hypocrisy within society and even within development methods. Improvisation often provokes laughter, not of the scatological or low physical type, but laughter in response to recognition of a social truth newly revealed. This laughter is often the result of a delight in liberation from some sort of tyranny, even if just a release within that theatrical moment. Something has been broken through with that laughter—some triumph of the human spirit, some freedom from oppressive forces. In that moment while laughing, the oppressed person stands outside her or his situation, sees it for what it is, and ridicules it as ludicrous. When shared, this laughter can increase the connectedness of a community and increase their joy.

Conversely, imagining a different reality can also be highly unsettling, as it can bring into question foundational belief systems that may be rooted in religion or culture. It can feel dangerous, isolating, unpatriotic, or even blasphemous to imagine change. Doing this imagining in a group setting that allows for these feelings to be a part of the process can help women to identify the costs and risks of imagining change and new behavior, *within* traditional roles and structures. Not only are these costs and risks identified, but they can be explored through improvisation to allow for a highly nuanced, embodied experience within participants' own cultural context. Through dialogue that ensues from dramatic representation, women can negotiate these potential changes in all their complexity, referring to lived experiences of these issues brought forth through the improvisation. Ultimately costs and risks can be weighed against benefits, so that the women—individually and in a group—can begin the process of deciding for themselves what kind of change is an improvement for their lives and the generations to follow. Women can understand the price they will likely pay for change.

Part of the process is imagining new ways in which power and resources could be shared for greater equity and the sustainability of life on this planet. Even those who would lose power or access to excessive resources in an old model could imagine ways in which their lives could be better in a new social model based on greater equity. Relinquishing or sharing a dominant position can sometimes create better relationships, relieve stress, or allow the weight of responsibility to be shared. At a conference on mothering at York University in Toronto, I heard a woman relate her husband saying that the greatest gift of the women's movement is that it gave men back their parenting. She went on to explain that what he meant by this was that men, who before the women's movement were supposedly above the menial task of direct care of children, now got to take on the role of nurturer, which many of them found profoundly gratifying. It resulted in closer relationships with their children and transformed their perspective to that of a nurturer.

Using theatre to actively imagine how gender equity could be realized can be extremely effective for relieving the apprehension some men may feel. Theatre for development scholar Emelda Ngufor Samba writes that women becoming empowered and assertive "would not entail transforming the society into matriarchy as is often misconstrued, but working complementarily with men towards the total eradication of gender inequity" (2005, p. 17). When dismantling hierarchies that are centuries old, using theatrical methods can put men and women on an even playing ground from which to negotiate these changes. Samba also writes that her theatre for development workshops with rural women in Cameroon proved to be "a medium through which men and women came to understand each other better and sought ways of living together more as partners then subordinates and superiors" (2005, p. 215).

Rehearsing change

In her book *Gone Primitive: Savage Intellects, Modern Lives,* Marianna Torgovnick wrote that "in any remaking of social orders and power relations, there must be two stages: first, the telling of the stories (the creation of myths) that make it possible to think new things, and then the painstaking transferal of the thoughts into actions" (1991, p. 69). This progression from new thoughts (or imagining) to action (or change) can be rendered less tumultuous by rehearing these changes in an applied theatre context. Applied theatre is an active way of *interrogating* change to test how viable it is by putting it into the living context of the specific community. Community members can witness an enactment of this change in real time and space to critique it, make improvements, replay it and, thus, continue to improve its design. When referring to change, this consideration is not limited to structural change of systems, roles, or allocation of resources. The focus of change can also be in attitudes and values that equally either restrict or allow for women's participation.

The attitudes and values associated with women can be linked to women's empowerment. Though it has certainly been the focus of much scholarly debate and attention, the term 'empowerment' is often not used clearly or consistently in the development discourse. A form of the term is used in the third of the Millennium Development Goals, which intend to promote gender equity and empower women (United Nations Millennium Development Goals 2000). In their article "Empowerment and Communication: Lessons Learned From Organizing for Social Change," authors Everett Rogers and Arvind Singhal write that "empowerment is the process through which individuals perceive that they control situations" (2003, p. 68). Feminist scholar Jo Rowlands describes empowerment as "processes that lead people to perceive themselves as able and entitled to make decisions" (1997, p. 14) and as "developing a sense of self and individual confidence and capacity, and undoing the effects of internalized oppression" (1997, p. 15). What emerges from all of these definitions is the prominent notion of empowerment as being a *process*. The popular belief of the development community is currently that one person cannot empower another person; individuals can only empower themselves. However, an outside agent can provide tools, encouragement, an invitation, practice, and instruction for how to further the process of empowerment. Applied theatre, with its focus on process, is a highly appropriate agent for cultivating empowerment among its participants.

It can be a profound experience for a woman who has been denied a public voice, rights, or freedom to first imagine an idea, and second, declare it with her own voice, and then to have actual people rehearse that idea in an applied theatre setting while being witnessed by others. This allows her to take various steps within the empowerment process. It allows her voice to be amplified within a supportive community. It gives her an experience of exercising her rights in a situation that acknowledges her dignity and worth. She can experience the joy and confidence that freedom brings, especially in relation to creative expression on something of great concern to her. In most cases, her mental capacity has been challenged to critically engage with the multiple factors at play. She has been challenged to analyze various components of her life and consider possible actions based on that analysis. But most importantly, it is a very different thing to *tell* a woman that she has a voice and is capable of authoring her own life, than it is for a woman to *experience* using her voice and to prove to herself that she is capable of authoring very real solutions to her own self-identified concerns. The proof of her ability is in the actual enactment and is witnessed by her supporting community.

It is also a remarkable experience for her to see and hear her concerns and her perspective represented through applied theatre. Whether it be a radio drama, a community performance, or a play produced by a professional theatre company such as Sistren Song, it all contributes towards an improved belief in her inherent worth and her ability to participate in the development of her own life, community, and nation. The theatrical event itself is proof of the worth of her perspective and experiences.

In practical terms, applied theatre is a cost-effective development tool. It allows an idea for change to be rehearsed so that obstacles or design problems can be encountered and identified before resources such as money, time, physical space, trust, and effort are invested. When facilitating applied theatre for a Women's Clean Energy Project in the Navajo Nation, we were exploring ways women could sell small-scale solar-powered lights to increase access to clean energy and improve the income of the women themselves. The group was most excited about the idea of selling these lights outside of the Walmart in a nearby border town where most people went to shop. When I asked what would need to be done first to rehearse this idea, one woman said that they would probably need to get permission from a manager of Walmart to set up a sales table. Before we even had the chance to attempt this scene, another woman said that the manager would never permit this since the top-selling items at this particular Walmart were kerosene for lamps and batteries for flashlights, which were in direct competition with the solar-powered lights. Everyone in attendance agreed that this was true. Thus, after a brief discussion, the women decided not to take on a giant like Walmart, but rather to explore options with less powerful obstacles. It was useful that the women decided against this idea before any resources were invested and to use our time focusing on what they considered to be more viable solutions.

Applied theatre as a development tool can also help make change safer for women. Any change can have unintended negative consequences. Disrupting the dominant narrative can trigger negative backlashes, such as increased domestic violence or loss of preexisting access to resource, freedom, or power for women who, when living in poverty, can be especially vulnerable. Once a possible new social arrangement is being witnessed in action, participants can often identify potential harm that women could incur through participation. At the same Women's Clean Energy Project gathering in the Navajo Nation, participants thought of selling lights door-to-door as a possible sales model. We set up a scene with two Navajo women acting out this scenario. One woman knocked on the door of the other, was invited in, and proceeded to introduce and demonstrate the lights. Everything seemed to be progressing very well, and the woman selling the lights actually got the other woman to agree to buy one of the lights. Then a Navajo man, shaking his head as he witnessed this scene, interjected that he thought it would look bad for a Navajo woman to be walking up to strangers' homes and knocking on their doors, noting that, "the hills have eyes." He said that he thought this would actually harm the reputation of this woman acting as the salesperson and therefore wasn't an appropriate option. Upon reflection, the other Navajo participants agreed that what he said was largely true. This doesn't mean that the women at the workshop dismissed the idea of door-to-door sales because of this new insight; it means that through the process of applied theatre they were able to identify the social cost of doing so, and could collectively and knowingly weigh the social costs of this door-to-door model for sales, along with the benefits.

One might think that these kinds of obstacles would be readily evident or would emerge from the discussion of an idea that most often precedes its enactment and, therefore, would not require that enactment to be identified. In my experience, participants are often only able to discover hidden obstacles once they are witnessing them embedded in a dynamic format such as applied theatre. This process seems to uniquely engender a process of reflection that allows participants to critically engage with an idea to imagine how it would play out in the long run. This could be due, in part, to the fact that the impact of applied theatre is direct, nuanced, and more immediate than other forms of expression.

Making change

There are many examples of successful efforts that are making change by using theatre for women's participation in sustainable development. Highlighted here are a few of the "super stars"—some of which have been doing work for decades—that have been proven effective, have been widely studied, and readily come to mind for those in the applied theatre field. Their work spans the globe, from South Africa and Uganda to India and Jamaica.

Soul City

A compelling example of making change for women's participation through applied theatre comes from South Africa's *Soul City Institute for Health and Development Communication*, an organization working to improve people's health and quality of life by harnessing the power of the mass media and by developing educational materials. Although they categorize what they do as edutainment—the weaving of social issues into entertainment (Usdin 2009, p. 578)—their work falls under the umbrella phrase of applied theatre. Previously in this chapter, domestic abuse was established as an obstacle to women's participation in sustainable development. The popular 1999 *Soul City* television series used performance to confront the prevailing social custom in South Africa to ignore domestic abuse, even if one heard it from a neighboring home, because it was perceived as a private matter. In this television drama the characters enacted how "neighbors collectively decided to break the ongoing cycle of spousal abuse in a neighborhood home. When the next wife beating occurred, they gathered around the abuser's residence, collectively banging pots and pans, censuring the abuser's actions" (Rogers & Singhal 2003, p. 68).

Evaluation research conducted by Soul City found that exposure to the program was associated with actual neighbors being willing to bang pots and pans outside an abuser's home. Patrons at a pub in a township of South Africa made a slight variation on this practice when they collectively banged bottles when a man in the establishment was abusing his girlfriend (Soul City 2001). After being exposed to this television program, both men and women throughout South Africa felt more empowered to act collectively, intervening as neighbors in situations involving domestic violence (Rogers & Singhal 2003, p. 68).

Stepping Stones

Originating from Uganda, *Stepping Stones* is a training packet focused on gender, HIV communication, and relationship skills that uses critical reflection, drama, and other participatory learning approaches to equip participants to build better, safer, more gender-equitable relationships (Welbourn 1995). It is a participatory tool that has been developed for working on HIV/AIDS issues from a gender perspective (Bhattacharjee 2000, p. 691). It is focused on process, not product. In its use of role-play—a form of applied theatre—no actual public performance ever results. Having been adapted for use in more than 40 countries and translated into 13 languages, Stepping Stones is possibly the most widely used HIV prevention program of its kind in the world (Jewkes, Wood, & Duvvury 2010, p. 1075). The author, Alice Welbourn, wrote *Stepping Stones* because she discovered in 1992 that she was HIV-positive and wanted to create a training package that would help protect others from acquiring HIV. Professor Rose Mbowa was the workshop coordinator in Entebbe, Uganda, where Stepping Stones was first introduced (Welbourn 1997). Welbourn has since gone on to develop *Stepping Stones-PLUS* (Welbourn 2008), a supplemental training packet designed to help individuals with HIV feel a sense of self-worth and to help communities recognize the importance of continual acceptance, support, and love for those among them with HIV.

A typical Stepping Stones program consists of 18 sessions over 9 weeks. Participants meet in peer groups of the same gender, that are led by a trained facilitator from their community. They explore sexual identity, facts about HIV, sexual behavior that increases vulnerability to HIV, and ways participants can change their behavior for health and overall well-being. An environment of acceptance and respect is established by the facilitator and encouraged among participants, so that different experiences and perspectives within the peer group are all honored and considered. Participants analyze their own experiences through creative exercises in order to consider alternative outcomes and develop strategies. Role-play is used to rehearse these strategies so that they can be critiqued by the group before trying them out in their actual lives. Welbourn emphasizes that "it is essential to recognize that Stepping Stones depends entirely for its success on its grounding in local knowledge and experience, explored and analyzed by participants themselves during the workshop" (Welbourn 2002, p. 54).

Instead of providing passive instruction of messages around HIV prevention from outside experts, Stepping Stones "views all the people involved as actors central to their own lives" (Welbourn 2002, p. 57). It leads participants to conduct research on themselves by providing active exercises for exploring behaviors and ways of relating to each other, while understanding how current behavior is rooted in their own particular culture and history. Key to this process is having participants rehearse and reflect on new ways of behaving and relating with others within their peer group. To keep it engaging, warm-up games and fun exercises are used in between the main exercises.

An example of an exercise used in *Stepping Stones-PLUS* is called *In the Spotlight*, the aim of which is to "illustrate how we have all felt left out or stigmatized at times about many things, how quick we can be to judge others without understanding things from their point of view, and how miserable this can make us feel if we are the ones being judged" (Welbourn et al. 2008, p. 17). Standing in a circle holding hands, the facilitator asks participants if any of them have ever felt left out or stigmatized because of a personal attribute, such as being too tall or because of a physical impairment. After being given time to reflect on this, individuals are asked to step inside the circle alone if they can think of such a time and to walk around the inside of the circle making eye contact with each person in the outer circle before rejoining the group. After each participant has identified a couple of examples and has physically walked inside the circle while being stared at, the group discusses how it felt to be stigmatized and singled out. To conclude the exercise, the group again stands in a circle holding hands and, in turn, singles out each participant by staring at them; then people are invited to say positive things about this person that distinguish them from the others, thereby giving an experience of being stared at for positive reasons that celebrate a community's diversity.

Though Stepping Stones was not shown to inspire participants to entirely dismantle the patriarchal structures within their communities—which may keep many, especially women, from participating—it did make improvements. Rachel Jewkes, Katharine Wood, and Nata Duvvury write that in South Africa, "there was no evidence of wholesale rejection of their patriarchal power, rather of notable steps towards molding a more benign patriarchy" (2010, p. 1083). On the island of Kiribati in the Pacific, spousal communication and relations improved after Stepping Stones. Before involvement in the program the accepted custom for men as head of the family was to order women around. After the training, men reportedly began to help the women more and were more willing to negotiate with the women about sex (FSPIMedia 2011a, b).

Of utmost importance within the Stepping Stones agenda is to improve negotiating skills. Applied theatre is used as a way for participants to work towards an agreement or compromise on issues such as condom use or alcohol use that can lead to physical abuse. The opportunity and invitation to critically reflect on issues of sexual behavior and HIV provided a base from which participants could begin to rehearse negotiating behavior. Placing this discussion in the semipublic setting of a peer workshop went a long way toward overcoming cultural barriers that classified these discussions as taboo. It proved to be especially helpful when faith communities were one of the supporting partners of the program; then participants understood that it was not against their religious faith to partake in such discussions and negotiate with their sexual partners and families about sexual issues.

In 2006 Stepping Stones was introduced into several South Pacific islands through a pilot program. In Fiji there was greater success with the programs in urban areas, due to participants' mobility in comparison with more rural areas where transportation to sessions was sometimes more of an issue. The amount of time the entire program takes, with its multiple meetings, is a major challenge. In the Solomon Islands many women had a difficult time attending because of traditional roles as mothers and homemakers. But the community took on this challenge and made it a success by creating a special peer group for the community's children. In other Pacific Island programs there is no children's peer group; the Solomon Islands are unique in seeing the need for a children's peer group within the Stepping Stones framework (FSPIMedia 2011). This considerably impacted the mothers' ability to participate in the program as well, since their children were occupied with the program and did not require supervision from the mothers during that time. Also the Solomon Island's pilot program gained strength due to the fact that support was coming from nongovernmental organizations (NGOs), faith-based organizations, and government agencies. This helped provide a wide base of support and resources necessary for the program to continue. The programs are most successful when they involve many organizations that can address the issues brought up and seek to supply services for all the needs related to healthy sexual behavior.

Despite the challenges, communities are showing that they can identify and address their problems and find solutions. Given the participatory focus of the program, it stands to reason that evaluation of impact and effectiveness should also be participatory, as noted in the lessons learned from Stepping Stones programming in Uganda:

> The discrepancies between the survey findings and the messages conveyed by people in open-ended focus group discussions, and the inconsistencies

between some of the answers given by survey respondents highlights the unreliability of the survey data and the critical importance of supplementing survey-based quantitative data with qualitative data collected using participatory methods. Where possible, this data should also be supplemented by additional data . . . It is only by triangulating all the data that one can begin to understand the complex dynamics affecting individual and community attitudes and behavior. (Hadjipateras 2006, p. 28)

For a behavior change program like Stepping Stones, a long-term approach is crucial for its success.

Sistren Theatre Collective

Sistren is a grassroots theatre project, originating in Kingston, Jamaica (Green 2004, pp. 481–482). It was born in 1977 when a group of 13 working-class women, assisted by Honor Ford-Smith of the Kingston Drama school, gathered to plan a play to present during the government-sponsored Worker's Week activities (Allison 1986, p. 4). Afterwards, the women continued the work by forming Sistren Theatre Collective, with, among others, Ford-Smith as the artistic director, Pauline Crawford as workshops director, and Rebecca Knowles as workshop leader (Allison 1986, p. 5). Run by and for Jamaican working-class women, Sistren's goal was, and is, to actively transform the status of women in society. Sistren seeks to examine the oppression of women and by "breaking down their isolation" help working-class women empower themselves to achieve a solution to their problems through collective action (Allison 1986, p. 5). Utilizing entertainment, collaboration, and humor, Sistren suggests sustainable methods through which the women can continue to confront future problems (Allison 1986, p. 4).

Sistren utilizes a number of applied theatre methods to explore the experiences of the members of the group. The participants start by sharing experiences from their own lives and identifying with each other's experiences and problems. Through improvisation, storytelling, and traditional cultural rituals, they then workshop the performance until they have created a solution to a problem, or until they have created a performance to share the issue with a wider audience. For Sistren, the *process* of creating the show is often more important than the end product (Allison 1986, p. 15). Frequently the participants in the workshop are empowered by the similarities they share with other participants—realizing they are not alone in their experiences and sufferings—and by the sheer fact that there is something they can do about their situation.

An example of Sistren's work is the creation of the show *The Case of Iris Armstrong*. In 1982 members of Sistren traveled to the sugarcane fields to interview the women working there to gather material for a new show (Green 2004, p. 479). While there, Sistren held a series of workshops in the evenings, attended by working women after their shifts. These workshops utilized Sistren's techniques of storytelling and improvisation to help the women come together to find a solution to a pressing problem in their neighborhood. This was the first time that anyone had paid particular attention to the tribulations of these women, and it was the first time they were really given agency to find a solution themselves (Allison 1986, p. 15). Through improvisation, the women were able to put together, rehearse, and finesse an argument to put before the local official. The women successfully convinced the official to fix the water pump, and went on to create a women's council in the community to continue working for women's concerns (Allison 1986, pp. 16–17). In this instance, not only did Sistren help the field workers figure out a solution to their current problem, but it gave them tools to find solutions to future problems.

In the 1980s Sistren members ended up traveling and performing globally more than they were at home (Green 2004, pp. 474–475). However, in 2009, Sistren returned to Jamaica to put together a show to present before Parliament with regards to the reproductive health bill soon to be deliberated. Parliament's Joint Select Committee on Abortion held a session to hear submissions from interest groups regarding the issue, and utilizing their techniques of personal experience, workshop and improvisation, Sistren put together a performance using local culture and personal experiences to highlight the importance of women's reproductive rights (Heron, Toppin, & Finikin 2009, pp. 45–46). Performed solely by women, the performance allowed for a female voice to be heard in the otherwise overwhelmingly male space of The Houses of Parliament. Sistren's involvement brought a practical and experiential element to the issues of the bill—otherwise overlooked in debates and rhetoric—reminding the politicians that the law, as it stands on paper, impacts large numbers of Jamaican women and their bodies (Heron et al. 2009, pp. 52–54). As of October 2012, the parliamentary committee still had not been able to come to an agreement about amending the existing legislation (Wilson 2012).

Grassroots theatre movements like Sistren can be successful among shifting political/economic climates, but it is imperative that they adjust and morph with the shifting political tides and continue to serve those whom they set out to serve, and who need them most (Green 2004, p. 488). Despite the challenges it faced in the 1980s, Sistren managed to survive by adapting to the changes in politics and economics and is still alive and well today. Now headed by Lana Finikin, a founding member of Sistren, some of its current projects include a Kingston Urban Renewal project, a Youth Leadership Training program, and educational projects regarding AIDS/HIV, Sexual Reproductive Health, Conflict Resolution, and Cultural and Historical Preservation. Sistren is currently funded by multiple organizations worldwide, and continues to travel around the world, spreading its techniques and expertise. However, by and large, Sistren's current work takes place at home in Jamaica with the working-class people whose lives it strives to better through theatre.

Jana Sanskriti

Jana Sanskriti (People's Culture) Centre for the Theatre of the Oppressed, based in West Bengal, India, is considered to be one of the largest and longest lasting Forum Theatre operations in the world. It was created in the early 1980s by

Sanjoy Ganguly. He and his fellow political workers traveled and worked in the village of Dahakanda intending to help mobilize oppressed people, but struggled to make themselves acceptable to the village people. Observing that music and performance was an important part of village life, Ganguly experimented with creating theatre in the villages. Although Ganguly had the greatest of intentions, he struggled to truly create a Theatre *of* the Oppressed, rather than Theatre *for* the Oppressed (Ganguly 2010, p. 17). Early on the movement leaders fought to overcome the tendency to give "advice and direction" to the audiences, because this was, as Ganguly explained, "casting shadows on our work" (Ganguly 2010, p. 66). Ganguly sought collaboration with villagers who could enrich the plays with their own experiences. In 1991, Jana Sanskriti's leaders met with Augusto Boal, which helped the movement continue to build and sustain true Theatre *of* the Oppressed in West Bengal. Jana Sanskriti was considered by Augusto Boal to be the chief exponent of his methodology outside of its native Brazil.

Jana Sanskriti has more than 30 theatre teams from 30 different rural villages throughout West Bengal. Although these teams are part of Jana Sanskriti, there are no monetary linkages, and it is truly considered Theatre of the Oppressed done by oppressed sections of society. The makeup of Jana Sanskriti theatre teams includes both men and women, who are typically agricultural workers. The experiences of the theatre team members directly influence the scripts that are created and performed, and although there is not monetary gain for the performers, many participate because Jana Sanskriti provides a space where they can express themselves, and where they have found the courage to point out the causes of oppression in their lives (Jana Sanskriti 2013a).

Each theatre team typically presents two performances a month in their village. The theatre team members develop campaigns, where they collect feedback from the people on various initiatives. Jana Sanskriti also has a core team that supports ad hoc satellite teams based in various villages. When Jana Sanskriti teams do Boal's style of Forum Theatre, a theatre team selects, constructs, and narrates a social problem from their daily life. Sanjoy Ganguly believes that "actors do not play the script, they script the play," and in this process, they "discover themselves" (Ganguly 2010, p. 120). After some fine-tuning by the artistic director, the theatre team presents the play to an audience, but a solution to the conflict is not present in the first performance. The second time it is performed the audience is given the task of finding a solution to the problem presented within the play. Audience members become spect-actors by entering the dramatic space to enact their solution (Jana Sanskriti 2013a). The trained theatre team members assist these audience spect-actors by asking questions about the solutions offered. A mediator, called the Joker, assists in this process, and attempts to lead the performers and spect-actors to a point of consensus. Jana Sanskriti believes that this consensus plays an important role resulting in social initiatives and community action (Jana Sanskriti 2013a).

Female roles were once portrayed by men in Jana Sanskriti, because women were not members of the movement, but women eventually came to play a strong role in the work of Jana Sanskriti, and this active involvement continues today (Ganguly 2010, p. 24). The first all-women teams were created in 2002, and these teams regularly conduct workshops and performances for their communities. Although the majority of these women have large families and intense domestic responsibilities, Jana Sanskriti has developed these teams from rural working-class families and has involved them in the theatre movement. Because men often have to leave the villages for work, women often take on all the responsibilities of the household. Female theatre team members must also overcome traditional values that do not condone women being seen interacting with outsiders. Many of these women must face violence when they return home from performances and rehearsals (Ganguly 2010, p. 33).

There are several performance pieces that specifically focus on gender issues that are frequently presented by Jana Sanskriti. *Sonar Meye* (*The Golden Girl*) presents a picture of the life of an average woman in rural India and the powerlessness women often feel because of the patriarchal system (Da Costa 2008, p. 299). Specifically, the audience is shown the disrespect a young woman must endure on a daily basis, specifically in regards to her educational pursuits as they collide with her role in the home. This performance is intended to encourage discussions of gender inequality and relations within their communities. Male spect-actors are encouraged to enter the scene and intervene, thus creating a situation in which gender inequality evolves from "women's problems" to an issue in which each party must claim responsibility (Da Costa 2008, p. 303).

Sarama is a play about the rape of a young woman who lives in a slum, and the ways in which her previously content life was devastated by the crime against her (Jana Sanskriti 2013b). While she is shunned in her own society as a ruined woman, political officials in their own quest for power use her case. The play follows how various forces in her society use the incident to serve their own interests. In the end she emerges from this demoralizing scenario, and, with the help of a sympathetic women's group, gets the support she needs to birth the child resulting from the rape. The performance of *Sarama* is done in a minimalist fashion with the actors' bodies used as the props. Teamwork and the agility of the performers, along with the sensitive use of music, bring this powerful drama alive.

Because Jana Sanskriti has such a strong presence in villages, the women of Jana Sanskriti have formed women's organizations in which they work to activate health systems, stop the illegal manufacturing and selling of liquor, and support education (Jana Sanskriti 2013a). Ganguly believes that when it comes to acting outside of the arena, women surely play the most important role in terms of number and leadership (Ganguly 2010, pp. 125–126). Jana Sanskriti's theatre has offered a significant opportunity for people to script power relations onstage and live new commitments offstage. Through this process, both women and men learn from, make sense of, and live the consequences of immediate, onstage interactions and experiences in their offstage lives (Mohan 2004, p. 203). This involves people in the process of reimagining and transforming the communities in which they live; working towards a more just and equitable future for all.

Climate Wise Women

Climate Wise Women (CWW) represents an expanded idea of applied theatre used for women's participation in sustainable development. CWW is a global platform for the promotion of women's leadership on climate change through the art of oral transmission. When CWW's rotating group of distinguished international community activists perform their stories publicly, they give a human face and voice to an issue that sits squarely at the nexus of the conversation on gender equality, environmental justice, food security, the eradication of extreme poverty, and public health (Climate Wise Women 2013). CWW presents these events—featuring women community leaders from around the globe—at colleges and universities, for community and business groups, and at major world events on climate, climate justice, and gender equality, engaging both panelists and audience members alike.

Pacific Gender Climate Coalition (PGCC) is one of the groups that partners with CWW to disseminate gendered knowledge about climate change for use in public policy. The coordinator of PGCC, Ulamila Kurai Wragg, shared her story at the event Rio+20 and Women's Lives: A Cross-generational Dialogue. I share a portion of her performed story to give an example of how CWW uses a form of applied theatre—oral transmission—to promote the inclusion of gendered knowledge in sustainable development.

> As people from a small island state, we are vulnerable to sea levels, and women always come out as the most vulnerable. We women plant, fish, raise children, and keep house. Because of what we do, we have a lot of gender-based knowledge. That's why gendered language is so important. I make sure my leaders stay committed to hearing the women. Climate Wise Women has given a platform for women to speak up, the opportunity and space for women to speak up and be heard. I'm here today for the many unheard voices back in the villages—women who have lived on the coast all their lives. They have traditional gendered knowledge that is priceless. We people from the Cook Islands are coastal managers. My brother has different gendered knowledge than I do because of his gender and the work he does as a man. When he is deep sea diving, if he feels cold water against his skin, he knows that is a warning. When I am fishing on the coast if I see certain urchins along the coast, I know a certain type of weather is coming. That is gender-based knowledge. Governments must be gender responsive to this kind of knowledge. (Wragg 2012)

Additionally, PGCC is training women on Participatory Video, a powerful and creative means of expression in which women document their own experience and disseminate their traditional gendered knowledge on climate change through the Internet (Lunch & Lunch 2006). Participatory Video provides a method for women to act on their own problems by communicating their needs, views, insights, ideas, and knowledge with decision makers and/or other groups and communities. Because the women themselves are the authors of their own videos, they are created in a manner that the women consider culturally appropriate to their communities.

Applied theatre in society and culture

One of applied theatre's strengths is disrupting hierarchical systems and the societal structures that perpetuate inequity and limit women's participation. It serves as an ideal tool for imagining new ways men and women can live together in community and plan together for their collective future. Women, especially those living in poverty, are most likely to be willing to engage in applied theatre techniques as a problem-solving or idea-generating tool because they have the least to lose in terms of actual or perceived power. Men with wealth or power—and even women with some privilege associated with wealth or power—may avoid applied theatre because of social risk. They want to maintain their dignity and avoid the many unknown variables within the process that may cast them as less powerful or as guilty for maintaining wealth while others suffer. Men living in poverty may be reluctant to give up what dignity they feel they have, due to what they perceive as the superiority of their gender. Even development practitioners could be reluctant to participate as the agenda of a given project could be questioned or destabilized, which could put funding earmarked for a specific purpose in jeopardy.

Not only may women be the most willing to partake in applied theatre, they may also be uniquely adept at the kind of improvisation inherent in applied theatre. In Hartmut Bossel's article "Indicators for Sustainable Development," he writes, "Sustainable development implies constant evolutionary self-organizing and adaptive change. For this the widest possible spectrum of adaptive responses to new challenges should be available for potential adoption. But this means that diversity of processes and functions is one of the important prerequisites for sustainability" (Bossel & Balaton Group 1999, p. 6). Women living in poverty, having already met the challenges from such forces as climate change, economic downturns, and changes in government, may just be the most adept and practiced sector of our world population in terms of diverse and adaptive response to new challenges. Often these women have little ability to use these skills to do much more than survive, such that the world has largely not taken notice of these skills and thus has not benefitted from women's ingenuity, perspectives, and approaches. Applied theatre could be a conduit through which women can communicate what they can offer to solutions for the collective challenges we face.

Applied theatre is a good match for this skill set based on life experience—the stuff theatre is made of—and therefore has incredible potential for being able to translate that hard-earned aptitude into an effective contribution towards sustainable development design.

When women do well, they tend to invest what they gain back into their families and their communities. Given this, to improve a woman's well-being is to improve the well-being of her community and, ultimately, our world. Author Rashmi Luthra writes, "Women at the margins of society—those bypassed or trampled by globalization and a knowledge-based economy—are strategically placed to imagine a just, equitable, and environmentally sustainable future that would benefit everyone in the long-term" (2003, p. 47). Drawing upon the eco-feminist approaches of Maria Mies and Vandana Shiva (1993), Luthra goes on to assert that, "Women of the South, who are disproportionately victimized by development and globalization by definition, are in a position to envision a liberating, sustainable future for all, rather than a future benefiting and privileging a select few" (2003, p. 47). Feminist scholar bell hooks describes this place in the margins as a "Site of creativity and power, that inclusive space where we recover ourselves, where we move in solidarity to erase the category colonized/colonizer. Marginality as site of resistance. Enter that space. Let us meet there. Enter that space. We greet you as liberators" (hooks 2008, p. 85). In my experience, the space created when women work together through applied theatre feels like the space described by hooks.

Women living in oppression can gain a point of access to share this liberating vision through applied theatre. In *Popular Theater, Development and Communication*, Mrinalini Thyagarajan writes that "theater does not require any level of education or literacy, as it works with feelings and sensations and translates thoughts and concepts into identifiable experiences" (2002, pp. 13–14). Action is the primary ingredient in theatre, so it is useful for getting sustainable development objectives and deliberations off the page and onto the stage—of applied theatre (literally) and of life (metaphorically). Since the action from applied theatre arises from the community, it is more likely to accurately reflect the community. Therefore, it stands to reason that the sustainable development that uses applied theatre as a tool will more likely accurately address the lived needs of the community in an acceptable way.

My position is that an appropriate use of applied theatre should *not* simply adjust or educate women to accommodate themselves within the current world systems—that is, to improve their well-being without altering traditional gender roles. Rather, it should involve women in a restructuring of our world away from systems that perpetuate the gender inequity, poverty, and environmental destruction that make sustainable development a necessary endeavor. The theoretical foundations for applied theatre that will be more deeply explored in the next chapter support this view. This represents a shift from viewing women as *beneficiaries* whose lives can be improved by sustainable development, to authentic participants and authors of a system which is considerate of local knowledges embedded in community practices and institutions (Beetham & Demetriades 2007, p. 202).

Using applied theatre to engage women's participation in sustainable development is a way of recognizing and utilizing a woman's culture as a method for her inclusion. However, the benefits of recognizing and utilizing each woman's culture extend beyond her inclusion; it works towards the foundational change that needs to occur for authentic gender equity and for our world to be authentically sustainable. Development efforts that disregard people's culture most often also disregard local communication processes (Mlama 1991, p. 5), and therefore, are often not inclusive or successful.

If development efforts seek to change structures without working to change culture, that culture will likely reproduce the same conditions over and again. Or as David Diamond, author of *Theatre for Living*, writes, "Working politically to alter the structures in which we live without changing the behavior that creates those structures is futile" (2007, p. 38). Culture is "a way of perceiving and doing things that identifies one people as distinct from another. A culture derives its qualities from the conditions—economic, political and social—existing in a society. But at the same time a culture determines the regeneration of these conditions" (Mlama 1991, p. 10). Therefore, culture not only reflects a given society's structures, it determines those structures as well.

Therefore, the goal is to interrupt culture, to break cultural cycles that lead to conditions in which women are restricted from participation in sustainable development. This book proposes applied theatre as one appropriate and effective tool for shaping a new version of a given community's culture so that women can participate in shaping their own lives. A United Nations publication, *Rethinking Poverty*, states that "creating the conditions that allow women to demand change and influence priorities of State institutions is vital if gender equality and the empowerment of women are to be advanced" (2010, p. 74). Mlama writes that "to effect change in the basic structure of a society, therefore, means changing a people's way of life, a people's way of perceiving and doing things to support the intended changes. Indeed, history has seen many societies evolving different cultures to support successive but different modes of production" (1991, p. 11). What this suggests is that change is possible, and that recognition of the importance of culture in relationship to that change is essential.

In the article "Drama and Theatre in Education," Gordon Vallins writes that "not merely can drama reflect and re-inforce our attitude in values, it can also attempt to change them, to shape the culture in which it exists: it can be used to suggest alternatives to the present systems, it can give warning, it can explore the relationship of people subjected to the complexities of the system and thus expose its prejudices and injustices" (1971, pp. 167–168). Applied theatre not only can unleash a wave of creative freedom, but also freedom from oppression and from restrictions to participation for women. Inequity always results in strife. Strife is a waste of any community's energy and resources and diminishes its people's basic enjoyment of life. Since applied theatre is an effective tool for eradicating inequity, then adopting applied theatre and becoming proficient in using this powerful tool is healthy for any community.

Conclusion

Humans have been capable of substantial and noble change in the past. The seemingly impossible has become possible as cultures change to recognize the ability, worthiness, and dignity of more or all of its members. Not only are humans capable of this type of change, we seem to delight in it, more than resist it. There is a joy experienced in evolving and growing in understanding or capacity. Given that societal structures are based on commonly held cultural values and are strengthened by historical precedence, gender equity requires deliberate questioning of these values and an interruption of historical precedence. Theatre has an established role for doing just that. The many examples in the pages of this book demonstrate that even in communities without a strong tradition of theatre, theatre-based methods can be an effective tool for imagining, reimaging, and making authentic change.

2 Historical and Theoretical Foundations

This book is interdisciplinary in scope—researching and reaching across the borders of applied theatre, sustainable development and women's studies. Hopefully its findings will likewise incite new thinking and practices in these distinct disciplines. One of the challenges of interdisciplinary research is that the readership also comes from a wide variety of disciplines, so basic subject knowledge of all the primary disciplines cannot be assumed. A theatre artist or scholar will benefit from a brief description of sustainable development, just as a development practitioner will benefit from a description of applied theatre. The *benefit* of interdisciplinary research is that it can get closer to representing the real lived experiences of women yearning to participate in their own sustainable development, as human lives seldom arrange themselves into tidy academic silos, but spill over academic boundaries. A broader academic immersion into lived experience can help all stakeholders—researchers, theatre artists, development professionals, and community members—to more accurately identify challenges and opportunities.

Since the inception of international development in the 1940s and 1950s, a number of theoretical and empirical traditions have converged on this field. This book complicates that even further by considering the use of applied theatre for women's participation within the field of development. One of the challenges in establishing and articulating an analytical framework for this book is that the three fields represented in this study are all emerging fields and lack clear, decisive definitions—even within their discrete fields. There is a great deal of controversy and evolution within each field, which makes them both lively fields for investigation and innovation, but also moving targets.

I will be focusing on the *intersections* of theories and approaches from sustainable development, women's studies, and applied theatre to give light to revolutionary reimaginings of how our society operates, can operate, and with what values. I will primarily draw upon feminist methodology for analysis (Armstrong & Juhl 2007; Beetham & Demetriades 2007). This assumes an emphasis on embodied knowledge; an effort to dismantle hierarchies; an acknowledgement of power and how it is shared; and an implied social justice aim. The writing of Paulo Freire (2000) will serve as the primary ethical and moral compass for the analysis. I will apply his educational theories to development, as a means to reveal how men and women deal critically with reality, and for them to discover how to participate in the transformation of their world (Mayo 1999, p. 5). Development theorists will help apply all of this to the need for effective and appropriate methods for supporting the participation of women through the use of applied theatre. The complimentary overlap between these many theoretical approaches will help to articulate a theoretical framework for analysis of the case studies in this book.

Applied theatre

Applied theatre is an umbrella phrase that has come into popular usage to collectively refer to various forms of theatre that engage communities—most often in nontraditional performance spaces—in transforming their own lives. It seems the best way to approach understanding applied theatre is to keep an expansive view of the spectrum of practices that it includes, rather than seek neatly defined criteria for inclusion or exclusion. It often starts with the urge that Sanjoy Ganguly describes in his book *Jana Sanskriti: Forum Theatre and Democracy in India*—"to help oppressed people organize themselves" (2010, p. 10) and culminates in a dialogic process in which the actors and the spectators are collaborators (2010, p. 23).

Applied theatre takes inspiration from people's theatre such as the work of Kenyan writer Ngugi wa Thiong'o, who staged his play *Ngaahika Ndeenda* (*I Will Marry When I Want*) (1982) in 1976 with the Community Education and Cultural Center in the village of Kamiriithu to liberate the theatrical process from what he held to be the general bourgeois education system (Thiong'o 1986). European models for theatre were used in colonial education to actively convey the colonizer's values, language, and culture to those who were colonized. Although this effort in Kenya by the community to reclaim theatrical expression in their own form, in their own language, and for their own aims was a commercial success, it was shut down after just six weeks by the authoritarian regime in Kenya. What is undeniable is that the aspirations of this effort were not quenched but, instead, find their continual expression in much applied theatre.

In *The Applied Theatre Reader*, Tim Prentki and Sheila Preston describe applied theatre as "describing a broad set of theatrical practices and creative processes that take participants and audiences beyond the scope of conventional, mainstream theatre into the realm of a theatre that is responsive to ordinary people and their stories, local settings and priorities" (2008, p. 9). According to Philip Taylor, professor of educational theatre at New York University, the phrase has been useful for "finding links and connections for all of us committed to the power of theatre in making a difference in the human life span" (2006, p. 93). As described in the book *Applied Theatre: International Case Studies and Challenges for Practice*, applied theatre differs from mainstream theatre when it is "played in spaces that are not usually defined as theatre buildings, with participants who may or may not be skilled in theatre arts and to audiences who have a vested interest in the issue taken up by the performance or are members of the community addressed by the performance" (Prendergast & Saxton 2009, p. 6).

Artist and scholar Nicola Shaughnessy, in her book *Applied Performance: Live Art, Socially Engaged Theatre and Affective Practice*, utilizes the descriptive terminology 'applied performance' as well as 'applied theatre' to be inclusive of a wider range of performance situations than just theatre, such as dance or performance art. She writes that "implicit in this terminology is the concept of 'care': practitioners of applied theatre and performance care about and/or care for the communities they are working with; the work is often politically or pedagogically motivated; it has conscience, integrity and commitment" (Shaughnessy 2012, p. xiv). The primary goal of applied theatre is to advance, explore, or resolve social issues, rather than to simply entertain—though, be assured, participation in applied theatre projects is often highly entertaining and deeply engaging for communities involved.

There is a variety of theatrical forms that are often included within this categorization of applied theatre that originate from a wide variety of fields and disciplines. Those working in public health who are engaging in behavior change communication often use applied theatre techniques to facilitate their process of intervention with individuals, communities, or societies, to develop strategies to promote positive behaviors (Lefevre et al. 2004). Development scholars from fields such as geography refer to applied theatre as theatre-based participatory development (McCarthy & Galvao 2004). Theatre in education is a field that uses theatre for education and radical participation, which has in turn influenced many applied theatre forms (O'Toole 1976). Popular theatre—which exposes contradictions within a given society to inspire its audience to question, reflect, and seek answers—is also included within the categorization of applied theatre (Thyagarajan 2002; Schechter 2003). Theatre for Development is most often, though not exclusively, used to refer to applied theatre work on the African continent (Boon & Plastow 2004; Epskamp 2006; Kamlongera 1986; Kerr 1995). There are also names for forms included under the phrase of applied theatre such as playback theatre (Rowe 2007), theatre of the oppressed (Boal 1985; Duffy & Vettraino 2010; Emert & Friedland 2011), community performance (Cohen-Cruz 2005; Kuppers 2007), and prison theatre (Balfour 2004).

The above list of formal names for types of applied theatre is by no means exhaustive, nor is it consistently referenced in publications on this subject, but it does provide a view of the expansive use of applied theatrical techniques for furthering work on social issues in communities around the world. What is remarkable is the variety of professionals—from educators to doctors—that have found applied theatre useful for reaching members of communities and authentically engaging community members in improving their own lives, according to their self-identified priorities, concerns, and values. As theatre artist and scholar Petra Kuppers writes of community performance work, "To nail it down, to define, is an act that opposes many of the principles of community performance work itself" (2007, p. 3). The relative newness of these techniques, and their recent applications within many fields and disciplines, accounts for some of the looseness in categorization and lack of consistency in how the phrase is used. Given the improvisational nature of this form—easily accommodating itself to various objectives and strategies—it seems entirely appropriate to retain a somewhat open and evolving definition for applied theatre.

Applied theatre in development situations spans a range from being top down to bottom up in perspective. A top-down perspective assumes that a funding organization, NGO, or government defines the objectives and subject matter for an applied theatre project and then works for or with a community to achieve their desired change. A bottom-up perspective assumes the subject group defines and acts on its members' self-identified needs and aspirations throughout the entire applied theatre process. From its theoretical origins in Paulo Freire and Augusto Boal, what is now referred to as applied theatre is intended to be bottom up.

The case-study in Chapter 5 focuses on an example of entertainment-education—which does not have its original theoretical foundation in Freire and Boal—in which educational content is woven into dramas on radio or television, animated cartoons, popular music, or street theatre. Entertainment-education influences social change and awareness, attitudes, and behaviors "by showing desirable behaviors rather than describing them, by addressing norms and beliefs that may be too controversial to confront directly, and by reaching populations who might otherwise be difficult to reach" (Salem et al. 2008, p. 6). What tends to distinguish entertainment-education from most other forms of applied theatre is that it tends to be more top-down in its messaging. This brings into question the extent to which entertainment-education should be classified as applied theatre. The case study in Chapter 5 explores this question and notes possibilities for increasing participation, especially by women.

It also should be noted, that for this study, mediatized versions of applied theatre forms—such as radio dramas, awareness-raising videos, and television programming—will be included, whereas other scholars may not include forms that are not 'live' in the category of applied theatre. For this work, the criteria for inclusion of theatrical forms that are recorded or digitalized under the descriptive phrase 'applied theatre' is that they include some participatory methods in the creation, design, and execution of the product, and/or some participatory methods for critiquing and engaging with the form afterwards, such as through listening groups (discussed in greater depth in Chapter 5.) Another criteria for inclusion is that these forms be an "ethically engaged aesthetic act," as Mindy Fenske describes in her article "The Aesthetic of the Unfinished: Ethics and Performance" (2004, p. 1). To be considered applied theatre, the impetus, intent, and focus of the mediatized theatre must be towards a social issue important to the community by whom, with whom, and for whom the theatre was created. In this article, Fenske states that dwelling on the ontological debates of whether a recorded or digitized performance should be considered theatre is not necessarily productive in a social justice context. Her reference to this distinction refers to an ongoing debate prompted by performance theorists Philip Auslander's response to and critique of Peggy Phelan's ontology of performance, which limits 'performance' to the ephemeral copresence of live performances and audience (Chvasta 2005, p. 157).

It should be noted that the inclusion of mediatized forms of applied theatre could likely be highly contested by some and a deal-changer for many. It could be held that benefits derived from 'liveness' and authentic contact cannot be duplicated by technology. The impact of applied theatre that utilizes technology is explored in the book *Applying Performance: Live Art, Socially Engaged Theatre and Affective*

Practice by Nicola Shaughnessy (2012). What seems unavoidable is that theatre is being transformed by the technology of our screen-mediated world. *Real Players? Drama, Technology and Education* (Carroll, Anderson, & Cameron 2006) is another book that looks at a form of applied theatre—educational drama—as it seeks to engage students in the digital environment. It is likely that a spirited conversation will continue among applied theatre practitioners regarding the costs and benefits of issues surrounding liveness and digital medias.

Applied theatre history and theory

Though there are numerous historical and theoretical influences that could also be credited as inspiring the development of what is currently referred to as applied theatre, the two primary influences most often cited are the writing and work of Paulo Freire and Augusto Boal. Both originated from Brazil, were influenced by Marxist ideology, and worked with each other in developing and realizing their ideas and theories. Freire (1921–1997) was an educator, philosopher, and influential theorist of critical pedagogy. Most applied theatre practitioners cite the pedagogical theories of Freire as the basis of their work. The three major features of Freire's pedagogy that have influenced applied theatre are conscientization, the banking system of education, and praxis. According to Freire, *conscientização* or conscientization is defined as "consciousness raising" and refers to "learning to perceive social, political, and economic contradictions, and to take action against the oppressive elements of reality" (Freire 2000, p. 35). This is closely related to awareness, which is a necessary precursor to effective action, and to empowerment, which provides the strength and confidence to act.

Since people are adjusted to function within their society significantly by the style of education in which they are educated—often for a decade or more during a formative time of their lives—Freire's insights on education are extremely relevant to applied theatre. The infiltration of the colonizer's educational models throughout the colonized world was a powerful force that still contributes towards the perpetuation of oppression and must be understood to begin to undo oppression. In his seminal book, *Pedagogy of the Oppressed* (2000), Freire questions the "'banking' concept of education" in which knowledge is deposited into students' minds (Freire 2000, p. 72) by oppressive educational systems that treat students as objects. In contrast, Freire advocated for a problem-solving style of education that encouraged dialogue between teachers and students, and that engaged students in critical thinking. For Freire, critical pedagogy is concerned with developing a critical consciousness or recognition of systems of oppressive relations and one's place within that system. Freire insisted that a dialogic relationship between teacher and student is necessary for transformation to a critical consciousness. As Freire states, "It is necessary, that is, unless one intends to carry out transformation *for* the oppressed rather than *with* them. It is my belief that only the later form of transformation is valid" (2000, p. 67).

Freire's theories of praxis deeply influence nearly all applied theatre. Freire argues that to overcome oppression, one must emerge from it and turn upon it.

"This can be done only by means of the praxis: reflection and action upon the world in order to transform it" (Freire 2000, p. 51). Freire differs from the Marxist views of praxis in that he disagreed with the practice of simply explaining to the masses their need for action (Freire 2000, p. 53). He felt reflection and action cannot lead to transformation if theory and practice are merely explained to the masses. As Freire noted, "The oppressed must be their own example in the struggle for their redemption" (2000, p. 54). Herein lies the basis for viewing those who have been oppressed: not merely as the beneficiaries of liberation, but as actors and participants in their own liberation from oppressive forces.

Augusto Boal (1931–2009) was heavily influenced by Freire's work, evident by the homage he paid to Freire by naming his book *Theatre of the Oppressed* (Boal 1985). In this book Boal argued that the audience's cathartic experience—based on emotion—contributes to maintaining the dominant patriarchal ideology by keeping the spectator passive and submissive. Inspired in part by the theatre of Bertolt Brecht (Boal 1985, pp. 83–85), Boal wrote, "If, on the contrary, we want to stimulate the spectator to transform his society, to engage in revolutionary action, in that case we will have to seek another poetics" (1985, p. 47). This new poetics Boal proposed transforms passive spectators into spect-actors. Boal's poetics of the oppressed focuses primarily on action. This consciousness-raising form of theatre encouraged dialogic opportunities for communities not usually engaged in critical analysis of their own lives, or the structures that influence and limit their lives. It provides a way for marginalized people to participate in the formation of their own lives.

Reviewing other models on which theatre has been based, Boal writes, "Aristotle proposes a poetics in which the spectator delegates power to the dramatic character so that the latter may act and think for him. Brecht proposes a poetics in which the spectator delegates power to the character who thus acts in his place but the spectator reserves the right to think for himself, often in opposition to the character. In the first place, a 'catharsis' occurs; in the second, an awakening of critical consciousness" (1985, p. 122). For Boal, catharsis is not a positive outcome of theatre, as it represents a purging of the revolutionary impulses within the spectator, leaving the spectator passive and obedient. Boal goes on to write:

> But the *poetics of the oppressed* focuses on the action itself: the spectator delegates no power to the character (or actor) either to act or to think in his place; on the contrary, he himself assumes the protagonist role, changes the dramatic action, tries out solutions, discusses plans for change—in short, trains himself for real action. In this case, perhaps the theatre is not revolutionary in itself, but it is surely a rehearsal for the revolution. The liberated spectator, as a whole person, launches into action. No matter that the action is fictional; what matters is that it is action! I believe that all the truly revolutionary theatrical groups should transfer to the people the means of production in the theater so that the people themselves may utilize them. The theatre is a weapon, and it is the people who should wield it. (1985, p. 122)

Boal's systematized his methods for transforming the spectator into a spect-actor in four stages (Boal 1985, p. 126). The first stage is *Knowing the body* and includes a series of exercises that heighten awareness of one's body and the socializing restrictions that are placed on the body, based on one's social class, occupation, and other factors. The second, *Making the body expressive*, is a series of games that encourage expression through the body. In the third stage, *The theatre as language*, participants experience theatre as language and as a process-oriented exercise, rather than a finished product. This third stage is divided into three parts that represent various degrees of direct participation on the part of the spectator in the performance. The first degree is *Simultaneous dramaturgy* in which community members improvise (with the help of a script) a scene about a local issue or concern. They perform the scene to the point at which the main problem reaches a crisis and needs a solution. Here, they stop the action and ask the audience to suggest solutions, improvising various ideas on the spot for the audience to critique and improve. For the second degree, *Image theatre*, participants are asked to use the bodies of other participants to 'sculpt' their expression of the given topic, such as imperialism or oppression. Without using any words, they are then asked to sculpt these same participants into their ideal vision of this topic. Finally, a transitional sculpture shows how to get from the current reality to the ideal reality. The final degree is *Forum theatre* in which a 15–20-minute scene about a local issue with a difficult solution is performed. Those who witness it are encouraged to critique the solution offered and suggest better versions that are then acted out. Anyone in attendance is invited to replace any given actor in the scene in order to act out his or her solution. The fourth stage is *The theatre as discourse*, an unfinished form of theatre that actively involves all in the area. An example of this form of theatre is *Invisible theatre*, in which a scene about a local issue is acted out in an environment other than a theatre, for an audience that is unaware that what is happening is a theatrical scene, but, rather, thinks it is real life.

The facilitator of this theatrical process is referred to by Boal as the "Joker" (1985, p. 180), who acts as a sort of trickster or master of ceremony. The Joker can stop the action at any time to engage the audience in analyzing a given actor's motivations or actions. The Joker is above the action, not bound by the fiction of any given performance. This original idea put forth by Boal has been applied, developed, and refined by many applied theatre practitioners for various purposes. Applied theatre practitioner Michael Rohd describes a good facilitator of applied theatre as someone who is energized and enthusiastic about the process, a good listener, nonjudgmental, who deepens the discussion, and who moves the event forward through questions (1998, pp. 113–114). Key to effective facilitation is posing questions to which everyone authentically wants to hear the answer, but not offering answers her or himself; rather, letting participants propose and consider various answers from multiple perspectives. The role of facilitator for applied theatre is extremely challenging, often requiring this person to both create a safe place for exploration, while simultaneously destabilizing old securities and challenging traditional views and assumptions.

Applied theatre is necessarily political because it challenges the current societal models, practices, and policies that have resulted in oppression, loss of freedoms, and inequity. Disrupting how the dominant cultural exchanges occur—from the local level to global markets—is a form of resistance. Also of interest is how much certain cultures (with less clout in terms of cultural capital) can survive and even thrive with their own integrity and character intact in the face of global cultural capitalism. The survival of local cultures, languages, and identity can be nurtured by applied theatre that is for, by, and of the people. As described by Rustom Bharucha in *The Politics of Cultural Practice: Thinking Through Theatre in an Age of Globalization,* theatre can provoke new modes of existence in the age of globalization. In this book he advocates for his reader to be critically alert to the vastly differentiated contexts of globalization (2000, p. 18). Applied theatre often involves some form of cultural practice across borders—whether as a form of interactive theatre evolved by a Brazilian theatre practitioner being applied in a country such as India, or facilitators from Europe or the United Kingdom facilitating an applied theatre project in an African nation.

All forms that fall under the umbrella of applied theatre, to varying degrees, involve people in critically engaging with issues important to their lives in an active, solutions-based manner. Boal's basic methods for involving people for scripting and rehearsing their own lives have been developed, enhanced, and applied in various countries for a wide variety of social aims and objectives.

Entertainment-education

Entertainment-education (EE) is the process of intentionally designing and implementing a media message that is both entertaining and educational so as to increase audience members' knowledge about an educational issue, create favorable attitudes, shift social norms, and change behavior (Singhal & Rogers 2004, p. 5). It is a communication strategy to bring about behavioral and social change. Soul City in South Africa (covered in Chapter 1) is a well-known example of entertainment-education used to create social change around issues such as domestic violence. Many EE projects benefit from extensive formative research, which is conducted while an EE project is being designed, or is ongoing in order to improve its effectiveness. This research-based information about the characteristics, needs, and preferences of a target audience sharpens the design of EE (Singhal & Rogers 2004, p. 6). Some EE projects are not as research-based and rely more on the intuition and creativity of the production staff.

The history and theoretical foundation for EE, often led by health communication experts, differs in significant ways from most other forms of applied theatre theoretically based on the work of Paulo Freire. The case study in Chapter 5 will explore those differences more fully while exploring Population Media Center's form of education-entertainment uniquely based on the Sabido Methodology, a form of behavior change communication (BCC). BCC is a process that motivates people to adopt healthy behaviors and lifestyles. The process of designing a BCC program typically includes analysis, a strategic design, development and pretesting of messages, implementation, monitoring, and evaluation. Research of the target audience is key for informing each step. Community members can help design and guide each stage of the process to ensure their needs are addressed and to strengthen the community itself through the process. The message ideally should be tailor-made for each community, and clearly convey the benefits of the recommended behavior change in a way that corresponds to the community's values. BCC works to inspire both individual and societal behavior change, seen as necessary for sustained improvement in health. A combined effort through several communication chains—such as mass media, interpersonal, and community drama—increases the influence on behavior change. These programs can be designed with a mind towards scaling up to reach more people with the BCC message in related areas and can build in mechanisms for the sustainability of the program by including trainings and partnerships (Salem et al. 2008).

A distinguishing feature of EE is the often expansive reach of such programming. For example, *Heart and Soul*—an EE radio and television soap opera produced in Kenya in 2002 through a collaborative arrangement among 25 UN agencies—reached an audience of over 50 million people in 23 African countries (Singhal & Rogers 2004, p. 8). Even with live theatre, EE can have an impressive reach. Over the period of several years, a South Indian street theatre group, Nalamdana, reached more than one million people (Singhal & Rogers 2003). EE programs often reach such numbers in developing nations that are not overly media saturated. What will be examined through the case study in Chapter 5 is what kind of participation for women is possible in such broad-reaching methods. Chapter 5 will analyze the costs and benefits of this method as well as where, and under what circumstances, its use seems most appropriate in terms of women's participation. It will also include suggestions for making EE more actively participatory for women who are in the target audience for the programming.

The first projects that can be identified as entertainment-education occurred in the 1940s, 1950s, and 1960s with such programs as: *The Lawsons* in 1944 by the Australian Broadcasting Corporation; *The Archers* in 1951 by the BBC radio series; and *Simplemente Maria* in 1969 in Peru. During this time, communication theory was not a part of planning or designing these projects. After the *telenovela* (television soap opera), *Simplemente Maria* was broadcast in Mexico in 1970, the creative writer-producer-director Miguel Sabido from Televisa (a private television network in Mexico) carefully deconstructed it to understand its theoretical basis, in order to replicate it at his own network. He drew upon Albert Bandura's social learning theory—a natural fit for entertainment-education—and created a method based on positive, negative, and transitional characters that were developed over a long period. As stated by leaders in the EE field, Arvind Singhal and Everett Rogers, "This theoretical approach has since tended to dominate most theoretical writing and research about entertainment-education, and Sabido's methodology for the design of E-E programs, especially soap operas, influenced most later work on entertainment-education by communication professionals around the world" (Singhal & Rogers 2004, p. 12). This method acknowledges the importance of emotions as triggers for changing behavior related to various health issues. The method also attempts to use drama to model both individual self-efficacy and collective efficacy, both needed for sustainable positive social change.

The Sabido methodology is a form of EE that is primarily used by the Population Media Center, the subject of the case study in Chapter 5. As stated, the theoretical foundation for the Sabido method is based on the work of Albert Bandura, a Professor Emeritus of Social Science in Psychology at Stanford University, who has been ranked as the fourth most frequently cited psychologist of all time, and as the *most* cited living one (Haggbloom 2002). Bandura's Social Learning Theory asserts that people learn from one another, via observation, imitation, and modeling. In particular, people learn through observing others' behavior, attitudes, and outcomes of those behaviors. Social learning theory explains human behavior in terms of continuous reciprocal interaction between cognitive, behavioral, and environmental influences (Bandura 1976).

Sabido also drew upon other theories as he developed his method. Claude Shannon and Warren Weaver's Communication Model (Shannon & Weaver 1998) provided a model for the communication process through which distinct sources, messages, receivers, and responses are linked. Eric Bentley's Dramatic Theory (Bentley 1990) provided a model for the development of characters and their interrelationships used in plot construction. Carl Jung's Theory of Archetypes and Stereotypes (Jung 1981) was used as a model for the universal human physiological and psychological energies that characters can embody. Paul MacLean's concept of the Triune Brain (MacLean 1974), supplemented by Sabido's theory of the tone (Salem et al. 2008, p. 6), was used to create a model for sending complete messages capable of communicating with various centers of perception. Together these theories provide a foundation for the structure and design of messages, settings, characters, and plots. These theories also provide a framework for predicting how and why the drama will affect the knowledge, attitudes, and behaviors of the listening audience (Salem et al. 2008, p. 7).

The basic formula for EE projects is the creation of a story that features positive, negative, and transitional characters. The audience develops strong emotional bonds with the positive characters, who eventually grow into role models for listeners. The negative characters become cautionary tales for where negative choices, attitudes, and behaviors lead. Audiences generally identify most strongly with the transitional characters as they, too, often vacillate between positive and negative values, attitudes, and behaviors. The consequences suffered by these transitional characters are deeply felt by audience members emotionally invested in the story, which takes over a year to be told. Audiences enthusiastically cheer victories gained by transitional characters. Through this journey, the audience witnesses the consequences and benefits for both positive and negative attitudes, values, and behaviors so that they can chose for themselves how to act. About this methodology, Dr. Negussie Teffera, the director of Population Media Center (PMC) in Ethiopia, writes that "unlike documentaries or single-episode dramas, serials allow the audience to form bonds with the characters over time as the characters evolve their thinking and behavior" (Teffera 2008, p. 33).

Given the melodramatic world created by these dramas, demarcations of good and evil attitudes and behaviors are clearly defined by the creators, with little room for ambiguity. However, the issues most often addressed through this methodology are not hotly contested issues, and the stance taken by PMC is overwhelmingly seen as aligned with bringing about the common good. An example of an uncontroversial stance held by a PMC serial drama is that behavior that spreads HIV/ AIDS is negative and should be avoided. PMC does preliminary work to build consensus by local governments and social leaders in deciding upon the messages being disseminated by the dramas. In addition, this methodology is combating ignorance and misinformation around an issue, such as birth control, by disseminating information from health professionals.

A research-based approach is one of the distinguishing characteristics of the Sabido methodology. This is based on extensive formative research on audiences, society, and culture. A communication plan is developed by working with in-country stakeholders in accordance with relevant laws and policies. The issues addressed in the dramas are officially sanctioned and represent an agenda articulated by national policy makers in a manner that adheres to national policies and strategies. Currently EE is a phenomenon whose methods are taught at universities around the world and are utilized by a diverse range of organizations, inspiring both enthusiasts and skeptics with its impressive reach and impact. In assessing the value and impact of BCC and EE, it is important to keep in mind the power of the creator's visions and evaluate each program for the intention and content of the creator's programming.

Development and sustainable development

Among contested views of what constitutes development, there is a "general agreement on the view that 'development' encompasses continuous 'change' in a variety of aspects of human society" (Sumner & Tribe 2008, p. 11). Development as it is used in this book assumes an intentional activity (Cowen & Shenton 1998, p. 50) to change a group of people's lives for the better. What is considered 'better' is often based on the values and traditions of the person or people setting the development agenda, which does not necessarily correspond with the values or traditions of the group of people whose lives are being intentionally acted upon, changed, or developed. This book puts forth that in an ideal development situation, the group being acted upon, changed, or developed would either be the same people setting the development agenda or, at least, participating in setting that agenda.

The concept of international or global development, as we understand it today, only came into existence in the second half of the twentieth century. The idea of development—which has been heavily criticized—has largely been seen as "a process by which 'backward' countries would 'catch up' with the industrialized world—courtesy of its assistance" (Black 2007, p. 10). In the decades following the conclusion of World War II, dozens of new states were formed, gaining independence from their colonizers. Many of these countries had enormous challenges to face as new nations in providing a decent life for their people just free from the exploitation of colonization. These efforts were often undermined by corruption within newly formed governments of these former colonies and the legacy of colonization that perpetuated inequity and exploitation.

The concept of sustainable development largely arose in the 1970s and 1980s from two concerns: "increasingly worrisome evidence of ecological degradation and other biophysical damage, both despite and because of the greater wherewithal provided by economic growth, and the largely disappointing record of post-WWII 'development' efforts, particularly the persistence, and in some places worsening, of poverty and desperation in a period of huge overall global increases in material wealth" (Kemp, Parto, & Gibson 2005, p. 13). The goal of sustainable development is to nourish and sustain the fulfillment of all life on earth.

Development/sustainable development history and theory

Historically, the initial players in international development efforts came into existence soon after World War II. The United Nations Monetary and Financial Conference, commonly known as the Bretton Woods conference, took place in 1944 to regulate the international monetary and financial order after the end of World War II. Here the agreements were signed to set up the International Bank for Reconstruction and Development (IBRD) and the International Monetary Fund (IMF). The creation of the United Nations occurred a year later in 1945. Since that time, the evolving understanding of what international development is, or should be, has been greatly contested by stakeholders from a wide variety of perspectives. Decades of international aid that did not succeed in improving the lives of the poor—and in some case saw the worsening of poverty and debt—have led to many revisions of the very concept of development and its practices.

The inaugural address by US President Harry S. Truman in 1949 conveys many of the development attitudes of the global North regarding the South when he stated that "we must embark on a bold new program for making the benefits of our scientific advances and industrial progress available for the improvement and growth of underdeveloped areas" (1949). Decades later, in response to this speech and its implications, postdevelopment advocate Gustavo Esteva wrote:

> 'Underdevelopment' began, then, on January 20, 1949. On that day, two billion people became underdeveloped. In a real sense, from that time on, they ceased being what they were, in all of their diversity, and were transmogrified into an invented mirror of others' reality: a mirror that belittles them and sends them off to the end of the queue, a mirror that defines their identity, which is really that of a heterogeneous and diverse majority, simply in the terms of a homogenizing and narrow minority. . . . Since then, development has connoted one thing: to escape from the undignified position called 'underdevelopment.'(2010, p. 2)

Another point made by Truman in his speech was that the poverty suffered by half the world's population was "a handicap and a threat both to them and to more prosperous areas" (Truman 1949). An understanding of the interconnectedness of the global community was ushered in by the world's participation in two world wars and by efforts to recover from those wars. Truman's speech implicitly communicates that the victors of the war should, and do—rather magnanimously from his point of view—see it as their responsibility to not only aid in recovery efforts for defeated nations, but to provide aid to all nations who may be suffering. It also could be seen as an effort to stabilize the international market in which prosperous nations hoped to prevail. In Truman's statement he also seems to be communicating that the stability and sustainability of prosperous nations depends upon the stabilization and sustainability of less prosperous nations. The unrest and deprivation of poorer nations threatens stability everywhere.

President Truman also alluded to the relationship between development, industry, and science when he went on to say, "The United States is pre-eminent among nations in the development of industrial and scientific techniques. The material resources, which we can afford to use for assistance of other peoples, are limited. But our imponderable resources in technical knowledge are constantly growing and are inexhaustible" (1949). This could be said to have ushered in the idea that technology could solve nearly all of our problems. In retrospect, it seems to have almost ushered in a mentality that one generation's legacy of environmental damage was somehow gifting the future with challenges that would inspire their ingenuity and maybe even stimulate their economy (by creating jobs for reparations). As it has played out, we see that this is not the case. The expense and seeming impossibility of reversing the environmental damage of past generations is much more a liability than any kind of a gift. Furthermore, it destroys earth's delicate ecosystems that support life.

The idea of development is linked with the seemingly unquestioned aim that we as a people all want to 'progress.' This assumption that progress is a universal value can keep the underlying values behind progress from being explicitly named and the costs of this progress from being identified as such. Ecofeminist Vandana Shiva writes that "somewhere along the way, the unbridled pursuit of progress, guided by science and development, began to destroy life without any assessment of how fast and how much of the diversity of life on this planet is disappearing," and that "a new awareness is growing that is questioning the sanctity of science and development and revealing that these are not universal categories of progress, but the special projects of modern western patriarchy" (1989, p. xiv). Indeed, the very definition of progress, based primarily on the values of economic progress, is being questioned by more recent views of development.

Early theories of development largely focused on economic and material progress of human beings, and the gain of economic and material resources as the key to accessing all other resources. Development researcher Hartmut Bossel writes:

> For ages people have been judged by a single indicator: their wealth. But that single magic figure of x million dollars, or y hundred hectors of land, or z head of cattle implicitly expressed much more than property: it expressed the ability to buy sufficient food, to build a comfortable house, to feed even a large family, to live in luxury, to educate children, to pay for health care, and to support oneself in old age. And it implied that under these circumstances one could be reasonably happy. . . . In real life we usually need more than one

indicator to capture all important aspects of a situation. A single indicator can never tell the whole story. (1999, pp. 11–12)

Bossel goes on to state that using the GDP as an indicator of national wealth and well-being is inaccurate, given the fact that the GDP is essentially an indicator that measures "the rate at which natural resource wealth is being depleted" (1999, p. 12), hardly an indicator of well-being. Vandana Shiva cites the industrial revolution as being an occurrence that "converted economics from prudent management of resources for sustenance and basic needs satisfaction into a process of commodity production for profit maximization" (1989, p. xvii).

In 1972 governments of the world came together in Stockholm for the United Nations Environment Conference, responding to the urgent need to consider the problem of environmental deterioration. As author Mostafa Kamal Tolba states:

> The Stockholm Conference clarified the link between development and environment, and suggested an approach that would recognize the socioeconomic factors behind many environmental problems and cure the effects by treating the causes. The Stockholm Conference redefined the aims of development, making a high quality of life, rather than endless acquisition of material possessions, the main criterion of success. It defined environment as the dynamic stock of physical and social resources available at any given time for the satisfaction of human needs, and defined development as a universal process aimed at increasing and maintaining human well-being, thus it became evident that environmental and developmental objectives are complimentary. (Tolba, Abdel-Hadi, & Soliman 2010, p. 22)

A year after the 1972 conference the United Nations Environment Programme (UNEP) was established to provide leadership and encourage partnerships in caring for the environment. In 1987, the United Nations appointed the Brundtland Commission, formerly known as the World Commission on Environment and Development (WCED), which in its final report, *Our Common Future,* defined sustainable development as it is still largely defined, "development which meets the needs of the present without compromising the ability of future generations to meet their own needs" (WCED, 1987). The commission's conclusion was that "ecological and social failures had common causes and demanded a common response" (Kemp et al. 2005, p. 13). This report ushered in an era of interest and debate as to what sustainable development was and how to best achieve it.

The next official advancement of sustainable development efforts occurred because of the first United Nations Earth Summit that took place in Rio de Janeiro, Brazil, in 1992. As author Felix Dodds writes of the conference, "There was much hyperbole around the Earth Summit, the biggest international conference ever, and in the end phase of preparations, most countries poured in their experts to ensure that there was a minimum rocking of boats at one's own expense. Responding to popular demands at the time, a number of countries seemed to favor environmental protection measures that would not disrupt domestic production lines or established patterns of employment" (2001, p. 255). Still, the event was the largest-ever meetings of world leaders, bringing together the heads or senior officials of 179 governments. It resulted in the publication and adoption of *Agenda 21*, the *Rio Declaration on Environment and Development*, and the *Statement of Principles for Sustainable Management of Forests* by more than 178 governments. Furthermore, Chapter 38 in *Agenda 21* called for the setting up of the United Nations Commission on Sustainable Development (CSD) to monitor progress on the implementation of Agenda 21 and activities related to the integration of environmental and developmental goals by governments, NGOs, and other UN bodies. A plan was developed to further implement Agenda 21 and was adopted at a Special Session of the United Nations General Assembly in 1997.

The great anticipation and monumental occurrence of the turning of the millennium culminated with the United Nations Summit in 2000, during which time the eight Millennium Development Goals (MDGs) were adopted (United Nations Millennium Development Goals 2000). They are:

1. Eradicate extreme poverty and hunger.
2. Achieve universal primary education.
3. Promote gender equality and empower women.
4. Reduce child mortality.
5. Improve maternal health.
6. Combat AIDS, malaria, and other diseases.
7. Ensure environmental sustainability.
8. Develop a global partnership for development.

These goals highlighted the centrality of gender equality to efforts to achieve truly sustainable development and honor the vision of the "platform for action" adopted at the 1995 Fourth World Conference on Women in Beijing, China. An important outcome in regard to the MDGs is the improvement of measuring indicators in regard to gender and women. It should also be noted that even before the date set for achieving these goals in 2015, a new set of goals referred to as the Sustainable Development Goals have been introduced (Evans & Steven 2012) that may either work in tandem with the MDGs or replace them.

William Easterly, in his book *The White Man's Burden: Why the West's Efforts to Aid the Rest Have Done So Much Ill and So Little Good*, expresses dismay at the very notion of any one plan to alleviate poverty. He writes that unless we address the failure of trillions of dollars of foreign aid to alleviate poverty,

> the current wave of enthusiasm for addressing world poverty will repeat the cycle of its predecessors: idealism, high expectations, disappointing results, cynical backlash. . . . All the hoopla about having the right plan is itself a symptom of the misdirected approach to foreign aid taken by so many in the past and so many still today. The right plan is to have no plan. (2006, p. 5)

Here, the understanding of the term 'plan' could be seen to entail a rigid agenda, as it seems Easterly is intending the use of the word. Much development funding comes earmarked for specific areas that often correlate with funding trends or donor interests. This can hamper organizations' ability to be responsive to the needs expressed in the field by community members.

Rio+20, or the United Nations Conference on Sustainable Development in 2012, was deemed by many to be a step backwards by multiple measures. Wording about women's reproductive and sexual rights were struck from the document, and pledges by participating countries were weaker than hoped for. Based on my impression of the event as a participant, many people working in the development field seem to have less faith and interest in what occurs at these high-level negotiations, and more hope in what can come of grassroots organizing that is not bound by restrictive interest groups and conservative factions within governments.

The text *International Development Studies: Theories and Methods in Research and Practice* puts forth several definitions of development. Of note for this book is a concept of development that is "policy related and evaluative or indicator led, is based on value judgments, and has short- to medium-term time horizons— developments such as the MDGs, for example" (Sumner & Tribe 2008, p. 11). In this definition, growth and success are measured by indicators, goals, and outcomes. Critics of this concept of development cite bureaucratic goals that may be paternalistically set by governments or agencies without sufficient contribution from, or awareness of, the people they intend to benefit. "In other words there is an issue over whose objectives and values are expressed within the context of this second approach to development, and whether the articulation of the objectives is in any sense democratic or involves the effective participation of civil society" (Sumner & Tribe 2008, p. 13).

An alternative definition described by *International Development Studies* criticizes ethnocentric, Western conceptions of development to offer a radically alternative approach that could be described as 'postmodern,' 'postdevelopment,' or 'postcolonial.' This approach, in opposition to other concepts of development, is characterized by the previously cited critique by Esteva to US President Truman's speech, and the writing of Shiva. It asserts that "development (and poverty) are social constructs that do not exist in an objective sense outside of the discourse . . . and that one can only 'know' reality through discourse. In this approach there is no such thing as 'objective reality'" (Sumner & Tribe 2008, p. 14). In this approach, development can be only carried out based on multiple realities created by those endeavoring to realize a more just and equitable world for their future within their own communities and nations.

In the book *Development as Freedom* Amartya Sen views development as "an integrated process of expansion of substantive freedoms that connect with one another" (2000, p. 8). He advocates for an expanded focus on human freedom in regards to development, rather than extreme focus on single measures such as the growth in GNP, which is merely a *means* for expanding human freedoms. He sees the purpose of development as being "the removal of major sources of unfreedom: poverty as well as tyranny, poor economic opportunities as well as systematic social deprivation, neglect of public facilities as well as intolerance or overactivity of repressive states" (2000, p. 5). As winner of the 1998 Nobel Prize for Economics, Sen applies a strong ethical framework to economics and puts human welfare central in his economic thought. This results in a highly integrated approach to development.

The concept of sustainable development has been widely embraced by many institutions around the world, though they do not agree on its exact meaning, nor the implications of the concept. Many of these institutions that claim to be following the path of sustainable development have been criticized as conducting activities counter to the goals of sustainable development. Development's focus on improving the lives of the poorest of the world runs counter to the economic interests of nearly every investment in the private market. Without enforced governmental regulations and international guidelines, it is naïve to expect the free market to voluntarily shoulder the cost of sustainable development or assert the political will to do so. Indeed, it seems a broad scale acknowledgement that our current practices and models are unsustainable is needed before real change will occur. Until the system is truly seen as broken, efforts to fix it will likely be underwhelming.

The road to sustainability will not be easy, nor without resistance, as those who are currently most powerful will have to give up the most of what they already have. As author Mostafa Kamal Tolba writes:

> Although these reforms will in the long-term alleviate poverty, meet basic human needs, and end economic conditions that promote environmental degradation, it will require imagination, determination, and courage to oust the rigidly unfair, protectionist international economic order, commodity price volatility, crippling debt, and chronic poverty that currently have a stranglehold on the South. Governments will need to set guidelines for them to achieve sustainable development, persevering in the face of the free marketers who will be dismayed by such an idea. (2010, pp. 26–27)

As The Real World Coalition writes in its book, *From Here to Sustainability:*

> Our world has seen, especially for the majority of citizens in the rich industrial countries, a spectacular increase in living standards, longevity and opportunities to fulfill potential. Yet this world has failed, despite having the knowledge, wealth and capacity to do so, to lift the absolute poor out of poverty, reduce the divisions within and between societies, and reverse the trends which threaten the global environment. We have the resources to create genuine progress for all; governments everywhere lack the will to implement the changes made urgent by mounting evidence of environmental degradation and widening gaps between rich and poor. We have grounds simultaneously for unprecedented optimism and pessimism about the human prospect. (Christie, Warburton, & Real World Coalition 2001, p. 2)

There seems to be a need to acknowledge the basic disconnection or gap between the priorities and policies of political decision makers, economists, big business and the rich, and the mass of citizens across the planet who are barely earning a living, raising families, and seeking to find meaning in living a decent life. "If we want sustainable development for the new century—that is, economic development that brings a higher quality of life for all, without doing it at the expense of future generations, the poor and the environment—we have to close the gaps" (Christie, Warburton, & Real World Coalition 2001, pp. 7–8). That challenge points toward clear priorities for decision makers in the 'sustainable transition' needed in the years to come. A common theme that emerges from writings and efforts surrounding sustainable development is that for it to be achieved, broad public participation is a fundamental prerequisite.

Women's studies

Women's studies is an academic interdisciplinary subject that began developing in the 1980s and has changed the landscape of knowledge production—challenging both what we know and how we know it (Armstrong & Juhl 2007, p. 11). The women's movement, or the feminist movement, is historically made up of multiple campaigns and reform efforts on issues related to women's realities, such as voting, reproductive rights, land ownership, sexual violence, and the more radical reformation of our societal structures. The theories of feminism and accounts of the women's movement that have evolved from Europe, the UK, and the US have been seriously challenged by women in the developing world and the Global South. Priorities of the movement vary greatly among nations, races, and economic classes. Radical feminist bell hooks, in her highly accessible book, *Feminism Is for Everybody,* defines feminism as, "a movement to end sexism, sexist exploitation, and oppression" (2000, p. viii). The focus on women's studies is concerned with the unequal treatment of women by various forces within male-dominated societies and the structures that result from these societies that perpetuate and enforce inequity. Within this field of study, there is an explicit commitment to social justice for women and the societies that suffer in multiple ways when women are oppressed. There is also an acknowledgement that major systems of oppression are interlocking.

Before discussing the history of women's studies, it is useful to unpack the meaning and usage of some of the terms that are key to this field. 'Gender' refers to the socially constructed roles of being either a man or a woman, and includes notions of what a given society considers to be appropriate behavior for both men and women. 'Sex' refers to the physical and biological characteristics that define men and women. Many feminist theorists believe that gender is not an innate condition, but, rather, something we do (West & Zimmerman 1987) and something we perform (Butler 2006). In her seminal work, *The Second Sex*, Simone de Beauvoir writes that "biological and social sciences no longer believe there are immutably determined entities that define given characteristics like those of the woman, the Jew, or the black; science considers characteristics as secondary reactions to a *situation*" (1953, p. 4). Therefore, it is the situation of being identified as a woman that is the focus of this book, complete with all the characteristics associated with that gender, outwardly by society and inwardly through internalized notions that some women begin to believe about themselves as women.

I would also like to explicitly state that I intend an inclusive use of the term 'woman.' Along the continuum of gender expression, I intend to be inclusive in my writing of people who identify as women always, *or* at given times in their lives. In my work with the movement I cofounded, Mothers Acting Up, we continually had men who self-identified as mothers and were active in our programs. The definition of mothers that we propagated through our movement was "mothers and others who exercise protective care over someone smaller" (Osnes & Forbes 2011, p. 744). In Andrea Doucet's book *Do Men Mother?* she cites many examples of instances in which men self-identify as mothers when doing the primary work of nurturing children (2006). Feminist theorist Judith Butler writes in her book *Gender Trouble* that "any feminist theory that restricts the meaning of gender in the presuppositions of its own practice sets up exclusionary gender norms within feminism, often with homophobic consequences" (2006, p. viii). Within each of the three case study chapters, the applied theatre program being considered will be understood within the unique gender norms and practices of each community.

When using a term like 'women,' which includes nearly half the world's population, there is also the danger of assuming an essential identity or nature to all women. Clearly women are in reality a richly diverse group who vary greatly due to such factors as geographic location, religion, economic status, race, physical ability, and sexual orientation. However, "although women, even in micro-societies, form a heterogeneous entity, they still share common problems that could be solved collectively on a global level" (Samba 2005, p. 215). The case studies and examples examined throughout this book explore areas where both specialized, local tools and approaches are needed, *and* where there is room for a solution or approach that may be effective globally for women's participation. In *The Drama of Gender: Feminist Theater by Women of the Americas* Yolanda Flores writes:

> Just as there is no universal "woman" subject, neither is there a single feminism. Yet, the framework of constructing a false universal woman is necessary because it allows the different feminists and feminisms to reach the consensus that women have been misrepresented in, when not completely excluded from, literatures, histories, and other forms of cultural productions, and to recognize that, with all their differences and particular goals, women need to build coalitions among the groups of feminists in order to be more effective in bringing about social change. (2000, pp. 3–4)

Likewise, there is sometimes an essentializing of a single force—patriarchy—as causing all of women's oppression or subjugation. In *The Creation of Patriarchy*, Gerda Lerner defines patriarchy as the "manifestation of institutionalization of male dominance over women and children in the family and the extension of male dominance over women in society in general" (1987, p. 239). Caution should be used in attributing all oppression to patriarchy, as it can result in an inaccurate assessment of the many varying challenges and obstacles women face in participation. Judith Butler writes that the "notion of universal patriarchy has been widely criticized in recent years for its failure to account for the workings of gender oppression in the concrete cultural contexts in which it exists" (2006, p. 5).

Though there tend to be many similar experiences by women of subjection, there are important differences too, sometimes based on economic status, religion, race, or class. However, as Adrienne Rich writes in *Of Woman Born*, "patriarchy is a concrete and useful concept . . . it is now widely recognized as a name for an identifiable sexual hierarchy" (1976, p. xxiv).

I prefer the wording "women living in poverty" to "poor women" because the later wording identifies women based on their economic status first and foremost. It also tends to infer that a woman's poverty *defines* her rather than *describes* her current situation. The phrase "poor woman" could also be seen to communicate that her poverty is an unchangeable condition of her life. Even Paulo Freire and Augusto Boal's way of referring to a group of people, such as women, as "the oppressed" seems a bit dated, given our evolving awareness of language. I am likewise sensitive to the overuse of the phrase "living in poverty" throughout this book, but believe it to be more readily understandable to alternative descriptive phrases such as "without adequate resources." Labeling can determine how women are viewed and, more importantly, how they view themselves. It can lead to a self-fulfilling prophesy such as "accepting judgments and prophesies which others make about you" (Winniefridah 2011, p. 317). In a book dedicated to the use of theatre as an agent of change, the language and wording throughout the book—though not perfect—was chosen to support the belief that change in women's conditions is possible.

Beyond the specific language used, my intention for this book is to resist a deterministic narrative in which human arrangements always result in men oppressing women. It doesn't have to be that way, and it isn't always that way. Lerner notes that when "feminist anthropologists have reviewed the data or done their own fieldwork, they have found male dominance to be far from universal. They have found societies in which sexual asymmetry carries no connotation of dominance or subordination. Rather, the tasks performed by both sexes are indispensible to group survival, and both sexes are regarded as equal in status in most aspects" (1987, p. 18). I resist polarizing language that is likely to deter men from engaging in discussions of gender equity, for fear they are being blamed or stereotyped as patriarchs or oppressors.

When presenting on the film *Pray the Devil Back to Hell* in my classes, I was deliberate in not alienating my male students. This is a powerful drama on the peaceful resistance of women in Liberia to the civil war (1999–2003) that ravaged their country and their lives. Most males throughout the film are portrayed as rapists, violent, and seemingly without conscience for their actions. In class, we discussed how the men are equally denied their full humanity in a situation in which they are forced to become soldiers at a young age, and are given free access to drugs and weapons. Rather than identifying men as the problem or the oppressors, we were able to discuss the underlying problems—such as greed—as the forces that compromised the humanity of citizens of Liberia during the civil war. This actual story from Liberian history stands as proof that a new story can be told; the women of Liberia successfully enforced peace treaties that eventually resulted in the democratic election of the first female leader of an African country,

Ellen Sirleaf Johnson. Indeed, another way of resolving war and returning to a more sustainable way of living is possible, as this dramatic film and Liberian history demonstrate. As this recent history tells us also, women can be the ones with the audacity to imagine and the skills to lead this new political reality.

Women's studies history and theory

Since the three case studies from this book focus on women from Central America, Asia, and Eastern Africa, histories and theories of women's studies from the perspective of theorists from these regions will be interwoven with more Western histories and theories throughout this account. The history of self-naming throughout the evolution of the women's movement is useful for understanding how women from various countries have negotiated both differences and common ground. The phrase "women of color" is a political term created to build coalition among American women who are Black, Chicana, and other non-White women to challenge the presumed homogeneity of the North American feminist movement of the late 1970s (Case 1988, p. 6). Central American feminist Yolanda Flores writes that it is "essential to contextualize this term in order to avoid grouping women from third world counties into this category or incorporating American women of color with third world women and feminism without establishing their differences" (2000, p. 6). The category of Third World women is described in Chandra Mohanty's anthology *Third World Women and the Politics of Feminism* as defined through geographical location as well as particular sociohistorical conjunctions (Mohanty, Russo, & Torres 1991, p. 2).

Feminist Emma Pérez writes that the work of Chicana feminist production and the intellectual production of other Women of Color "rejects colonial ideology and the by-products of colonialism and capitalist patriarchy—sexism, racism, homophobia, etc. The space and language is rooted in both the words and silence of Third-World-Identified-Third-World-Women who create a place apart from white men and women and from men of color . . . from deconstructing male centralist theory about women to reconstructing and affirming a Chicana space and language in an antagonistic society" (1991, pp. 161–162). A theme of struggle seems to emerge as a unifying agent from literature on both women of color and Third World women. More specifically this struggle seems to focus on attaining interpretive power (Flores 2000, pp. 8–9). As Pérez writes, "We have not had our own language and voice in history. We have been spoken about, written about, spoken at but never spoken with or listened to. Language comes from above to inflict us with western-white-colonizer ideology" (1991, pp. 175–176).

As an alternative term for feminism, the term 'womanism' was made widely known by American writer Alice Walker and is described from the African perspective as "the totality of feminine self-expression, self retrieval, and self-assertion in positive cultural ways" (Kolawole 1997, p. 24). Some female theorists from the African continent have resisted both the terms feminism and womanism as not representing their realities, values, or perspectives. According to scholar Mary E. Modupe Kolawole, "Many African women resist subscribing to feminism as a rejection of the imperialist attempt to force them to accept a foreign 'ism' that is superfluous to the needs of the majority" (1997, p. 20). Africana woman-ism is an ideology that was created and designed for women of African descent that is grounded in African culture (Hudson-Weems 2004). As stated by literary critic Molara Ogundiepe-Leslie, "African women in general wish to retain certain features of their traditions; those which are positive for women" (1994, p. 13). To avoid the uneasiness some African women (and men) feel about the term femi-nism, scholar Molara Ogundipe-Leslie advocates for the term Stiwanism, which stands for *Social Transformation Including Women in Africa* (1994, pp. 209–230).

The two dominant ideologies that have evolved from the inception of the feminist movement are liberal feminism and radical feminism. They needn't be thought of as binaries or in opposition, but, rather, as different approaches that can cross over and influence one another. There are other approaches to feminism also, such as materialist, lesbian, black, and Lacanian (psychoanalytic). I focus on liberal and radical because they are most pertinent to the development of this book's analytical framework.

Liberal feminist reform

The liberal feminist reform movement began in the nineteenth century, and was retroactively termed the first wave of the women's movement. It sought equality for women within the existing social structure, believing that if women "obtained the right to an education, the right to own property, the right to vote, employ-ment rights—in other words, equal civil rights under the law—they would attain equality with men" (Taylor, Whittier, & Pelak 2007, p. 506). This view, which continued into second wave feminism, holds that women lack power because they are not allowed equal opportunity to compete and succeed in a male-dominated society, and, instead, are relegated to domestic and subservient roles within soci-ety. The strategies for change within this movement tend to focus on changing women individually and collectively to make them qualified for full inclusion and securing greater levels of participation by training women for high government positions or executive jobs.

Julieth Timoth Kabyemela's book, *Theatre for Women Empowerment and Development: Experience of Politics in Rural Tanzania,* is based on her applied theatre fieldwork that was conducted using a liberal feminist theoretical frame-work. She used Theatre for Development to promote "equality by advancing women to be equal with men and within the existing structures" (Kabyemela 2012, p. 14), focusing on equal opportunities for participation in management of the society. She used her study to examine the use of theatre for development as "an alternative strategy to increase women's participation in local politics and decision-making organs, especially in rural Tanzania" (Kabyemela 2012, p. 27). Basically she was examining the use of theatre to prepare women for public office.

Another example of this feminist approach can be seen in the recent work of The Whitehouse Project, a nonpartisan and nonprofit organization working to advance women in business, politics, and media in the United States from 1998 to

2013, when it closed its doors (Franke-Ruta 2013). Along with leadership training for potential young female leaders, The Whitehouse Project created the EPIC (Enhancing Perceptions in Culture) Awards to honor innovators who bring positive images of women's leadership to the American public. In 2006 the actress, Geena Davis, was given this award for her portrayal of President Mackenzie Allen on ABC's television show *Commander In Chief*. The Whitehouse Project's awards celebrate artists who create characters who serve as positive role models in popular culture for women, and artistic efforts that normalize the presence of women in leadership roles in society's collective imagination. They even partnered with Mattel to create a 'Barbie for President' doll and website to inspire younger girls to self-identify as leaders (Mattel 2013). Given the unrealistic female body type propagated by the Barbie doll through the decades, this effort has problematic elements, as well as likely positive outcomes. As previously stated, women need to first be able to imagine themselves in these expanded, nontraditional roles before they can even conceive of trying to achieve them. Also, society can be aided in imagining and accepting women in new roles when experiencing this possibility first in a form of culture, such as a television program or a theatre performance.

Radical feminism

Emerging largely in the 1960s and 1970s, but inspired in part by the 1950s writings of Simone de Beauvoir (Beauvoir 1953), radical feminism holds that "in all societies, institutions and social patterns are structured to maintain and perpetuate gender inequality and female disadvantage permeates virtually all aspects of sociocultural and personal life" (Taylor et al. 2007, p. 507). Therefore, a radical transformation of society's dominant ideology and structure needs to occur to usher in authentic change for gender.

Feminist scholars such as Valerie Bryson (Bryson 2003) and Chris Beasley (Beasley 1999) link capitalism and the patriarchy as dual systems that mutually reinforce the oppression of women. As gender studies scholar Matsa Winniefridah writes:

> Women provide their labour power and reproduce the next generation of workers for the benefit of the capitalist and patriarchy. Drawing women into wage labour market represent an increase in the exploitation of womens' [sic] unpaid labour. However, wife role is as strategically important in the home as it is at factory work. In both the home and the workplace, the woman has no economic power. Economic power and decision making lies with the capitalist employer and the patriarchal capitalist man in the home. There is a symbiosis relationship between capitalism and patriarchy. (2011, p. 316)

In her book *The Real Wealth of Nations: Creating a Caring Economics* (2008), Riane Eisler offers a bold economic model that assigns worth to the act of caring (and other assets not commonly assigned an economic value), which is disproportionately carried out by women and is severely undervalued in nearly all current economic systems. This caring economics is in keeping with the aims of radical feminism.

All women in male-defined societies, regardless of their culture, struggle to improve their lives. However, due to cultural differences, a solution that works in one culture may not be effective or appropriate in another culture. As men and women throughout the world work towards a more sustainable and equitable future, making peace among the different "isms" working towards change would significantly improve the likelihood for success. As Mary E. Modupe Kolawole writes, "Perhaps the combative attitude will be eliminated with new terms but better still with a new attitude that accommodates diversities through a dialogic stance" (1997, p. 23).

Feminist or womanist research

The subject position of women is primary in feminist and womanist research. This entails studying women from their own perspective and from their experience. In the case of women participating in their own development, it must be recognized that it is often a major paradigm shift for women to even claim the position of subject when communicating in public. There may be little or no former experience in doing this for women without access to education or power, necessitating that appropriate actions be taken before expecting women's participation in declaring what they think, want, or value. In terms of research, this also entails recognizing the subject position of the researcher and acknowledging that the researcher's beliefs, attitudes, and values shape the research. It also recognizes the power imbalance between researcher and the subject of the research, in this case, women who are living in poverty. As much as is possible, this means trying to remove the hierarchical relationship between researcher and participant.

This can be realized by involving women in as many levels of the research process as is possible and continually asserting that women are the experts and authorities of their own experiences. This also requires appropriate methods for involving women that honors the knowledge and skills they do have. Since methods that are more active and embodied tend to more accurately serve effective communication, applied theatre is a uniquely useful tool for dismantling hierarchies and putting researcher and participants on an even playing field. The location of much applied theatre work is often a space in which the participants are familiar and comfortable, giving them a 'home team' advantage at times over the researcher. Also, given the theoretical foundation for applied theatre work, the entire process is set up so that the participants are the experts and the researcher is merely the facilitator guiding the process that acknowledges the participant's expertise.

Gender similarities between the researcher and the participants or subjects do not transcend all the many other differences that may exist between them. Though differences will always be there, recognizing and addressing these differences allow all to draw upon that diversity and recognize that these differences can facilitate and permit different knowledges to be put forth. Although all research has as its aim to assert new knowledge to improve society's collective understanding, or ability to deal with pertinent challenges, feminist and womanist research aims to improve the lives of the women it studies, and, secondly, their surrounding families, communities, and world. Therefore, ideally feminist and womanist research is not extractive, but, rather, results in knowledge that benefits the women with whom it was conducted. Indeed, the research process is often designed and intended to empower women and change the existing power inequity. New knowledge can emerge when inequities in society are challenged; this entire process can validate new perspectives and ways of defining experiences.

There is a strand of feminist research that is engaged in making up reality with the women who are the subjects and the authentic participants in the research. This approach is known as social constructivism, which suggests that "knowledge about the 'world out there' is produced in a complex process of interaction. There is no one 'reality'; rather, people perceive the world in a multitude of ways, which gives rise to multiple realities" (Farnworth 2007, p. 273). This implies that there is not one single truth about a given issue that the researcher is out to discover. Related to this is feminist epistemology, which is

> a branch of feminist theory which argues that 'truth' is strongly shaped by our social conditions, and that the idea of value-free knowledge is a false construct, biased towards the male experience of the world. While approaches to knowledge and its production continue to generate many internal disagreements within feminisms, in general, feminist epistemology attempts to raise the volume of excluded voices, specifically women's, and ensures that knowledge distortions that erase women's experiences as legitimate are unpicked and investigated. (Hochfeld & Bassadlien 2007, p. 221)

By attending to the focus of this research—using theatre for women's participation in sustainable development—methods for research and analysis are being chosen that best include excluded women's realities, and support the researcher and the participants in being co-creators of reality.

Specific to gender and women's studies in development, there are two specific approaches that have developed: Women in Development and Gender and Development. Both are related to and influenced by liberal feminism and radical feminism. Women in Development (WID) originated in the early 1970s by women who grew critical of the dominant framework for approaching development that focused on men's prosperity, largely leaving women out of the entire development process. "Based on a 'liberal feminist' framework, primarily developed in north America, 'women in development' (WID) . . . assumed that women's subordination was directly linked to their exclusion from the formal marketplace, and therefore stressed the integration of women into the market economy through development programmes focusing on women" (Beetham & Demetriades 2007, p. 201). Gender and Development (GAD) was created from critiques of this approach, largely by feminist development scholars of the South who used a postcolonial analysis to determine that WID was based on Western values not applicable to women living in the South. They advocated for an approach that gave consideration to the realities of women in the South, based on their participation (Parpart, Connelly, & Barriteau 2000). Beyond the market economy, "the GAD approach recognized that gendered subordination is constructed at many levels and through many institutions, including the household, the community, and the state" (Beetham & Demetriades 2007, p. 201).

Theoretical framework for analysis of case studies

The theoretical framework for this book is constructed from common ground among the three disciplines examined in this chapter. Its purpose is to serve as a structure to support the analysis of the three case studies of applied theatre for women's participation in sustainable development. I will be working with theories from applied theatre, sustainable development, and women's studies; focusing on a revolutionary reimagining of how our society operates, and from what values.

The ideology influencing this work is primarily revolutionary. I resist the narrative necessity that revolution is brought about only through violence; and I believe theatre and art can be a creative catalyst for transforming our world. Boal himself refers to his Theatre of the Oppressed as a *rehearsal* for the revolution. I join other feminist and womanist theatre scholars in evolving the theoretical work of both Freire and Boal—who at times marginalized the role of gender—to make it applicable for advancing the participation of women (Armstrong & Juhl 2007, p. 18). Although the theoretical framework for this book leans towards radical feminism and Gender and Development (GAD) ideologically, it also includes both liberal feminist ideas and Women in Development (WID), and intentionally resists binaries that tend to divide those working towards shared values and goals by different means. My own stance, as informed by a decade of work with the international movement Mothers Acting Up, is to bring creativity to this revolution and express it as a joyful act. I have found that is it more productive to stress opportunities over negativity, and to utilize language that unites with shared values over language that polarizes through differences.

Theoretical approach

Feminist beliefs and concerns are the guiding framework for this research process, which means being continually informed by the standpoint and experiences of women. I use the term 'feminist' to acknowledge my particular origins in the United States and to communicate that basis for my work, but wish to express my respect for other terms claimed by women around the world for the work they do to better the lives of women. Feminist research is an engaged process in which the researcher discloses her or his own "subject position" throughout (Hesse-Biber & Yaiser 2004). This book's preface shares my background and experiences that have informed the values and preconceptions influencing my work. The only way I felt I could appropriately write from a feminist position, is if the analysis on my case studies was anchored in direct experience. Therefore, I have chosen organizations for analysis that I have worked with through applied theatre, so that my understanding and writing can be grounded in experience. In that way I can give a more embodied testimony to the place and all other descriptive aspects. This personal association and involvement also allows me to incorporate the local women's views—as best as I can—often through their own words.

Through this approach I situate myself as a scholar, teacher, and practitioner of applied theatre for women's participation in sustainable development. I will draw upon each of those positions throughout this book when needed to give an account of the work being analyzed. For myself as a university professor and an applied theatre artist, a book is a culturally appropriate and effective manner for communication. Yet I am communicating about people for whom this is largely *not* an appropriate or effective mode of communication. I am writing about where our two realities meet, that place where we try to work together towards sustainable development. This requires that scholars and development professionals acknowledge the hierarchy this situation almost invariably sets up, and work to resolve and dismantle those in whatever ways possible. This is mitigated primarily in the forms of communication—most often through applied theatre techniques—that allow women to be the experts of their own realities in the communication that ensues.

Here I draw upon the theoretical work of Edward Said in his seminal work *Orientalism* in order to make the comparison between Orientalism and development in order to mine the postcolonial associations in both. According to Said, Orientalism is a way of coming to terms with the Orient that is based on the Orient's unique place in the European Western experience. More specifically, in academic fields it includes "anyone who teaches, writes about, or researches the Orient," engages in "a style of thought based upon an ontological and epistemological distinction made between the 'Orient' and (most of the time) the Occident," and finally as an institution of domination which makes statements about it, authorizes views of it, describes it, teaches it, settles it, rules over it—in short, "a Western style for dominating, restructuring and having authority over the Orient" (Said 1979, pp. 2–3). What is also key to his work is the idea of the Orient as being both "Other" from and inferior to the Occident or the West. Given that it is so often the case that development is the project of Western people who—like this book—author statements and views about it, there is an awareness to be gleaned from Said's work. I am continually attempting throughout this book to render it less an exercise of power and authority over, and more an exercise of partnering with and witnessing. By being sensitive to the human experience, academics and development professionals can begin to break the bonds of history and question biased vocabulary by reflecting on their own practice, and in this way guard against colonial attitudes and repetition of received ideas (McCarthy 2010, p. 85).

I acknowledge that development work is done in relationship across many divides: economic status, unequal access to education, race, culture, and sometimes nationality. It is necessary to tend to any confusion or unanticipated needs that arise on both sides of these divides. A hierarchy is maintained, in part, based on who holds the power and agency within the relationship. It is often thought to be the researcher's job to articulate and disseminate the meaning that emerges from the process of applied theatre. However, women can be engaged in evaluating their own experiences and articulating the meaning through culturally appropriate methods through applied theatre. In the framework for this analysis, ways for sharing power and agency that emerge from the case studies will be explored and prioritized.

In the writing itself, I include the voices of the women I have worked with or have researched whenever I can, and sometimes in unconventional ways, in terms of standard academic writing. This calls for the creation and use of mixed research methods that includes the "subjugated knowledges" of women who largely have not had access to participation (Hesse-Biber & Yaiser 2004). I acknowledge the imperfect transmission of this knowledge through multiple translations, but assert that the continual effort is of worth. An example of a mixed research method is the inclusion of stories and photographs to communicate the content and spirit of an interaction. I am attempting in various ways to include the voices of the women being written about, to avoid what Carol Gilligan refers to in her seminal book *In A Different Voice* "where those spoken about have no voice" (1982, p. xix).

Including voices of women who are not from the academy in an academic book requires that multiple realities are acknowledged. It also requires openness to embodied ways of knowing and an acknowledgment of traditional gendered knowledge as a valuable source of knowledge. A point of common theoretical ground from all three fields is an acknowledgment of there being no one fixed truth or reality.

There is an old theatre adage which states that you can only improvise when truly prepared. This relates to Easterly's call for there to be "no plan" in development, but, rather, for it to be responsive to the needs of each community. For the applied theatre facilitator, this means preparing by conducting research, establishing partnerships, and preparing possible exercises and approaches that could be utilized, but, then, being ready to have "no plan" and be responsive to the needs of the given moment. This resembles the artistic process undertaken by theatrical directors who likewise often prepare for directing a show, but once rehearsals start, abandon their preparations and respond to the creative moments presenting themselves (only able to do so proficiently because of their extensive preparation). This needn't mean that previously established objectives for the project are abandoned, but that *how* those objectives are best met can change in the moment.

A key aspect of applied theatre methodologies is their ability to adapt to different circumstances and situations. What this entire book seeks to emphasize is that there is not one specific method or a single combination of methods that is superior, but that there are useful approaches, methods, and tools that have been effective at involving women in their own sustainable development. Some tools work effectively within a specific culture and not as effectively within another culture. For example, radio dramas have proven to be highly effective for Population Media Center in Ethiopia because the majority of the population regularly listens to the radio, but this would not be so in cultures with lower listening rates. Conversely it may be that some tools or approaches seem to be effective and appropriate in nearly every cultural application. For example, with my Vocal Empowerment Workshop, I have found that there are a few warm-up exercises that are fun and effective with every group of women I've ever worked with. Exposure to and familiarity with this variety can help the development professional be adaptive and responsive to the lived reality of the women who are seeking to participate in their own development.

Although the effectiveness of certain methods can vary based on the nature of the community, there are some fundamental principles in the work of applied theatre that should be constant and bear stating explicitly for certain clarity. These principles—such as respect, trust, full disclosure, and equality—are essential characteristics of applied theatre that reflect both its purpose and the way in which it is practiced. These principles are so primary to the form, that without them, applied theatre could not effectively operate. Although these ideals are not always fully attainable, they function as an important beacon guiding the work.

These principles call for development professionals to fully disclose to all participants the complete development agenda, funding arrangements, and limitations of resources. This should not be a paternalistic arrangement where development professionals—believing they have the best interest of the community members at heart—do not divulge relevant information. An ideal situation is one in which the women also share their lived realities to the fullest extent possible. Applied theatre offers many exercises that can intentionally nurture the trust this entails (Boal 2002; McCarthy & Galvao 2004). Often these are fun games that position all involved on an even playing field, dismantling real or perceived hierarchies and engaging everyone in activities that provide an experience of working together towards a very short-term objective. These games increase familiarity, trust, and respect. Without trust and respect in place, it is unlikely applied theatre as described throughout this book will successfully achieve the desired objectives.

Sometimes the person facilitating the applied theatre for women's participation is from outside the community, but this is clearly not always the case. In the case of Stepping Stones from Chapter 1, it is community members who lead the peer sessions. Even when someone from within the community is facilitating the applied theatre, it is extremely likely that that person has undergone advanced training and has some actual or perceived position of power within the community, due to their position as facilitator. By nature of their role, that person is at least partially setting the agenda and leading the action. The same principles for applied theatre pertain to any facilitator, regardless of whether or not they are members of the community or outsiders.

Indicators for monitoring and evaluation

Throughout our lives we use various indicators to guide our decisions and actions. When trying to achieve an effective and appropriate use of theatre for women's participation in sustainable development, there are naturally things to watch for that indicate to what extent women are able to participate in their own sustainable development through theatre. Indicators are "quantitative or qualitative measurements of the state of something that is important to us" (Bossel & Balaton Group 1999, p. 25). For the indicators to measure what is important to everyone involved, the indicators should ideally be decided upon by all stakeholders together. Therefore, the process of finding an indicator set for women's participating through theatre "must be participatory to ensure that the set encompasses the visions and values of the community or region for which it is developed" (Bossel & Balaton Group 1999, p. 7). Once indicators are set, it is important to establish baseline data—the level at which this participation currently occurs—so that any decrease or increase in participation can be identified and measured.

There is much literature on monitoring and evaluation of development projects that can be drawn upon to measure impact (International Institute for Environment and Development, Sustainable Agriculture Programme 1998; Kusek & Rist 2004). Some works are particularly focused on participatory methods, such as Marisol Estrella and John Garventa's book *Who Counts Reality? Participatory Monitoring and Evaluation* (1998). In practice, much applied theatre work is not formally monitored. Funding for external monitoring and evaluation of theatre programming can be prohibitively expensive and baseline measurement can be complex and take a long time. I am interested in exploring how applied theatre itself can be utilized as an accessible monitoring and evaluation tool—potentially facilitated by applied theatre artists—for women to monitor and evaluate their own progress. In response to how difficult and expensive it can be to provide outside monitoring and evaluation, gender and development researchers Tessa Hochfeld and Shahana Rasool Bassadien write, "Baseline *estimation* which is done with the participation of the beneficiary group is a more realistic goal. Changes attributed to the programmes or services offered can then be measured against this baseline estimate, using the indicators" (2007, p. 226).

By using active techniques, women can participate in establishing both baseline data and in measuring any growth or advancement that occurs as a result of a project. For example, in Nicaragua as part of a "training of the trainers" for the Vocal Empowerment Workshop I developed, I introduced an active tool for women to participate in establishing a baseline measurement of how confident they felt about their own voices before the training, and to measure any improvement in confidence after the training (Osnes 2012b). I created a vertical chart with the numbers 1 to 10 and a correlating drawing of a woman on top near the numeral 1 with her mouth wide open speaking confidently; a woman near the numeral 5 looking moderately confident speaking; and a woman near the numeral 10 not speaking at all (see Photo 2.1). Each woman was asked to use her hand to indicate where she would rate her confidence in using her voice on the chart. The chart was large enough for everyone to see in the circle, so I walked around to each woman with the chart to have her indicate how she felt.

Each woman seemed to give it a lot of consideration as she marked her level of confidence on the chart, and a lot of conversation emerged at the end of this exercise as to their generalized feelings about their voices. One woman noted that because there is so much domestic violence, the level of confidence felt at home

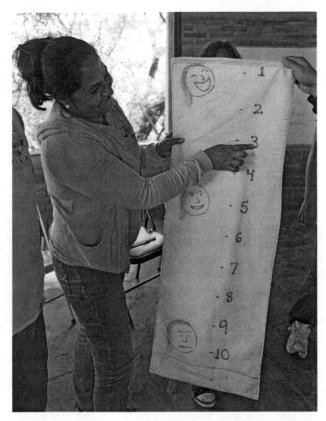

Photo 2.1 Nicaraguan woman marking her level of confidence using her voice on a chart.

could be hard to determine. A woman might be thinking of talking with her kids, her sisters and mother, or an abusive husband. The use of this chart for women to measure their own vocal confidence resulted in quantitative numbers that could be used for analysis, as well as qualitative information that grew out of the discussion that followed. Combined, they contributed to a deeply nuanced measurement of the vocal confidence felt by these women before and after the vocal training.

The practice in some applied theatre is to provide a narrative account of the perceived impact by one of the applied theatre artists, often the one with an academic affiliation or the one responsible for demonstrating impact to some granting or supervisory entity. Nicola Shaughnessy writes in her book, *Applying Performance: Live Art, Socially Engaged Theatre and Affective Practice*, "as applied theatre and performance generally takes place outside of the public space of theatres and galleries and is often 'bespoke,' developed for particular communities in a particular context, the work is not readily accessible, is difficult to document (due to ethics of participation-centered practices) and hence requires 'thick' description as a means of making the material visible" (Shaughnessy 2012, p. xix). Given the theoretical foundation for this type of work, this description is nearly always claimed to be only one perspective on the work, even as practitioners seek to take into account the experiences of others involved at every level. As Jane Plastow writes after such an evaluation of her work with the Adugna Community Dance Theatre in Ethiopia, "Although I have consulted and interviewed in the course of writing this chapter, there are inevitably differences of understanding and interpretation on certain points relating to the project. The chapter as written and the views it expresses are entirely my responsibility" (2004, p. 153).

Development professionals, unsurprisingly, seem to be more schooled in monitoring and evaluation techniques than applied theatre professionals, who often more strongly self-identify as artists. This is where the boundaries get murky between viewing applied theatre as a work of art—thus requiring aesthetic critique— or as a development program, and thus appropriate for conventional monitoring and evaluation. Clearly there is crossover between the two, but this distinction can be part of the reason that not enough applied theatre gets evaluated to demonstrate the impact it often has. In *Applied Theatre: International Case Studies and Challenges for Practice,* Monica Prendergast and Juliana Saxton write that "many practitioners do not pay much attention to assessment because, in the end, they know that whatever they may value and offer in proof, they can often be wrong," but go on to assert "the need and the importance of considering project assessment as a fundamental component of effective practice and, importantly, central to advocating for the field itself" (2009, p. 197).

In the article "Drama for Change? Prove it! Impact Assessment in Applied Theatre," Michael Etherton and Tim Prentki distinguish between "monitoring and evaluation," which happens within the scope of a project design and is concerned with assessing its immediate impact, and "impact assessment," which is concerned with measuring impact months and years after a project has ended (2006, pp. 139–140). They go on to advise that appropriate indicators be devised (2006, p. 147) and, more generally, that programs be designed to gather appropriate qualitative and quantitative data with which to conduct an evaluation. Applied theatre practitioner, Sheila Preston, advises that "in order that such research is not extractive (and contrary to the aims of the programme), this needs to be a fully people centered process" (Prentki & Preston 2008, p. 305).

I will be analyzing the three case studies in this book to detect what indicators they are utilizing and how they are using those to monitor and evaluate the impact of applied theatre for women's participation. The ways in which this is done in a gender-sensitive and participatory manner will be especially noted. It is my hope that this will contribute to an ongoing scholarly conversation of how we can continue to advance accessible tools to monitor and evaluate the impact of applied theatre for women's participation. I am especially interested in ways that applied theatre itself can be used as a tool to involve women in their own monitoring and evaluation. For resource-poor NGOs, this could be an accessible way to measure if they are achieving their goals and verify that their projects are improving lives.

Analysis of case studies

In this book, I analyze three organizations that have utilized applied theatre for women's participation. Each chapter will establish the context for the applied theatre; examine how the applied theatre was designed; identify outcomes; examine monitoring, evaluation, and impact; and conclude with lessons learned and recommendations. Each chapter will also use these case studies to illustrate and expand on some of the underlying issues, challenges, and problems facing the use of theatre to support the participation of women in their own sustainable development.

Though I will include in my writing many examples of applied theatre beyond my direct experience, the three primary case studies will be drawn from organizations with whom I have direct experience: Starfish One by One in Guatemala; the Appropriate Rural Technology Institute in India; and Population Media Center in Ethiopia. When writing about the three case studies, I will be writing about their work far beyond the extent to which I was involved. Representing three different continents, the organizations are all established and successfully making impressive progress for women in development. Each uses applied theatre in a different manner and to a different extent. Starfish One by One in Guatemala has only had outside applied theatre artists come to work with them, but wants to incorporate it more into their core programming. The founder and many staff members within the Appropriate Rural Technology Institute in India have used applied theatre as a tool to further their programming *and* have had an outside applied theatre facilitator come to further them in their efforts. In Ethiopia, the Population Media Center primarily uses education-entertainment for its programming, which I include as a form of applied theatre. The hope is that readers will find multiple entry points within this continuum, and that a wide range of approaches in which applied theatre can be used by individuals and organizations will be demonstrated.

My analysis of each case study will be structured as follows:

1. Description of the organization's mission, background, and programs; their stance on gender; their sustainable development aims; how the organization is funded; and a description of how I worked with this organization.
2. Site description, including relevant local gender information, religion, language, political climate, history, culture, and other factors that are relevant for situating the work of the organization.
3. Description of the applied theatre; goals, and indicators for measuring if those goals are achieved; design of the applied theatre; and outcomes.
4. Monitoring and evaluation of the applied theatre project or program, and the impact assessment measuring the impact of the applied theatre months and years after the project's completion.
5. Recommendations; lessons learned from their work; successes and failures; my observations; and comments and recommendations from key personnel and program participants.

The concluding chapter to the book will reflect on the general lessons ꞏ from the case studies and the numerous other programs examined to a lesser e. throughout the book. These lessons will include (a) characteristics common programs that successfully use applied theatre for women to participate in their own sustainable development, (b) strategies that have proven effective, (c) useful approaches or tactics, and (d) areas where further research and innovation are still needed.

Conclusion

In reference to Theatre for Development in Africa, author Osita Okagbu writes, "Central to my thinking is a basic concern with the issue of whether an appropriate methodology and conceptualization of the form has been theorized or developed to ensure a successful realization of the objective of the genre. Is there, for instance, a need to articulate a unique methodology and practice that takes into account the peculiarities of the African context? Which practices and methodologies work and which do not and why?" (1998, p. 23). Likewise in this book I develop and theorize an appropriate methodology and conceptualization of applied theatre for women's participation in sustainable development. Attention is given to what unique methodologies and practices need to be taken into account in this context. The ultimate goal of this book is to ensure a successful realization of the objective—women's participation in sustainable development—through the specific genre of applied theatre.

3 Starfish One by One

Education for young women in Guatemala

When I was working with the girls in Starfish One by One, I often heard the girls referring to the state of becoming a 'professional' in a reverent, slightly dreamy way. It was this singular word that seemed to propel these girls along to try new things and sacrifice immediate comforts for a better future.

Journal, July 2009, Osnes

Starfish One by One is a small, and relatively young, nonprofit organization dedicated to serving as a catalyst for the education of rural Mayan girls in Guatemala (see Photo 3.1) by enhancing the educational opportunities as well as the spiritual and emotional well-being of children and their families (Starfish One by One 2010). Starfish One by One awards scholarships to high-achieving girls in the sixth grade who would otherwise not be able to continue their studies due to financial and cultural obstacles. They partner with each girl's parents, mentors, and other organizations in creating support groups for mostly female students. These young women will become the agents of change for their families and their communities.

Photo 3.1 Students at Starfish One by One.

This organization is named after a parable that encapsulates this organization's mission and philosophy. Though versions of the story vary, the basic story is of a child on a beach at low tide throwing beached starfish back into the water. An adult accompanying the child points to the beach, which is littered with thousands of starfish, and says that she should give up the effort since there is no way she can save all of the starfish. The child's response, as she picks up another starfish and throws it back into the ocean, is, "But I can save this one."

Background

Starfish One by One was created in 2007 by the original cofounders of Friendship Bridge (www.friendshipbridge.org), Ted and Connie Ning, and Mimi Schlumberger. Friendship Bridge conducted microcredit for women in Vietnam and more currently in Guatemala. Though Friendship Bridge continues to operate in Guatemala, the three founders decided to offer their assistance farther upstream in a woman's life, before she missed out on the opportunity for an education. Starfish focuses on girls precisely at the age when many are not allowed to continue their schooling, and works primarily in communities near Lake Atitlan.

Programs

Starfish One by One's program consists of three tiers: academic scholarships for attending middle and high school; mentors for support throughout this time; and the bridge program that helps the girls transition into a life as a professional.

1. Academic Scholarships. Costs related to school and the time a girl spends at school studying represent a double burden for families living in poverty. Starfish provides scholarships for a limited number of qualifying girls to ensure six years of secondary education. Without scholarships, these young women would not be able to attend school past sixth grade. Girls are selected according to their aptitude, leadership qualities, their family's lack of financial ability to pay for schooling, and the family and student's willingness to commit to the requirements of the program. These requirements include meeting rigorous academic standards, attending weekly mentoring sessions, and doing community service work. Once in the program, the girls are formed into groups of 15, which stay together through middle and high school. The strong bond created by the girls helps sustain their journey on this new path (see Photo 3.2).

2. Mentors. Starfish employs mentors to guide young students through their education. Each female Mayan mentor meets with a group of 15 girls on a weekly basis for the duration of middle and high school. In addition to providing academic support, the mentor works with each girl to strengthen her talents and leadership abilities. Each girl receives information pertaining to a wide variety of subjects, such as reproductive education, personal finance, social responsibility, and environmentalism. For instance, for personal finance development each girl is guided through the process of opening and maintaining a bank account. This simple task is extremely intimidating to the girls at the onset, since few of their families—and

Photo 3.2 A Starfish One by One student receiving direction from Norma Bajan, In-Country Director for Starfish One by One.

certainly not the women in their families—have ever had a bank account or can even understand how it functions. With guidance from the mentors, girls gain confidence from these kinds of accomplishments and the skill and experience they will need to forge a new life.

The mentor is a woman who is from the same community as the girls and shares their dialect. She also shares the experience of poverty, a large family, and parents who never attended school. Mentors are university-level professionals who model the behavior and skills that each girl needs to be an effective professional and leader in her community. They serve as mighty champions and fierce advocates for these girls in the face of obstacles to this new path for Guatemalan women. The mentors are truly recognized as being at the center of all the work done by the organization.

3. The Bridge. To help the girls transition into their unique career paths beyond graduation, Starfish assigns experienced guides to support each in applying her unique skills and passions into a profession. The Bridge program begins in the girl's tenth grade, the year she starts high school. Since these girls are forging new ground with new behavior for women within their families and culture, they benefit from a guide who will help them identify and navigate attending university, doing an internship, or exploring a business opportunity. Although Starfish had originally conceived of these guides as business-oriented people from outside their organization, the bond between each girl and her mentor has proven so strong that they now have the mentors also serving as these guides. The guides bring practical experience that they can share while guiding girls in planning their career trajectory. Each guide is singularly focused on ensuring that each young woman applies her unique talents for the betterment of herself, her family, and her community. The guide supports each girl in creating and following a life plan that outlines her short, medium, and long-term goals. This is done to provide entry into the professional world that was previously a mystery to the young women in the Starfish program. Upon graduation from high school and the Starfish program, each young woman is equipped with a plan that makes possible her transition into the role of a professional and a leader (Starfish One by One 2012b).

The mentor's role is to be the connector of each girl with the different opportunities around her, coaching her but not doing it for her. For example, a Starfish student named Yolanda did her formal internship with Starfish as an administrative assistant. She is very interested in starting a small business. Her mentor, Norma Bajan, has been working with Yolanda on the launch of a small business that produces and sells washable sanitary napkins, since there is a big demand for viable alternatives to disposable sanitary napkins in their community, and all over the developing world. Norma has been working individually with Yolanda as they have researched different designs and locally available materials. Now that Yolanda has graduated, she is pursuing this full-time. With a small loan, she and another Starfish girl have started production. They will lean heavily on Norma for contacts to women's cooperatives and other possible marketing opportunities, but Norma will only make the connection and prepare the girls for the actual sales pitch. Norma will not engage in any of the actual production or sales.

Stance on gender

Although the founders of Starfish have a long record of working towards gender equity for women through their work with Friendship Bridge, it was learning about the Girl Effect that (in part) inspired them to refocus their efforts towards girls (see Photo 3.3). Travis Ning, the current executive director of Starfish, cites the Girl Effect as providing Starfish One by One with its theoretical foundation and its evidence base for their programming.

The Girl Effect identifies girls as one of the most powerful and untapped forces on the planet, and works systemically to invest in their futures (NoVo 2013). It is now a prominent international social movement of which Starfish One by One is informally a part. This movement is comprised of programs on the ground, and a powerful network of organizations cooperating to add expertise, build the knowledge base, raise awareness, and drive investments to adolescent girls (Nike 2013). The Girl Effect was started through the sponsorship of Warren Buffet's NoVo Foundation and the Nike Foundation. It is based on a now common belief in the field of international development that when given the opportunity, women and girls are more effective than their male counterparts at lifting themselves and their families out of poverty. When women and girls earn income, they reinvest 90% of it into their families, as compared to only 30 to 40% for a man (Fortson 2003).

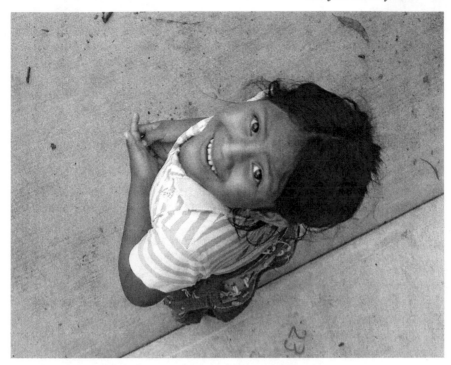

Photo 3.3 A Guatemalan girl.

The Girl Effect asserts that to end poverty, the best strategy is to invest time, energy, and funding into adolescent girls, because girls are uniquely capable of investing in their communities and making the world a better place. They also list what they identify as the top 10 things that stand in the way of girls reaching their full potential:

1. **Let's See Some ID**—Many girls in the developing world do not have a formal birth certificate, which then makes it near impossible for them to prove their age in order to avoid child marriage, open a bank account, vote, or even get a job.
2. **Illiteracy Does Not Look Good on a Resume**—A majority of the world's children who have left school are girls. This makes it hard for them to learn and advance as well as threatens their personal safety.
3. **Pregnancy Does Not Look Good on a Little Girl**—Child marriage is a common practice in the areas where girls are marginalized. Their bodies are not considered their property and thereby are subject to violence and abuse.
4. **The Face of HIV Is Increasingly Young and Female**—Educating girls in HIV prevention has shown considerably positive results, but the girls also need to be supported to make empowered choices.

5. **A Nice Place to Work Would Be Nice**—Girls need to be trained on financial literacy and given the proper opportunities to work in a safe environment, which can provide training for their future endeavors leading to economic independence.
6. **The Check Is in the Mail But It's Going to Your Brother**—A small percentage of the world's aid goes to girls, but when they are given the opportunity, they will reinvest in the community at a much higher rate than their male counterparts.
7. **Adolescent Girls Aren't Just Future Women**—Girls are living now, so they deserve programs designed for them in the present, not for their future as mothers.
8. **Laws Were Made to Be Enforced**—Many of the world's nations have laws to protect girls, but the key is ensuring that governing bodies are enforcing these laws.
9. **She Should Be a Statistic**—Girls have been consistently left out of research. Annual statistical reports need to be produced concerning the welfare of the world's girls.
10. **Everyone Gets on Board or We're All Overboard**—For this campaign to be effective, everyone needs to understand and buy into the campaign (The Girl Effect 2013).

Investing in girls tends to set a positive cycle in motion that can interrupt the usual progression of a woman's life that locks her and her family into a life of poverty. This usual progression includes an early dropout rate from school, early marriage, and a large number of offspring. Education can be key in setting a girl's life in a different, more positive direction. If girls are in school, they have less of a chance of becoming pregnant, as education is directly tied to birth rate (National Center for Health Statistics 1997). If they stay in school they will very likely be able to get a better paying, more secure job, or to know how to secure financing to lift themselves out of poverty. When they do have children, they will understand the importance of education and health care, all of which will continue the positive cycle (Banerjee & Duflo 2011).

Sustainable development aims

Starfish's primary focus is the education of young Mayan women. They are focusing on the prevention of negative influences impacting women's lives, rather than treatment of those negative influences. Their no-nonsense approach is simply that the odds for success are better with prevention than treatment. Given limited resources, Starfish identifies this approach as being able to leverage resources for the most positive social change. Education is the focus of this effort because of the overwhelming evidence that this primary factor unleashes so much change for girls' futures and the future of their families and communities.

Woven consistently throughout Starfish's programming is an emphasis on commitment to the community, not just personal ambition. Starfish is focused on quality

Photo 3.4 Mentor Vilma Saloj (woman on the left) with a Starfish student.

over quantity and adheres to the philosophy for change "through one, change many." If some indigenous Mayan girls are able to reach high heights of achievement, they will raise the level of what is possible for all. As stated by Travis Ning, "We have a conviction that comes from data. It's not just what feels good; the Girl Effect works. For a small organization with limited funds, it is the best bet for making an authentic impact" (Ning, Bajan, & Saloj 2012).

For one of Starfish's mentors, Vilma Saloj (in Photo 3.4), her aim is for the first female president of Guatemala to be a Starfish graduate. She mentioned one of their students, Irma, as an example of a girl who has such qualities. Irma ran for president of her class and wants to get a regional government position someday, but Vilma wants her to go to the top. For herself, Vilma shared that she also would not mind aspiring to the office of president, perhaps starting with running for mayor or senator first.

Funding

Starfish does not receive Girl Effect funding from NoVo or Nike Inc., but rather is supported by individual and institutional supporters. Roughly 30% of costs are supported by foundations, and 70% by individuals. Individual sponsors pay for a partial scholarship (and sometimes mentorship—depending on the amount) that ensures school access for each girl. Unrestricted funding and foundation support covers the other costs like mentorship, supervision, transportation, innovation, monitoring. and evaluation (Ning et al. 2012).

Description of how I worked with this organization

I first met the Starfish cofounders, Connie and Ted Ning, when a mutual friend brought them to my original solo performance, *M-other* (www.mothertour.org) in 2008 when it was premiering in Boulder before touring as a part of the *MOTHER tour*. Given our shared focus on women in sustainable development, Connie and I met to decide how the *MOTHER tour* could work with Starfish One by One. Meanwhile, the Philanthropiece Foundation (Philanthropiece 2013), which was partnering with Mothers Acting Up in supporting the *MOTHER tour*, expressed their desire for me to take the tour to Guatemala in 2009 to work with another of their partners, Limitless Horizons Ixil (discussed at the beginning of Chapter 1). Therefore, in addition to working with LHI in Chajul, we expanded the *MOTHER tour* in Guatemala to include several weeks in the Lake Atitlan area where Starfish's programming takes place.

Connie also worked with Sue Patterson, the founder of Women's International Network for Guatemalan Solutions (WINGS), which works to improve the lives of Guatemalan families by providing them with education, access, and advocacy in family planning, reproductive health, and other public health programs and services. We wanted WINGS to also benefit from the *MOTHER tour* being in Guatemala (WINGS 2013). With Philanthropiece, WINGS hosted the performance of *M-other* on July 2, 2009, in their Antigua headquarters for a group of about 70 people, primarily English-speaking staff members and student interns of NGOs working in Guatemala. The codirectors and the program coordinator for Philanthropiece were in attendance at the performance as well. The postperformance discussion with this group created—as they do in diverse groups around the world—"occasions for interpersonal communication" (Samba 2005, p. 25) on shared concerns. Later that month, after working in Chajul with LHI, I traveled to the Lake Atitlan area to present four Vocal Empowerment Workshops for Starfish. Participating in these workshops with me were two University of Colorado (CU) undergraduate theatre students, Chelsea Hackett and Kelly Gibson.

Upon returning from this trip, Chelsea formed a student group—Performers Without Borders—at CU and was able to secure funding from the Philanthropiece Foundation for her and several other students to return to Guatemala in 2010 to work with Starfish One by One and several other organizations using applied theatre. Though I did not travel on this trip with these students, they consulted with me before going and used the framework of the Vocal Empowerment Workshop from the *MOTHER tour* for much of the work they did.

Site description

Guatemala is a country of contrasts. It boasts beautiful mountains and lakes, mighty Maya ruins such as Tikal, and a rich cultural heritage. Yet it also is marked by extreme poverty, illiteracy, and disease. Guatemala is a country in Central America bordered by Mexico to the north and west, the Pacific Ocean to the southwest, Belize to the east, the Caribbean Sea to the east, and El Salvador and Honduras to the

Southeast. Before the Spanish invasion in 1524 and independence from Spain in 1821, no nation called Guatemala existed (Grandin, Levenson, & Oglesby 2011, p. 11). What we now identify as Guatemala is part of what was once an expansive Maya civilization. Since at least 15,000 BCE, people in these areas had thrived until Maya city-states appeared in what is now the Valley of Guatemala around 250 BCE. Great city-states arose in the CE 200s and "then declined precipitously after about CE 800 for many interwoven reasons, including land overuse, drought, and endemic internecine war. Scholars still vigorously debate the causes of the Maya city-states' decline" (Grandin et al. 2011, p. 11).

Through the 1500s and 1600s, the many native tribes of the area were conquered by the Spanish, who brought the Catholic religion along with their rule. Guatemala finally gained independence from Spain in 1821. At the onset of the twentieth century, the US United Fruit Company started becoming a major force in Guatemala and set the stage for conflict between foreign capitalist interests and the indigenous people. This tension became most violent during the Guatemalan Civil War, which ran from 1960 to 1996. It was fought primarily between the US-backed military government forces of Guatemala and leftist rebel groups mainly supported by the Maya indigenous people, who mostly lived in poverty. During this time Guatemala experienced extreme unrest through mass terror and human rights abuses, and extreme violence. More than 600 massacres occurred, one and a half million people were displaced, and more than 200,000 civilians were murdered, most of them Maya (Sanford 2004). Daniel Wilkinson, author of *Silence on the Mountain,* writes that "the war in Guatemala had been one of the most brutal conflicts in the hemisphere in the twentieth century . . . with a military government allied with the United States battling a guerrilla movement" (Wilkinson 2004, p. 4). Wilkinson's book tells the story of how decades of terror led many Guatemalans to adopt a survival strategy of silence so complete it is said to verge on collective amnesia.

Although Spanish is the official language, there are 21 Mayan languages that are spoken, primarily in rural areas. Nearly 60% of the population is Ladino, or mixed Amerindian and Spanish, and the remaining 40% is primarily various Maya people, such as the K'iche, Kaqchikel, and Mam (Central Intelligence Agency [United States] 2013). For the indigenous Starfish girls, speaking Spanish with mistakes is a significant source of shame and shyness. For Starfish students, most only learn Spanish once they are in school and don't speak it fluently. Even in the senior year of high school, most cannot write Spanish and are challenged in speaking Spanish. Starfish students from Panajachel speak Kaqchikel; students from Santiago speak Tzutujil; while students in Chicacao speak Spanish.

Roman Catholicism is the dominant religion in Guatemala, and among the Maya it is often heavily infused with beliefs of pre-Columbian origin. Since the mid-twentieth century, there has been a surge of conversions to Evangelical Protestantism. According to Starfish Program Director Norma Bajan, the area where Starfish works is about half Catholic and half Evangelical, with the latter experiencing very recent growth. Bajan states that religious attitudes significantly influence the work they do with the students in a wide variety of ways. Since it is believed that God will provide and that whatever is happening is God's will, assertiveness is drained away almost to the state of apathy. People don't view themselves as having any personal agency. In addition to this, Norma states that there is a culture of not being able to complain, which serves to reinforce the status quo (Ning et al. 2012).

According to Starfish One by One's website, Guatemala continues to be one of the northern hemisphere's poorest countries. Child malnutrition is among the highest in the world; one out of every two children in Guatemala is chronically malnourished. High illiteracy rates and fertility rates keep families trapped in cycles of poverty (Starfish One by One 2012). One of the factors driving this level of poverty is extreme economic disparity within the country, with 80% of Guatemala's arable land being owned by wealthy ladinos (Starfish One by One 2012).

It should be noted that because Lake Atitlan—around which Panajachel and Santiago are situated—is a popular tourist destination, it is comparably more cosmopolitan and less isolated than other parts of Guatemala, such as Chajul. The allure of learning Spanish and English is higher due to the presence of tourists. The influence of this can be seen in a variety of ways: the students see different types of behavior; have more career opportunities; and benefit from better infrastructure, access to NGOs, and good roads. However, Chicacao, where Starfish also works, is hours from the lake and certainly not a common tourist destination.

Local gender information

The *Global Gender Gap Report 2010* ranks Guatemala as the lowest-ranking country in the Latin American and Caribbean regions and describes Guatemala as remaining "disadvantaged in the rankings because of a high gap on education, low political empowerment and low labour force participation" (Hausmann et al. 2010, pp. 26–27). To understand the Starfish girls' gender situation, a useful point of departure is demonstrated through the data collected from their mothers. For mothers of Starfish students, the average age at marriage is 18. The average age at first birth is 19. The average number of living children is six, and the average years in formal schooling is one and a half years (Starfish One by One 2012).

When interviewing Vilma Saloj and Norma Bajan—a Starfish mentor coordinator and the in-country director, who are both from the area where Starfish works—they described the local gender attitudes using the word 'machismo,' and described their community culture as very conservative. They described women as being quiet with no opinions of their own. They just take care of the kids, cook food, and clean the house. Starting in school, the children are taught to repeat what they are told with no personal opinion. Norma believes that local and national politicians take advantage of that characteristic of indigenous people. Vilma describes the lack of vision that comes from living in poverty. Poverty makes people live day to day so that they don't have the capacity to look up. Starfish works with the girls to build a concept of personal opinion and vision.

Starfish has found that dropout rates rise dramatically when a girl turns 12. This is when the "double burden" (higher costs of education and the fact that she is not generating income) of educating her becomes more acute. Likewise, as she enters puberty, families are far more reluctant to let her travel to school or be alone. The world of a girl past puberty becomes significantly smaller and she becomes increasingly isolated (Starfish One by One 2012). Menstruation becomes a barrier for participation in school, due to cultural attitudes and lack of adequate supplies such as sanitary napkins. Beyond that, Vilma notes that there is a lot of shame associated with puberty for girls that makes them go inside themselves and renders them less expressive. She said that these changes that girls go through physically and emotionally are not spoken about in families. When a girl has her period, there are many restrictions put on her, such as not being allowed to go outside, to play with younger children, or to talk with boys.

Another local gender factor that influences the work of Starfish is that young women in rural Guatemala frequently lack professional role models and guidance to help them identify their unique talents and apply them to a professional field. Prior to entering Starfish, the students usually only know of two or three professionals, such as a doctor, a teacher, or a nurse (Starfish One by One 2012b). This is one of the reasons that the close relationship between the students and the mentors is so important. Through the mentor, the student can begin to imagine the life of a professional and understand the path that professional woman took to get to that level of achievement.

In the description of the applied theatre workshop with the Starfish girls that is to follow, the girl's initial composure is characterized as somewhat closed with their arms wrapped around their torsos protectively, eyes downcast, and their voices soft. It should be noted that this seems to be the physical stance taken by these girls in what they perceive to be a public situation in which they are being asked to be expressive. When in their private moments—even the moments before the workshops started—the girls were chasing each other, laughing, and speaking with fuller voices; being effectively and much more broadly expressive. This workshop was attempting to give these girls the skills, experience, and confidence to begin working towards a strong *public* voice.

Local theatre history

Though there is a history of theatre in Guatemala, it should be made clear that the population reached by the applied theatre programming described in this chapter has likely had very little to no exposure to theatre or even knowledge of its existence. Most theatrical activity has centered around Guatemala City—the capital of Guatemala and a huge urban center—which is very foreign to most rural indigenous Guatemalans. It still may be useful to touch on some highlights of the theatrical history and practice of Guatemala, as it may grant some insight into the national character and culture of which the Starfish program is a part.

An indigenous Maya drama, the *Rabinal Achi,* exists from centuries before the arrival of the Spanish. It is a commemorative drama that enacts a conflict between two city states and is still performed in the city of Rabinal (Tedlock 2005). The area's first Dominican Christian missionaries—charged with evangelizing the territory that included Mexico and Guatemala—taught traders songs and verses and asked them to disseminate them in their travels, which suggests a rudimentary kind of theatre (Damasceno et al. 1993, p. 55).

Throughout the twentieth century, Latin American popular theatre moved away from entertainment and toward the socially relevant, consciousness-raising—intended to result in calls for action. An article by Michael Millar entitled "Popular Theatre and the Guatemalan Peace Process" examines the development and performance of the play *No hay cosa oculta que no venga a descubrirse* in the Guatemalan community of Santa María Tzejá. Recounting the memories of refugees who returned in 1992, this play was produced for the purpose of collective social transformation (Millar 2006).

In his book *Grappling with Atrocity: Guatemalan Theater in the 1990s,* John Shillington writes, "The atrocities committed in the civil war have become a prominent subject in the theater in the 1990s. The theatre in the 1990s has changed its emphasis from the provocative, revolutionary style characteristic of the late 1960s and 1970s. Instead, this theater seeks a balance between acknowledging the atrocities of the war and fostering a national reconciliation" (Shillington 2002, p. 13).

Proyecto Payaso, of Quetzaltenango (Proyecto Payaso 2012), is a clown troupe based in Guatemala that performs shows about HIV and AIDS to indigenous communities throughout Central America (Dempsey 2009). This nonprofit organization sees clowning as a powerful way to address issues surrounding sexuality, such as condom use, safe sex, and what is important in a relationship. By collaborating with health educators in rural health clinics, Proyecto Payaso provides education in an entertaining manner and breaks down boundaries of what can be spoken about in the community. The clowns use indigenous language in their performances and workshops, after which they distribute educational materials and condoms.

Vilma Saloj told a story about when Proyecto Payaso visited her high school years ago. She remembers how they made everyone in the audience turn to a partner and look into each other's eyes, which she said everyone found very difficult. Next, after blindfolding and giving a scarf to each student, they asked the students to creatively move the scarf, suggesting such images as being in a forest with the scarf as a snake that was running away. The fact that they were so expressive was so inspiring to Vilma that she reports using that experience to inspire one of her girls who had to do a monologue for school and was terrified. Summoning her creative courage, Vilma said she modeled performing the piece with a full voice and grand gestures for the girl. After that, the girl nailed it, although it was difficult to get her to do some of the gestures (Ning et al. 2012).

When traveling in Guatemala in 2009 we were told about a rather recent governmental mandate that required theatre to be taught in all public schools. It was unclear how many teachers were actually doing this, or had the skills or experience to lead these kinds of activities. Staff members at LHI in Chajul said that they did not believe it was being taught at all, since there was no training or materials provided by the government for teachers to fulfill this requirement. It is interesting to note the political will at the national level to increase exposure to and participation in theatre. This certainly opens up opportunities for theatre artists of all kinds wanting to work in Guatemala. Though this mandate will not likely result in funding for theatre in Guatemalan schools—which are woefully underfunded—it does provide incentive for teachers and school administrators to be open to theatre.

Description of applied theatre

Thus far, the formal use of applied theatre within the organization Starfish One by One has primarily been through outside facilitators working with the staff and students. In this chapter, I will focus primarily on the Vocal Empowerment Workshops that I led in 2009 with the two CU students—Chelsea and Kelly—for the students of Starfish. I will also briefly touch on two other experiences Starfish had with applied theatre: the work led by Chelsea in 2010 and work done by an outside consultant named Rebecca who worked with Starfish to teach them about Invisible Theatre. Norma and Vilma of Starfish did not remember Rebecca's full name or much about the visit, but referenced that work in our discussion of applied theatre.

Goals of workshop

Through discussions with the Starfish staff in the months preceding our visit, together we articulated the goals of the workshops on several levels. The overarching goal for the workshop was—as stated from the girl's perspective—"to make our voices strong so we can reach our dreams." Supporting that was the goal for the girls to have a physical experience of their public voices as strong and expressive. Integral to that goal was for each girl to experience her voice as coming from her entire body and for that body to grow in its expressive range. From these experiences, the goal was for each girl to gain an increased sense of individual vocal confidence, which they could use to communicate decisions they would make about their own lives, which relates to empowerment. We also wanted the students to consider various ways in which they could use their voices, singularly and communally, to advance them in their desired life trajectory. Connie Ning had specifically mentioned in the planning stage that she would like the workshop to support the girls in steering away from gossipy or negative use of their voices, towards a more supportive way of being and speaking about and to each other. From this emerged another goal for the workshop: to help students increase the solidarity between themselves and to realize how they could use their voices to mutually support each other.

Given these goals, the indicators to measure if goals had been met were as follows. The first indicator was an increase in the strength of each girl's voice, as experienced by each girl and observed by those present. Strength was measured by volume, physical support of the voice for fullness, bodily composure, and directedness or eye contact while speaking. Observations of girls' physical range of motion—such as how far they were willing to raise their arms—could be observed, and indicated any increase in range of physical expression. To measure how long these girls would be able to sustain this increased vocal strength and expressive range, we relied upon continued correspondence with the mentors.

That is why it was important to have the mentors participating in the workshops so they could draw from the workshop to sustain the work towards a strong voice in the years to come. Indicators for increased confidence with their voices was measured in part by their ability and willingness to participate in the more advanced improvised portions of the workshop. This also indicated their ability to apply their strong voices and expressive ranges to their individual dreams for the future. Their increased ability to support each other's strong voices in a positive way was indicated by their willingness and ability to apply new tools and methods towards that purpose throughout the workshop experience.

Design of workshop

The base design of the Vocal Empowerment Workshop from the *MOTHER tour* was used to design the Starfish workshop (MOTHER tour 2011). We called the workshop *Making Our Voices Strong to Help Our Dreams Come True*, to represent the design and intent of the workshop. I changed from the use of the phrase "vocal empowerment" to "strong voices" because it is difficult to translate the word *empowerment* in many languages, including Spanish. We did the workshop four times for four different groups of Starfish girls. The workshops for the girls in Santiago were three hours long each, and two hours long each in Panajachel. Both towns are located on Lake Atitlan. Many of the girls in their program live in outlying areas and have to bus to their weekly Starfish mentoring meetings. Each workshop had at least one mentor also in attendance participating. We conducted these workshops in the open space in which the mentoring groups usually met—an open rectangular room with chairs or benches along the outside walls. There were approximately 15 girls in each session. I co-led the workshops with Kelly and Chelsea, with Chelsea doing the majority of the translating. One of the mentors, Candelaria, also did some translating at two of the workshops. I spoke some rudimentary Spanish, and it should be remembered that even the Starfish students were not completely fluent in Spanish. We certainly relied upon movement, gestures, and leading by showing to also communicate with each other. Although each of the four workshops we offered varied and evolved slightly, I will be describing the experience primarily as a sort of compilation of the experience of all four workshops as one. I will note any differences or changes that we made when necessary, to make a point and convey a lesson learned.

We began the session by all standing in a circle doing warm-up exercises, intending to establish a safe and comfortable tone, energize the space, get to know the girls' names, and nurture a feeling of community in the group. Although these girls were accustomed to being in community together, they were *not* accustomed to having three American women be a part of that community. With the mentor, we briefly introduced ourselves and the goals of the workshop, and explained that this would be an active time together. With the 'name game' we began by throwing a ball to a person while saying that person's name. Then that person passed the ball to a different person while saying her name, and repeated this pattern until everyone had caught and thrown the ball. That pattern of throwing continued to be repeated until I eventually added another ball into this pattern to make the exercise even more challenging.

For the next warm-up exercise we had each girl say her favorite color and add a motion that involved her whole body. Directly following each girl's motion, the entire group imitated that motion in a wave around the circle. Then Kelly led an exercise called 'the human knot' for which we started with all the girls standing in a tight bunch. Kelly directed the girls to reach across the circle and grab another girl's hand. Then they were to reach with the other hand and grab a second girl's hand. Then the challenge is for the group to untie themselves working together as a community (without releasing each other's hands).

Next, I led the group in what I called 'the 1, 2, 3 for a strong voice.' I began with number one, getting your body relaxed. In the first relaxation exercise, I instructed them to stand with their legs apart and knees slightly bent and to swing their arms up as they inhaled and to swing their arms down as they exhaled. I asked everyone to exhale on an open "ahh" sound. I added that the release of breath should feel like a release of tension or nervousness. We then 'shook' out tension by doing eight shakes with the left hand, then eight with the right, eight with the left foot, and lastly eight with the right foot. Then we decreased the number of shakes to four, then two, and finally one. I asked the girls to imagine they were shaking any tension or nervousness they felt out of their bodies.

To get the girls to open their throats for strong voices—number two of the '1, 2, 3 for a strong voice'—I asked each girl to force a yawn saying, "Look around at each other; they're contagious." I asked each girl to notice how her throat opened when she yawned. While maintaining that open throat, I asked everyone to let out a yawn on an open "ahh" sound while stretching her arms outward. Holding my hand on my stomach over my diaphragm and abdominal muscles, I asked them to also feel how these muscles had to support their sound when their throat was open. "Listen to the quality and the strength of the sound you can make when your throat is open," I prompted before asking them to all make an open "ahh" sound while imagining they were also yawning.

To give direction to their strong voices, number three of the '1, 2, 3 for a strong voice,' we focused on authentic contact. I had everyone break into groups of two and asked partners to stand facing each other at an arm's length. I asked them all to establish eye contact with their partners and—while maintaining that contact—to shake out their bodies while standing in place, like shaking dust out of a rag. While still shaking themselves out, I asked them to add an open "ahh" sound. Next, while still maintaining eye contact, I asked everyone to simultaneously stretch and yawn. After that was done, I asked them to repeat this yawn, adding to let the yawn out on an open "ahh" sound while still stretching. Then, while still maintaining eye contact, I asked each girl—one partner at a time—to declare her dream for her future profession to her partner with a full voice, from a relaxed state, with eye contact. Once that was completed, we moved back into our full circle, and I asked each girl—one at a time—to declare this same dream to the entire group, all while staying relaxed, keeping their throats open, and scanning the entire circle to make authentic contact with each person.

Our intention with the next exercise was for each girl to realize the strength she *already had* within herself, evident by the fact that she was already part of a program to change her course in life, and to show her how that strength could be drawn upon in the journey ahead. Sitting in a circle, we explained this goal and asked each girl to use her voice to tell a one-minute story of her past that explained how she had the strength to be where she was today. A secondary goal for this activity was to simply commence getting the girls to use their strong voices in a semipublic setting, such as a workshop.

When the above exercise did not work, we improvised another way to achieve that secondary goal. We thought that providing a more direct question or prompt for them might help their ability to speak in front of the group. Thus, we identified situations in the future for which the girls might have to use their voices in public. The first was during an interview to progress to the next level of school, which the mentor said each girl would have to do. We did this by putting two chairs in the center of the circle and having the mentor portray the school official and one girl sit opposite her and answer the questions. The next prompt we did increased the challenge of the exercise; we had a girl stand alone and face us all and pretend she was invited to speak about the Starfish One by One program at a school assembly. The final prompt we devised was for a girl to pretend to speak with the first lady of Guatemala about the importance of education for girls.

This exercise in particular elicited a lot of giggling from the girls. There had previously been giggling too, but it had been a more shared expression of excitement and nervousness. The difference in the giggling here was that it seemed to be directed at the girl who was trying out new behavior by using her strong voice in a public setting. The effect of the giggling on the girl trying new behavior was that it most often made her retract and either curl in on herself *or* also get infected by giggling and lose the composure needed to attempt the exercise. Therefore, though this was not part of the plan we had created for the workshop, giggling was clearly a significant obstacle to everything we had intended for the workshop, so I improvised a way to address giggling. I stopped the scene in which the girl was pretending to talk about Starfish to a school assembly, and asked her if the giggling made it harder for her to do what she was attempting. She, of course, said yes. Identifying giggling as an obstacle to having a strong voice, I led the girls in an exercise that might help them to work through their giggles so they could be more supportive of each other. Since giggling is often a nearly uncontrollable response to nervousness, I suggested a way that they could take back control over themselves. We all took in a deep breath together, and slowly let it out, focusing on relaxing to regain composure and let the giggles subside. If the giggles reemerged at any point during the workshop to the point where it seemed to obstruct a girl's ability to try something new, I would simply identify the obstacle again and once more lead everyone through the breathing exercise.

For our next activity, called "Overcoming Obstacles," we asked the girls to arrange themselves in groups of similar occupational dreams, such as doctors, secretaries, teachers, or nurses. We asked each girl to think of realizing her dream as a journey from point A to point B, along which she would almost certainly encounter many obstacles. Starting with the nurses, we put them all at the starting line at point A. The others sat to the side as observers who could offer their ideas when appropriate. Our assumption in splitting them up was that similar professions would likely encounter similar obstacles, so they could travel the journey together. It was also a practical necessity since there was not sufficient time to have each girl enact the journey separately, nor would a solitary journey accurately depict how they would likely travel.

In the room we marked an imaginary line to indicate point A where the girls were now, and, on the opposite side of the room, another imaginary line to indicate point B, the fulfillment of their dreams—thereby mapping out the journey to becoming a professional. I challenged the girls to identify three potential obstacles to their dream. When one girl said that money would be a problem, I asked the girls how we should represent that obstacle. One girl suggested it could be a bank from which the girls would have to try and borrow money. A mentor suggested it could also be a relative from whom a girl might try and borrow money. So we had two of the observers represent the banker and the relative. We had those two girls stand together a few steps from the starting line, point A. The next obstacle the girls identified was a father who would want the girl to stay at home to help with chores and generate income instead of attending school. Thus we had another observer portray a father and placed her a few steps further from the starting line. They identified a sick mother as the final obstacle, so we had a girl portray the mother just a few steps before the finish line, point B.

With the likely journey set up, we had the group of girls begin their journey together from the starting line until they encountered the first obstacle blocking the path. After fully engaging with and attempting to resolve this obstacle to all the girls' satisfaction, the girls were allowed to progress to the next obstacle. We had the girls act out an improvised scene with the given obstacle, and stopped the action to suggest and critique possible alternatives (the mentor led this conversation for the most part). An important aspect of this exercise is that the girls on the journey were individually challenged to come up with ways to get over each obstacle, but, beyond that, the girls observing were helping to critique the viability of the solutions offered. Everyone was allowed to share suggestions or make slight adjustments to the solutions put forth by the girls on the journey. The intent was to make this representation of the journey realistic and rigorous.

With the group of girls who all dreamed of becoming doctors, we replicated this same structure with a slight variation that was intended to help the girls understand how they could support each other through obstacles. This time, instead of having each obstacle obstruct all the girls who wanted to be doctors, we had the first obstacle only be in the way of *one* girl in the group. In this example the obstacle for the one girl was pregnancy. The girls were challenged to devise ways that they could work together to help this one girl still journey towards her dream, while having to deal with parents who wanted her to get married and the added responsibility of caring for a child. At the next obstacle, a different girl was challenged with a difficult situation for which she needed the support of her friends. The girls were given the opportunity to experience supporting someone else in overcoming obstacles, and in receiving support themselves.

To strengthen the ideas brought forth by the last activity, we had the girls form two rows facing each other. We had them lock arms across the two rows, some letting their arms hang low, and some holding their arms up high, like the roof of a house. Then one by one, we had each girl travel through this tunnel, which spatially was set up so the start line and the finish line were the same as the previous exercise, with the arms as the obstacles. Some girls climbed over the arms blocking their way, some under. Then trying a variation on this last exercise, we had the girls pass through the two rows again in a similar way, but this time they had to use their voices to gain passage beyond each obstacle. To get past the arms blocking her way, a girl had to say in a strong voice—with full eye contact—to each person blocking her way, "Con permiso" ("With permission?"). Only if this was spoken as such would the girl be allowed to pass.

One of our last activities was to have each girl take 14 beads of her favorite color (or however many girls there were in the workshop). Then, one by one, they were invited to go around and collect a bead from each girl. When a girl gave someone a bead, she had to use her strong voice and say, "I give you one of my yellow beads." Then, eventually, they ended up with one bead of each girl's favorite color. Giving each girl a piece of twine, we instructed them to string the beads to make a bracelet (see Photo 3.5) representing their Starfish community. Then we invited the girls, one at a time, to tie their string around the wrist of another girl while simultaneously gifting that girl with a statement of what quality the giver admired in the person receiving the bracelet. Then the whole group repeated the positive thing, so that everyone acknowledged each girl. We deliberately stretched the exchange from a private one between two people, into a more public chain of giving.

In closing the workshop, we asked the girls to each put their arm with the bracelet into the center of the circle. Joining hands, we invited them to say, "We have strong voices," and then raising that hand, turn, and extend the arm out as

Photo 3.5 Starfish girls with bracelets made in the workshop.

far out from the circle as possible, saying, "And we are taking them out into the world." Our intention here was for the bracelets to serve as a physical reminder of the workshop and of the experience and lessons learned. Another variation on this closing was to have all the girls cross their arms, right over left, in a big circle, and join hands while all facing the inside of the circle. Then we all said together, "We are women with strong voices," and then spinning outwards while still holding hands, we said, "and we are taking them out into the world." We ended with our hands clasped and our arms fully extended upwards.

Outcomes of workshop

One outcome of our warm-up exercises and workshop was that all the girls spent several hours in community with three American women. They all participated in the workshop and were expressive—to varying degrees—within this expanded community; this, in and of itself, is an accomplishment. It gave them experience in using their voices in the presence of people from outside their immediate community, even from outside their nationality.

During the initial ball-toss exercise, the girls giggled extensively when they missed the ball and scurried to retrieve it quickly—seemingly to avoid prolonged attention. Compared to the exercises that followed, the girls were willing to have their arms move away from their torso when throwing and catching the ball; indeed, the task of throwing and catching a ball demands it. They seemed relatively confident doing a familiar activity—such as throwing a ball—with only the minor added challenge of having to say the receiver's name while throwing. Once there were two balls in the game, their focus was definitely challenged, as they had to prepare themselves to receive the next ball soon after having thrown the last.

The girls seemed to enjoy the chance to share what their favorite color was, though creating a movement to express that color seemed to be very challenging for them, and most resorted to a simple wave of the hand and forearm, with the elbow still held close to the torso. This was true even though Chelsea and Kelly went first, and each devised widely expressive movements to express their color. As Chelsea and Kelly's movements traveled around the circle in a wave, their movements were expressed much less expansively by the Starfish students.

The human knot exercise got the participants to expand their range of movement, since reaching across the tightly packed group of girls required them to raise their entire arm. The task of untangling themselves was extremely physical and required them to move their bodies on different levels. Each time we did this exercise, the mentors, Kelly and Chelsea, assisted the girls in figuring out who should go where to untangle themselves. The interesting thing about this exercise is that when the girls hold a different girl's hand in each of theirs, they mostly end up in one complete circle when they ultimately untangle themselves.

An overarching outcome of these warm-up exercises is that it got everyone to use their bodies and their voices together in a playful way. Having a specific and consuming task—such as the two balls going at once—helped to override self-consciousness. Having to cooperate to do some of the exercises—such as the human knot—is a skill that can be carried over into other shared activities among the girls in the future. Also, the fact that the girls simply had fun together while being physically and vocally expressive gives them a positive experience from which to draw when attempting to be expressive during the increasingly more challenging activities in the workshop, and later in life when making their dreams come true.

It should be noted how difficult it was for the majority of the girls to be expressive both vocally and physically, especially at the beginning of each workshop. For some it was quite severe, such as for a girl named Maria who appeared to be trying to back out of the circle into a corner with every cell in her body. If she was forced to speak, her hand involuntarily reached up to cover and protect her mouth. She was barely able to look up to meet another person's eyes. Observing her discomfort, I wondered if this was too much for her or inappropriate, given her stage of development. Here I looked to the mentors to guide our progress and would verbally check in with them when such questions arose. As a mother of a daughter the same age as many of these girls, I felt very comfortable nurturing what I perceived to be their needs and gave praise and encouragement generously. My own daughter Melisande—who was 14 at the time—was present at all of the workshops to take photographs and participated such that the girls could see I was her mother. However, I also realized it was my obligation to push them in learning new skills and trying new things. I was aware that I did not know the back-story to each girl's life and what trauma she may have been through or currently was enduring. I was keenly aware of the common axiom in development, "Do no harm," in these moments of negotiation, and relied upon the front work I had done with the mentors in planning for these workshops to feel comfortable asking what I was asking of the girls.

The exercise for relaxation—with the arms swinging upwards while inhaling and then released down on an open "ah" sound—was challenging for many of the participants, the majority of whom seemed to want to avoid having their elbows leave their torsos. However, as we repeated the exercise and continued to coax and then quickly praise each girl's wider expansion of movement, they did make significant progress and seemed to be proud of their accomplishments. They also seemed to be led by each other's expansion, and one girl's arms raised high over her head seemed to encourage another girl to do the same. Likewise, when one girl would let out her voice on a slightly louder "ah" sound, the others would increase the volume and strength of their voices.

The relaxation exercise—with hands and feet shaking out the tension—seemed easier and much more enjoyable for the girls, perhaps because of its silliness. It required the girls to count out loud together and move in quick succession; keeping track of how many shakes and with what hand or foot. Both of the relaxation exercises demonstrated how movement and voice combined can be used to release tension or nervousness. They also showed how a person can be relaxed and generate more energy simultaneously; how a person can be expressive and active and still be relaxed.

The yawning exercise is a great tool for overriding the censoring throat muscles that often constrict a full voice. This exercise gives the experience of using the voice without it being held back by the throat. Imagining you are about to yawn is also an easy trick for releasing the throat muscles. The girls seemed to enjoy this exercise since it was something familiar to them, but with a different purpose than expressing sleepiness or boredom.

In my experience, making authentic eye contact with a partner is extremely difficult for people the world over. It was especially difficult for the Starfish girls, who generally avoided eye contact by looking down and nearly crumbling into fits of giggling when trying to make contact. It took firm yet gentle persistence to get them to continue attempting to do the exercise. Giving them specific tasks helped them to maintain eye contact, as it seemed to lessen the intensity of contact or at least distract them from that intensity. Once in the big circle to declare each girl's dream, we explained that we would invite each girl to repeat her attempts to share her dream *until* she seemed somewhat relaxed, used a full voice, and made eye contact. The girls seemed to make a serious attempt once they realized they would be made to do it again if they did not. Since the mentor was the participating adult who knew the girls best, we had her take the lead enforcing and leading this portion.

As stated previously, it did not work when we asked each girl to tell a one-minute story about her inner strength that got her to where she was. When doing this at the first workshop—which was the only time we attempted this—the mentor, Candelaria, went first. She told a very moving story about her childhood. Only her father believed she could become a professional. Everyone else thought he was foolish and that she was stupid for trying. They kept telling her at every milestone, "Just because you made this one, doesn't mean you will make it past the next." Once she did become successful, they were proud of her and were glad when she started making money for all her brothers and sisters to go to school. The girls were very attentive and seemed involved in her story, but once asked to tell their own, there was silence and uncomfortable fidgeting. One girl tried but just said how happy she was to be a part of the Starfish program. So, at that point we took a small break and talked with the two mentors present to decide how we could get the girls to practice using their voices. That was when we decided we should ask the girls questions or give them a scenario instead of asking them to tell their own story. Once given the prompts, the girls managed to use their voices in this improvised scene, although giggling proved to be an unavoidable obstacle.

The outcome of the giggling was that it seemed to send a rippled message throughout the group that using a strong voice was not possible and, perhaps, that a single girl was foolish for even trying. My own impression of the giggling was that it was being used to shame those who tried to be other than meek and uncertain, and that it was an unconscious mechanism—perhaps even a manifestation of internalized oppression—for keeping others small and afraid. There are different kinds of giggling and laughter: some is an expression of amusement or a shared release of built-up tension or nervousness. Some kinds of giggling and laughter

Photo 3.6 A Starfish student uses her voice to improvise a school interview.

are targeted at an individual or behavior and are often shaming or censoring in their intent. To me, this giggling felt like a combination of both.

Simply identifying the giggling as an obstacle in a very matter-of-fact way seemed to interrupt the shame loop by *not* shaming the gigglers. The girls were willing to try the breathing exercise to disperse the giggling impulse, especially as they seemed to fear being giggled at themselves or losing their composure due to giggling. By the end of the workshop, we could mostly disperse the giggling by firmly but kindly insisting that we stop an exercise each time giggling obstructed an activity, in order to do breathing exercises to compose ourselves. We also talked with the students about how relaxation and full breath not only help disperse giggling, but also help maintain the composure that renders them less vulnerable to a fit of giggles. For girls especially, there is a need for peer support—rather than peer ridicule—of new behavior and attitudes. The new attitude underlying the use of a strong voice (see Photo 3.6) could be expressed as, "I am worthy and able to speak and use my voice to reach my dreams."

Once we had addressed the issue of giggling, we had a few volunteers improvise using their voices in public. The mentor Candelaria enacted interviewing two different girls for passage into the next level of school. Each time I interrupted the scene after a few minutes and asked the watching girls what they thought the student might do to have an even stronger voice. They gave suggestions such as, "Look up to Candelaria's eyes when answering her question," and "Hold your hands together in your lap so they don't fidget." Trying to keep these few suggestions in mind, we had them continue the scene for another minute or two. It was useful for the student to experience making adjustments to her manner of communicating with her voice and body, and for the watching girls to witness the marked improvement gained from small adjustments. The girls, in general, took the next two prompts very seriously: presenting at a school assembly about

Starfish and talking with the first lady about girl's education. Unsurprisingly, it was the girls who displayed the most confidence throughout the entire workshop who volunteered to do these rather challenging improvisations. We repeated the same format as before: having them improvise for a few minutes on the given prompt, stopping to give constructive suggestions, and then restarting the scene for another minute or so to incorporate those suggestions.

The outcome of the "Overcoming Obstacles" activity, in which the girls dreaming of similar professions journeyed from point A to point B together, was that the girls identified likely obstacles to achieving their dreams and experimented with solutions for overcoming them in a variety of ways, both collectively and singularly. Through this, they experienced how it took a strong voice to stand up to obstacles, such as a father who wants his daughter to stay home and help with chores rather than continue school. In one scenario, the girl convinced her father to allow her to stay in school by explaining how she would be able to help the family far more in the future if she was allowed to continue her education and secure a high-paying professional job. She could pay for her brothers and sisters to go to school, which in turn, would allow them all to provide for the father in his old age. While performing this scene, the girl's voice grew in volume, physical support, and composure—as her determination increased. Right when she broke from the scene at its conclusion, self-consciousness tinged with shame for being so forthright seemed to sneak back into her demeanor. When the entire group clapped and congratulated her on her achievement, some of her original confidence seemed to return. In a society in which women are neither expected to nor congratulated for confronting authority, she was truly looking to this new community for assurance for this new behavior. By witnessing and critiquing each other's performances, they learned that their physical presence was a part of their overall voice and included direct eye contact, planting their feet where they stood, and holding their bodies confidently.

It was powerful to witness the girls needing to work together to help the one facing an obstacle to her dream. In the example where the one girl dreaming to become a doctor was obstructed in her journey by an unexpected pregnancy, the other girls worked with her to devise ways to continue her studies. After much deliberation, they enacted approaching the head mistress—played by the mentor—to ask if she could go on leave and have her friends bring work to her so she could continue her studies at home. The mentor concurred that this was sometimes done in rare instances and was a viable solution. More than that, they helped the girl negotiate long-term childcare for her baby with an aunt, trading childcare during the week for childcare on the weekends. This entire activity required high-level critical engagement from the girls, both those witnessing and those journeying towards their dream. Through active dialogue, they improved upon their ideas until each one was deemed to be an authentically viable solution around a specific obstacle.

Since the previous activity was by far the most challenging and demanding on the girls, it was fun to reiterate lessons learned in an easier way. Having to crawl through, dip under, or step over the arms of the girls in the two rows was fun, and was more physically than mentally challenging. The second variations of this activity—where they verbally had to ask permission to pass through—got them all engaged in listening and rewarding each other for using a strong voice with direct eye contact. It set up a practice of them encouraging and rewarding each other's strong voices.

The first closings, in which the girls declared taking their strong voices out into the world as they extended their arms and bracelets outwards, was designed to symbolically represent how they could take their qualities out into the world. Indeed, they literally walked out of the workshop wearing the bracelet. The many colored beads represented each girl's unique qualities and dreams, and the bracelet itself represented their support of each other. The bracelets also served as a catalyst to help the girls integrate the experience of the workshop into their lives, since the colorful beads are likely to draw attention and cause others to ask about the bracelets, providing an opportunity to talk about the experience and incorporate it into their lives. The ceremonial gifting of the bracelets, and the personal recognition of each girl's qualities, brought an uplifting and affirming conclusion to the workshop. Since these girls will be encountering significant obstacles and challenges in breaking century-old patterns for Guatemalan women living in poverty, they need to nurture all the strength within themselves and their supporting communities to make their dreams come true.

The second version of the closing—in which participants spin out from the circle while holding hands declaring that they are taking their strong voices out into the world—changed the girls' focus from their insular community to the outside world, which they would all eventually graduate to. However, the fact that they were still holding hands reiterated that they would still have their supporting community to keep them strong. The last stance—in which the girls were all standing tall with their arms fully extended upwards, having just joined their strong voices in a declaration—was a testimony to how far each of them had increased their expressive range during the course of the workshop (see Photo 3.7).

Photo 3.7 Starfish girls and a CU student (second from the left) fully extending their arms during an applied theatre exercise.

Overall, the expansion of the girl's expressive range throughout the course of this two-to-three hour workshop was remarkable. Girls who at the beginning of the workshop seemed incapable of raising their arms to the point where their elbows would have to leave their torso were raising their arms fully extended over their heads by the closing. Eyes that only flittered upwards in timid glimpses from their downward cast were able to make direct contact with their classmate's eyes, while the girl asked for permission to pass through the obstructing arms towards her dream. These are determined girls who seemed fully cognizant of the audacity of their dreams to become professionals. In being chosen for this program, they had already overcome and achieved much. They knew their journey would be blocked on multiple occasions by many obstacles. Although still young girls who could be distracted and silly, they were likewise determined to push themselves at this opportunity to get the skills and confidence they will need to complete their journey. All of this was evident by their willingness to take risks and their positive attitude throughout the workshops.

Monitoring and evaluation of workshop

I have already provided my own thick description of the outcomes of the workshop design in the preceding section, which I acknowledge as coming from my own perspective but with an attempt to include multiple viewpoints. At the conclusion of several of the workshops, the girls themselves spontaneously gave us feedback on their experiences when they were formally thanking us for having come. One girl said, "I didn't know that I had to open the back of my throat to have a strong voice." Another said, "I was glad to learn how to work through the giggles because it is not always appropriate in every situation." These comments demonstrate that they understood the relevance of several intended lessons from the workshop. As an overall comment, one girl added, "It was good to learn how to use our voices because we do not think of our voices as strong." This attests to the value of workshops focused on vocal strength to spur participants to reconceptualize their ideas of their own voices. A final comment was, "It was good how we used our voices to have fun with the exercises in the beginning, and how we used our voices for very serious purposes too." This conveys that the girls felt free to simply enjoy the beginning exercises without fully realizing they were purposefully designed to support the serious portions that followed.

The only baseline set to measure what was important to us—vocal strength and expressive range—was our perception of the strength of the girl's voices and their expressive range at the beginning of the workshop in those initial exercises. Given that, I wonder now if we could have returned to some of those initial exercises near the end of the workshop for the girls themselves to witness and reflect on their growth and advancement as a result of the workshop. Related to this point, it is my belief that an improved workshop design would include the girls themselves setting the indicators used to measure if our goals had been met, and, if so, to what extent. I think that would have helped increase the critical engagement of the participants throughout. However, some of the girls were quite young and culturally immersed in a top-down educational system, so it may have proven to be overwhelming or incomprehensible. Working this aspect out with the mentors beforehand would help balance these factors. Including the girls in more of their own self-analysis could be a way for sharing power and agency throughout the workshop as well.

In the months following the workshops, the program coordinator, Amanda Flayer, held an informal focus group with all the mentors to ask them the questions I had provided, and sent me a summary of their responses. When asked what the most effective aspect of the workshop was, they responded that the relaxation exercises were very helpful, as were the vocal exercises. The girls liked the scenes they enacted and had a lot of fun with them. They said that the eye contact activity was important for the girls to gain confidence. They added that they were still using the exercises in their group meetings. When asked what they would change about the workshop to make it even better, they responded that they would have liked an even bigger variety of activities. The mentors responded to the question of how the workshop helped their community as follows:

> The workshops definitely helped our scholars to express themselves without being afraid, and this in the future will help them to reach their dreams. We believe that the girls are practicing what they learned from the workshop at school when they are asked to make presentations and talk in front of their classmates. We also hope that they will share what they learned with their families and friends. (Flayer 2009)

When asked for any other comments, they said, "The workshop was a beautiful experience. The girls had a lot of fun and we did too! We enjoyed that the activities were not theory based, but rather focused on participation. Hopefully we will be able to continue to use the activities and exercises with our scholars. We really feel that our girls have a 'bigger' voice now after the workshops" (Flayer 2009).

The positive comment about the exercise encouraging eye contact helped assuage some worries I held about the cultural appropriateness of women making direct eye contact in their culture. The word 'appropriate' is an interesting one to examine in this context, as what is deemed appropriate by a given culture could simultaneously be considered oppressive to women within that culture. Many cultural norms, which are deemed 'appropriate' by leaders in a given community, are regularly challenged by applied theatre practices. The lesson here seems to be that it is up to the women of that culture themselves to decide how and if they want to veer from 'appropriate' behavior. They are the experts; they uniquely understand the costs and likely consequences of straying from the status quo, as well as potential benefits. Indeed, applied theatre can be used as a tool for communities of women considering behavior change to explore costs and benefits of that change.

There were several mentions of how much fun everyone had during the workshop, and I would add that Chelsea, Kelly, and I also had a lot of fun. Being able to have fun while working towards program objectives simply makes the task lighter and the entire journey more enjoyable and perhaps more deeply received.

Vocal empowerment requires practice, and if that practice is fun, it is only natural that the girls and their mentors will gravitate towards that practice in the future. Looked at in this light, having this process be fun substantially contributes to its sustainability.

The mentors commented that the girls gained confidence and overcame fear while expressing themselves. The repetition of lessons—in slightly different forms—and the variety of activities seemed to help the girls overcome fear of using their voices and generally increased their confidence, though it was also noted by the mentors that they would have liked an even larger variety of activities.

The comment that they did not see the activities as theory-based—but rather as focused on participation—made me wonder if the mentors would have benefitted from more exposure to the theory that is the foundation for these activities. By their comment, I believe they were expressing their preference for an interactive, rather than a pedantic form of instruction, but I can see how a transparent theoretical framework could inform their perspective of the workshop. I imagine their deepened theoretical understanding would translate directly into even more valuable feedback on the structure of the exercises, general support of the workshop, and essential follow-up work.

Impact assessment

When attempting to measure the impact of these Starfish workshops in the months and years following, there are several aspects to be examined. There has been staff turnover since we facilitated the workshops in 2009, and none of the mentors we worked with are still with Starfish. However, Norma was with Starfish when Chelsea returned to Guatemala to give a similar workshop for Starfish in 2010. In September of 2012, I was able to interview and attend events with the new Executive Director Travis Ning, Country Director Norma Balan, and Vilma Saloj—a relatively new mentor (and now in 2013, a mentor coordinator)—during their visit to Colorado in 2012. During the interview, Vilma and Norma said they use some role-play in regard to their current focus areas. In using this technique, they said they do it in layers: first starting with the mentors, and once the mentors feel comfortable and confident with it, they attempt it with the students. It was not made explicitly clear if their use of role-play here was a direct result of the workshops offered in 2009 or 2010, but it seems likely that the workshops helped nurture an environment where such a technique would be attempted.

Vilma told a story about using applied theatre to address the issue of punctuality. She was utilizing a form of applied theatre known as Invisible Theatre developed by Augusto Boal, and taught to the Starfish mentors by a guest applied theatre facilitator, Rebecca. At a mentoring session with her group of girls, Vilma told the students who had arrived on time that they were going to do some Invisible Theatre to further a discussion on the consequences for being tardy. She said that she was going to tell the girls who came in late that they had lost their scholarships because of their habitual tardiness. After exposing it as an exercise to the tardy girls, she asked the girls who had been late how they felt, and they responded that they were afraid and felt terror. She said that the result was that the girls could understand the impact of being late. We discussed how this kind of an exercise worked in tandem with their effort to also build trust between the girls and their mentors. Norma replied that in this case, it caused worthy self-reflection and that this technique was just one tool in the tool chest. It took wise timing to know when to use it effectively.

Due to the live nature of applied theatre and the manifold factors playing into it, it can be challenging to make appropriate judgment calls in the moment. Norma described an experience she had with the workshop in 2010 where Chelsea had each girl in turn get into the center of the circle and simply yell as loudly as she could. Norma said that one girl, Maria, had a particularly difficult time with this and that Chelsea continued to encourage her to try. Norma, knowing Maria's extremely unstable home life and the trauma she had faced, felt uncomfortable with the situation and considered rescuing Maria from the activity. In the end, Maria found the courage to yell before Norma acted upon her urges. Norma said that now this girl is doing extremely well. She wonders what turned the switch for Maria and wonders if it could have been that moment. She said that now that girl even wears pants, which she and Vilma concurred was a very big deal in their culture. Norma said that she doesn't feel as though she has the experience to know how far to keep pushing or when to rescue the girls in regard to applied theatre activities. As our discussion progressed, we all seemed to agree that this kind of adeptness could only come from practice and would always contain an element of risk.

Vilma explained how she and the other mentors use role-play to help the girls rehearse new behaviors, such as interviewing for a professional job. She said it has proven useful for the girls to be able to give feedback to each other, such as "bad posture" or "too quiet," but that it often dissolved into silliness, even among the staff. After that, she said it is extremely difficult to regain the needed serious composure or attitude to make the exercise productive. In addition, Vilma noted that giggling was a continual frustration, and that once the girls started, that she as a mentor couldn't bring them back to being serious or productive. Here it seems clear that the technique for overcoming giggling as an obstacle that we worked on in 2009 was not handed down by the mentors who left Starfish, making evident, perhaps, the need for continual training to accommodate the reality of staff turnover.

Vilma stated the desire to gain more expressive skills *herself*, in order to be able to support the girls in increasing their confidence. She said that she doesn't feel that she can lead them in confident physical expression if she doesn't have it herself. Two of Vilma's students are the only indigenous students in an elite private school. She said that they ditched dance class because it was so hard for them. She felt limited as their mentor since she doesn't feel as though she can dance either. It seems evident that being able to be expressive through dance and theatre is becoming a necessity for academic success for students in Guatemala. With the relatively new governmental mandate to include theatre in the curriculum, Vilma said that many teachers—since they don't know how to direct or create theatre themselves—will simply arrange the students into groups with the request to "make up a play," and leave the students with no idea of what to do. It seems here that experience with applied theatre techniques could equip students with useful tools for academic success.

When I asked Norma and Vilma what it would take for Starfish to begin utilizing applied theatre in a more consistent way in their programming, Norma said that besides more training, there would need to be someone from within the organization who was a torchbearer for applied theatre. For example, she explained how the mentor Mariella was a torchbearer for family planning. Whenever the staff meets all together, Mariella champions family planning as a priority, and suggests how family planning objectives could be integrated into other goals and projects. Vilma said that Norma is a torchbearer for small businesses. She is always scheming how an idea or a need could be made into a small business. Vilma expressed interest in being a torchbearer for applied theatre, and so after this meeting, Travis, Norma, and I began planning for a year-long "training of the trainers" program, to support mentors in using applied theatre for vocal empowerment.

The outcome of this planning is that I have designed a year-long Vocal Empowerment Program for Starfish that began with a week-long "training of the trainers" in June of 2013, facilitated by myself and Chelsea Hackett with subsequent training trips planned. This program includes applied theatre exercises for empowering the physical voice, an affirmational song that touches on the primary aspects of an empowered voice, daily vocal exercises for the students, and applied theatre rehearsal of solutions to student's self-identified vocal obstacles that the mentors will faciliatate at each mentoring session. We are hoping to use participatory video techniques to engage the Starfish girls in creating an instructional training video from this project for all new staff members.

One useful outcome of the multiple experiences Starfish staff has had with applied theatre is that they recognized the complexity of applied theatre and had a beginning embodied understanding of its potential—evident in their desire to design an ongoing "training of the trainers" project. With the support and enthusiasm of key staff members, Starfish One by One is advancing their use of applied theatre for reaching their program objectives. An organization's ability and desire to adopt applied theatre can take a while to gestate and can benefit from a few 'one-off' external facilitators, or guest presentations. It leads to relationships that can grow and develop, during which time mutual understanding can unfold.

Lessons learned and recommendations

I recommend starting a workshop like this with active and fun warm-up exercises that are physical and require an increasingly expansive range of motion. Good choices could include the human knot or the ball-throwing exercises, as they get the participant's arms away from their bodies and expand their range of motion. Beyond that, these exercises are fun, give a positive impression of the workshop to come, and allow for trust and comfort to develop. I recommend holding off on exercises that require participants to compose something themselves until they are more comfortable and confident in this new situation.

The more consuming an exercise is mentally and physically, the less room there is for self-consciousness. However, this is a delicate balance since if an exercise is too challenging, participants may get frustrated, be unwilling to try, or disengage from the entire process. It is best to set participants up for success so they feel encouraged to try increasingly challenging exercises to expand their expressive range and strengthen their voices. A facilitator must sensitively assess participants before and during a workshop. It helps to arrive over-prepared with a wide variety of exercises to choose from, and from which to improvise in the moment. An effective facilitator needs to be ready to abandon an exercise when it does not seem to match the group's readiness, character, or ability. Likewise, a facilitator should be ready to dial up the intensity or expectations of an exercise towards a given aim when needed, to make the most productive use of the time allotted the workshop.

Participants can be asked to reflect and try to articulate what they learned from each exercise. Although reflection can deepen the lessons from the exercises, it can also interrupt the momentum and get participants back into their heads when trying to encourage their physical expression. What I have found is that moving from one exercise to the next within a given section can be useful to achieve flow in the workshop and capitalize on the expressive range gained. Then, at the conclusion of a section—on relaxation or direct contact, for example—reflection by the entire group can be beneficial.

It is obvious that for participants' strong voices and expressive range to be sustained, an active focus on these goals needs to be sustained by the organization on a regular basis. If not consistently beckoned out and supported with encouragement and praise, any expressive growth gained in a two-hour workshop will likely curl back in on itself. Conventional wisdom in the field of applied theatre holds that one-off workshops are not effective for obtaining long-term goals. Our intention at the time was to introduce the notion of using applied theatre to support strong voices. Our hope was that the mentors, who also participated in the workshops, would be able to carry on some of this focus if they felt it supported their work with the girls. The lessons learned from the workshops significantly informed the design of the year-long Vocal Empowerment Program.

The workshop showed that applied theatre was effective and appropriate for the girls in this program—evidenced by responses from both girls and mentors in 2009, and the attitudes they expressed in the 2012 interview. This case study underscored the importance of having a champion for applied theatre within the organization, in order for applied theatre to be actually utilized consistently to meet program objectives. Repeated and varied exposure to applied theatre can inspire someone to want to become that champion, as in the case of Vilma with Starfish.

In the context of Guatemala, the imperative for gaining vocal strength and expressive range is intensified since the girls need to have these skills to succeed academically in school, given the national mandate requiring the presence of theatre and dance in the school curriculum. As was obvious from Vilma's testimony in her interview, for indigenous women and girls, this is an extreme challenge;

all participants could benefit from some outside support. Even the Starfish mentors currently lack the confidence and skills to guide their students in this type of expression.

While in Guatemala in 2009 I also led a three-hour Vocal Empowerment Workshop for a group of mothers in Chicacao, which is about a two-hour drive from Lake Atitlan. At the time, Starfish was working to extend its scholarship program to this town (which they have since done), and was laying the groundwork by facilitating a mother's group. The group was made up of mothers who were interested in having their girls be considered for the Starfish program. During this session, the mothers had a chance to work through many of the challenges they faced in trying to support their children to escape the poverty they felt trapped in. A single mother named Rosa was concerned because a few months ago when she was sick, her 17-year-old daughter had to leave school to help out at home with the younger siblings. Once the mother had recovered, she wanted her daughter to return to school, but the daughter felt bad for the heaviness of her mother's load and wanted to stay and help. As a group, we rehearsed various ways the mother could talk with her daughter to convince her to return to school.

Based on the powerful experience of working with these mothers, I recommend—when focusing on girl's scholarship programs like Starfish (see Photo 3.8)—to offer applied theatre techniques to the mothers of the girls in the program. Providing these mothers with an active forum for resolving the challenges they face while trying to support their girls can be extremely beneficial to the overall success of the program. Also, providing some form of vocal empowerment training for the mothers could dramatically increase the likely success of their girls, by supporting the girls' primary advocate with the skills and confidence to empower *her own* voice.

Photo 3.8 Starfish One by One girls with their mentors.

Conclusion

The case study of Starfish One by One shows that aiming at women early in their lives provides them with opportunities for development, before they are locked into oppressive life situations from which it is much more difficult to make positive life changes. Starfish invests in girls to set a positive cycle in motion that interrupts the usual progression for an indigenous Guatemalan woman that would lock her and her family into a life of poverty. Providing educational support for high-achieving girls in Guatemala can allow these girls to break down age-old gender barriers within their society. It allows girls to lift themselves and their families out of poverty. The multifaceted changes brought about by supporting a girl's education are richly explored on the Starfish One by One website page entitled, "Why Girl's Education?" It explores what it means for her community and her country:

> In addition to mothering fewer but healthier, more capable children, Maria will have a higher likelihood of finding paid employment in the formal sector (as opposed to laboring in the informal sector doing tasks like washing laundry or making tortillas). She will be the most educated woman in her community, and pave the way for other young women to continue their own education. Maria will question bad government leadership and policy, and vote accordingly. She may perhaps decide to run for office herself. She will bring a voice that has never been heard, a set of unique ideas and perspectives that Guatemala has never experienced. She will not be a bystander, but rather the proactive agent of change that her community needs. (Starfish One by One 2012d)

What does Maria need, among other skills, to do all of this? What do all girls need to advocate for themselves against the obstacles they face when changing the culturally prescribed course for their lives? There is evidence that education is the primary factor that unleashes overwhelming change for the future of young girls, but how will they express all that they have learned? They will need an empowered voice. They will need a community to witness, affirm, and applaud the first tentative attempts to stand and be heard. Using applied theatre, vocal empowerment can serve as a powerful tool to help unlock the girl effect.

4   Appropriate Rural Technology Institute

Clean energy access in India

One of the longest and busiest roads through the city of Pune, India is named Karve Road. At the end of it stands a statue of Dhondo Keshav Karve, who started the first university for women in all of India. It seems fitting that the tribute to him is a long and congested road, since the journey to women's equality is likewise long, congested and full of stops and starts.

Journal, March 2011, Osnes

The Appropriate Rural Technology Institute (ARTI) is an internationally acclaimed research and development institution working in the field of rural development through innovative appropriate technologies. ARTI aims to develop, standardize, popularize, and commercialize these innovative rural technologies to improve the quality of life and standard of living in rural communities throughout India, and other developing communities in Asia and Africa. By introducing novel technologies that improve the life of rural people—such as fuel-efficient cookstoves and biogas systems—ARTI helps traditional rural business be more profitable and generate new business and employment opportunities in the rural sector (Appropriate Rural Technology Institute 2012a). Currently ARTI has about 35 members, all of whom have lived and worked in rural areas. It is a primary value of the institute that they work closely with the people for whom they develop solutions, testing their innovations in the field in partnership with rural people.

The main administrative and business offices for ARTI are in the city of Pune, in the Maharashtra state of Western India. ARTI's Rural Entrepreneurship Development Center is a few hours' drive away in the more rural setting of Phaltan (also in Maharashtra). This center has dormitory facilities to house about 40 trainees at a time, a lecture hall, live demonstrations, and audiovisual equipment. Wandering the grounds, it is a kind of inventor's wonderland, with various technologies in different stages of development, testing, and production. One can look into a plastic-lined garden bed in which the roots of a plant weave themselves into a mat that can be removed, dried, and used in the home. There are rows of cookstoves of many styles in various stages of completion. One can also witness the making of char briquettes from a kiln designed by ARTI that converts crop waste from sugar cane into a highly efficient fuel for many of their cookstoves. There is a bamboo solar food drier for use by Indian women who don't sell all their vegetables at market so they can preserve what is left hygienically rather than on sheets of plastic on the side of the road. ARTI's goal is to harness energy in situations during daily living where energy potential is wasted, by developing technologies to gather that energy for productive use.

Background

ARTI is a scientific society that was established in April of 1996 under the leadership of Dr. A.D. Karve and was originally comprised of a group of scientists, technologists, and social workers. National and international support has allowed ARTI to complete more than 50 projects that develop innovative appropriate technologies for rural development.

Dr. A.D. Karve, who led the founding of ARTI, is the grandson of Dhondo Keshav Karve (1858–1962), a famous social reformer for women's welfare in India who championed widow's rights and women's education (D.K. Karve 1936). Popularly referred to as Maharshi Karve—meaning a great sage—Dhondo Keshav Karve was first married at the age of 14 to an eight-year-old girl who died in childbirth at the age of 27. She was survived by their nine-year-old son, Raghunath Karve (1882–1953). This occurrence greatly influenced Raghunath's views on pregnancy and women's rights in regard to sexuality. Raghunath went on to become a professor of mathematics like his father, but was asked to resign by conservative administrators when he publically expressed his views about family planning, population issues, and women's rights to experience pleasure from the sexual act. Devoting himself full-time to these causes, he opened India's first birth control clinic in 1921 and published a Marathi magazine on these subjects, *Samaj Swasthya*, from 1927 to 1953. He advocated for the use of contraceptives for the prevention of unwanted pregnancies and, with his wife, Malati, chose to not have children.

An Indian actor turned director, Amol Palekar, made a film *Dhyaas Parva* (*An Era of Yearning*), which traces the life of Raghunath Karve, highlighting his incredible contribution to Indian society. The film was released in India and the United States between 1999 and 2002, and has won national accolades, six state awards, and acclaim in international quarters. About Raghunath, Palekar is quoted as saying, "As early as 1923, he talked about gender equality and women's empowerment—ideas that were nonexistent at the time. When he stood up for these concepts, there were legal cases against him and he was socially ostracized. Such a great man and his life, I think, can only inspire us" (Ramanan 2003).

Dhondo Keshva Karve, upon being widowed in 1891, insisted that since he was a widower himself, that he should marry a widow—something unthinkable given society's view of widows as outcasts. He shocked public opinion in 1893 by marrying a 23-year-old widow named Godubai, who even before this marriage had studied at Sharada Sadan (Home for Learning), a progressive facility for the education of Hindu women who were widowed young. Although Karve taught mathematics at Fergusson College in Pune 1891–1914, his passion was as an advocate for Indian widows. He founded numerous institutions and associations that directly assisted widows by providing shelter, schooling, and advocacy for them and their children. Though born into the Brahmin caste—the highest caste in Indian society—he was ostracized for his reformatory activities. In 1916 Karve went on to establish the first university for women in all of India, now known as the Shreemati Nathibai Damodar Thackersey Women's University. Karve wrote an autobiography in English entitled *Looking Back* in 1936 (D. K. Karve 1936) and on his hundredth birthday was awarded India's highest honor, the Bharat Ratna ("Gem of India") (Encyclopedia Britannica 2012).

With his second wife, Dhondo Keshva Karve, he had three other sons, Shankar, Didkar, and Bhaskar. ARTI's founder is the son of Didkar and Irawati Karve (I. Karve 1960), the principal of Fergusson College and an anthropologist respectively. Dr. A. D. Karve credits his mother for his social development mindset. As an anthropologist, she often had him accompany her on fieldwork, since she didn't have to pay him a wage. He says his mother talked with him and explained many things, which he otherwise never would have learned. Because she was a sociologist and anthropologist, she had an entirely different way of looking at things (A. D. Karve 2013).

Dr. A. D. Karve (shown with his daughter, Dr. Priyadarshini Karve, in Photo 4.1) founded ARTI when he was 60 years old—the standard age in India at that time for retirement. He had been working for an organization and explained that by starting

Photo 4.1 Dr. Priyadarshini Karve (left) and her father, Dr. A. D. Karve.

his own institute—ARTI—he was the boss and could do what he wanted. He was inspired to act upon ideas he had heard about in agriculture to help improve the lot of rural people. He was no longer interested in ideas hatched in sophisticated laboratories by scientists who received information by reading journals, but didn't know what was happening for people out in the fields. He saw that technologies developed by these disconnected scientists were not accepted by the rural people. To his mind, ideas should emerge among the rural people in order to develop more appropriate technologies around these ideas. Dr. Karve remarked how rare it was to develop technologies that are appropriate and are accepted by the people who will use those technologies. The word 'appropriate' was in vogue at the time of ARTI's founding, used to discern what would be actually useful in practice. Many technologies are very expensive, and difficult to put into practice, given certain financial constraints, so they are not appropriate. Dr. Karve described an article someone wrote about the Karve family who noted that they have always done what is appropriate given the time they were living. "When my grandfather was alive, the appropriate thing to do was to help women get education, for my uncle it was to promote family planning, and for him, to develop useful technologies" (A. D. Karve 2013). Dr. Karve said that at ARTI they were open to ideas from the people, but also developed some of their own. What is unique about ARTI is that they share what they develop with the rural people to see if it is useful to them. In addition, ARTI started a cooperative that sells their technologies, thereby showing that money can be made doing this. ARTI finds that this approach is more convincing than just showing the technology to the people

Programs

ARTI describes its activities in terms of projects and trainings rather than programs. The sphere of ARTI's research activities and ideas is reflected in its projects and training activities undertaken since its inception in 1996. Many of these projects have ultimately become successful technologies in rural areas. A major focus of their research has been on monitoring indoor air quality in households with, and without, improved cookstoves. ARTI has established norms for kitchen architecture and cooking devices for pollution-free cooking in Maharashtra, and the standardization and commercialization of compact biogas plants for domestic use. They have also developed many methods to improve agricultural yields. Awareness of the technologies developed by ARTI is generated through lectures to rural audiences, participation in rural exhibitions, articles written in local daily papers and magazines, and through live demonstrations and field days.

   ARTI also offers training for many of its technologies. Although these training programs are directed towards training potential rural entrepreneurs, they are also open to the interested layman (Appropriate Rural Technology Institute 2012b). ARTI has developed training modules on such topics as: nursery techniques, crop production on permanent raised beds, and biomass burning chulhas (clean-burning cookstoves) and fuel from light biomass. ARTI trains a wide variety of people across communities in rural areas throughout the country. These trainings are organized by ARTI, as well as various other NGOs and organizations with whom ARTI partners. There is a range of different trainings conducted, depending on the needs of the particular community. Generally speaking, the trainings have two main foci: technology and entrepreneurship. The technology side focuses on training around a given technology—through theory, practice, and film screenings. The entrepreneurship side seeks to give the trainees a working knowledge of how to start businesses using the technologies, either through sales or direct use (Deshmukh 2013).

Stance on gender

Dr. Karve does not profess to have started ARTI specifically for the participation of women in their own development. Nor does Dr. Karve claim to have been directly influenced by his grandfather's commitment to gender equality in the founding of ARTI. Rather he cites being influenced by growing up in Pune, which he describes as the cultural capital of Maharashtra, where a lot of new and liberal ideas were being talked about. Dr. Karve said that when he was still a child, his 85-year-old grandfather came to live with his family. Dr. Karve remembers many people would visit who wanted to talk with his grandfather, so he was exposed to many people with forward-thinking ideas. He said that gender equity did not seem revolutionary in this context, but rather something you were supposed to work for.

Around the same time ARTI was founded, there was a movement of women's self-help groups throughout India associated with the ideas surrounding microcredit (Ramesh 2007). Whereas formerly women had to ask their husbands if they wanted to get anything done, now they had their own money, so the staff at ARTI started thinking about what the women could do. Dr. A. D. Karve stated, "We were developing the technologies independently, but then we said, look—there are some of these that you can do even in your own back yard" (A. D. Karve 2013). That's how these two movements loosely merged with each other, but unintentionally, according to Dr. Karve. He says, "It was just an opportunity for us. In the women, we found a client who could take on our technologies" (A. D. Karve 2013).

Because these women's self-help groups had become the fashion in India at that time, the government of India gave ARTI a grant to conduct special courses for these women's groups. For seven years ARTI conducted trainings exclusively for women trainees. Dr. A. D. Karve reports that, "Now that the program has stopped, we are getting a lot of men also for our trainings. Some of the technologies that we are developing—that we *thought* would be very women-specific—are being taken up by men. For example, the whole idea of running a plant nursery; we thought this was ideal for women. But now we are finding that big nurseries are being run with men as the heads" (A. D. Karve 2013).

All of ARTI's trainers are male. Dr. Karve noted that even among ARTI's staff, there are hardly any women left. He explains that this is true because the job requires a lot of fieldwork. He said it is difficult for women to go and live in the field conditions where things are rather primitive. Explaining further, he said that many times trainers may have to sleep in a temple or spend the night on the platform of the railway station. That is the kind of life that women find unsafe. That could be one of the reasons that women don't take jobs like these. Being a teacher is a sort of a job that is socially safer for a woman, according to Dr. A. D. Karve (A. D. Karve 2013).

R. D. Deshmukh, president of ARTI, highlighted a few ways in which ARTI improves the lives of women in rural areas: agricultural production, entrepreneurship, health, and family. In regards to agricultural production, ARTI's technologies can help produce higher yields and more money, thus helping the entire family involved in agricultural production. Secondly, in some cases, women have engaged in starting their own agricultural businesses or selling ARTI technologies to the communities. To this end, he mentioned that ARTI could allow women to become self-sufficient income generators through their agricultural business or entrepreneurial endeavors. Mr. Deshmukh mentioned the drudgery and negative health impacts created by traditional technologies, specifically cookstoves (that are not clean burning). In regards to health, the pollution created by cookstoves can have significant long-term health effects (Global Alliance for Clean Cookstoves 2013). ARTI's cookstoves burn much more cleanly—greatly reducing these health impacts. In terms of drudgery, Mr. Deshmukh seemed to be referring to time spent on tasks related to homes without a cookstove: gathering materials to burn, cleaning the house of smoke, and the excessive buildup of black soot on cooking utensils. With ARTI's cookstoves, this drudgery is reduced, and allows women more time to engage in other activities. Principal among the activities Mr. Deshmukh cited were family and income-generation. With more time on their hands, women can spend more time on income-generating activities, as well as spending more quality time with their family (Deshmukh 2013).

Sustainable development aims

Given ARTI's projects and trainings, their sustainable development aims could be described as focusing on the efficient production of food and other agricultural products, and the efficient use of energy for cooking. ARTI's aim is to monitor and lessen indoor air pollution levels through clean-burning cooking technologies—such as clean-burning cookstoves—and biofuel digesters. Women are the primary beneficiaries of many of the technologies developed by ARTI, especially the work related to cooking, as that is almost exclusively done by women in rural parts of India. The use of open fires that burn solid fuels (wood, dung, crop wastes, or coal in some areas) in poorly ventilated indoor conditions results in high levels of indoor air pollution, most seriously affecting women and their youngest children (Bruce, Perez-Padilla, & Albalak 2000). There are 1.5 million premature deaths annually associated with exposure to such air pollution (Granderson et al. 2009), and millions more suffer every day with difficulty in breathing, stinging eyes, and chronic respiratory disease (Rehfuess 2006). Improved cooking techniques can also result in environmental benefits since women who have access to char briquettes are less likely to take as much wood from forests for burning, leaving more trees intact. More efficient combustion of cooking fuel also results in less black soot or black carbon being released into the atmosphere (Global Alliance for Clean Cookstoves 2013). Though many sustainable development efforts focus on urban and peri-urban areas, currently ARTI's focus is on rural populations. As knowledge of ARTI's innovations spread, some of their products are being used in urban and refugee settings.

Funding

The many projects that are the focus of ARTI's work are funded by a variety of sources both nationally and internationally. Core support comes from the Indian government's Department of Science and Technology in New Delhi. Support from the Shell Foundation in the United Kingdom has enabled ARTI to focus on monitoring indoor air quality in households with and without improved cookstoves, and to advance the commercialization of improved biomass fuels and cooking devices in India. ARTI was able to establish its Technology Resource Centre with support from the Council for Action by People and Rural Technology in New Delhi.

Description of how I worked with this organization

I first met the program coordinator for ARTI, Dr. Priyadarshini Karve (whom I will refer to as Priya), the only child of Meena and Dr. A. D. Karve, in the United Arab Emirates at the World Renewable Energy Congress (WREC) in 2010 (World Renewable Energy Congress/Network 2012). She assisted Dr. Barbara Farhar in coordinating an all-day preworkshop for WREC entitled "Engaging Women in Energy Enterprises: A Workshop on Energy and Gender-Equitable Development." Over our days together at the workshop and the conference, I was able to attend Priya's presentation during the WREC technical sessions on "Novel Strategies to Reduce Fuel Wood Consumption at Household Level," and she was able to attend my presentation on "Engaging Women's Voices through Theatre for Energy Development." I was also asked to present on a film for which I was the "human thread"—*Mother: Caring for 7 Billion* (Fauchere 2011)—at the conference during which I showed some prerelease footage. Priya also expressed great interest in this project since the film proposes that the solution to stabilizing population is through the empowerment of women worldwide. In our conversations I was intrigued by her family's story and deeply impressed with the work she was doing. Priya mentioned that she was interested in having me come to India to work with ARTI on engaging rural women in the development work they do, and we parted ways with hopes to someday find a way to make that happen.

Less than a year later, I had funding for a Women's Clean Energy Project in Peru, but that project fell through. I approached my funders to ask if I could use the resources to travel to India to work with ARTI instead, and they approved my revised proposal. In March of 2011, I traveled to Pune for several weeks to give multiple Vocal Empowerment Workshops at organizations in Pune, such as the Academy of Political and Social Studies and Co-operative Housing Foundation.

In attendance at these various workshops were members of the KKPKP (trade union for waste pickers), social workers, university students, women activists for the labor unions for railway sweepers, NGO interns, factory workers, and several members of a street theatre group, Sadak Natya Mandali.

When I arrived at the location for these workshops and saw that an equal ratio of men to women had come to participate, I wondered if ARTI had misunderstood the description of this workshop for supporting women's voices, and had promoted the workshop in a misleading manner. However, once we got to the point in the workshop where each participant was declaring her or his most passionate concern, most of the participating men expressed their passionate concern for the value of women's voices, or for women's equality in other ways. Indeed, it seemed as though the workshop had been promoted accurately and that the men had come hoping to learn ways to help women support their voices for participation in public life. Though I have often had men participate in public workshops for supporting women's voices in other communities—such as in the Carama Ngbe in Panama, or in Kuala Lumpur in Malaysia, or Hanoi Vietnam—they were much more the minority and not so verbally expressive of their commitment to supporting women's expressive capacity as I witnessed in India.

ARTI had also arranged for multiple screenings of the film *Mother: Caring for 7 Billion* at such venues as the Open Space: Centre for Communication and Development Studies, and the ARTI headquarters. Events were open to the public and were widely advertised through an article in the local newspaper, and through invitations. The film had been released in the United States in February of 2011 (a month prior to my trip to India), and I had been invited to lead a few postscreening discussions at US film festivals. It was fascinating to participate in postscreening discussions with Indian audiences. My general impression was that Indian audiences were much more comfortable with the topic of population and did not experience the subject in as controversial a way as in the United States. In fact, many people in India didn't understand why population was such an uncomfortable topic in other countries. In our postscreening discussions we considered how many people, especially in the United States, associate any promotion of population stabilization with coercive measures that limit personal freedom for procreation. We also discussed the sensitivity of issues such as family planning due to religious pressures in countries around the world. The topic of population will be further explored in Chapter 5, which focuses on the Population Media Center's work in Ethiopia.

The primary reason for the trip, however, was to conduct a two-day "training of the trainers" Vocal Empowerment Workshop for the staff of ARTI in Phalton at their Rural Entrepreneurship Development Center. Here a core of 18 people participated in in-depth training on how to use applied theatre to support women's participation in their own development. Also participating were several local women from self-help groups that work closely with ARTI and three Co-Operative Housing Foundation social workers from Pune, who wanted to receive deeper training than the three-hour workshop I had done for them in Pune in the preceding days. Priya's mother and father traveled to Phalton with us for this training; her mother, Meena

Karve, participated in the entire workshop, and her father, Dr. A. D. Karve, observed several portions.

One of the great surprises during my time in India occurred when Priya had arranged a showcase by engineering students at the Smt. Kashibai Navale College of Engineering (SKNCOE) in Pune, where Priya used to teach. Received as a guest of honor, I was seated in a front-seat chair in the audience among the other students, and was entertained by more than 40 engineering students who were all members of their SKNCOE College Art Circle. They sang ballads, pop songs, rap, and soul; danced traditional forms as well as hip-hop; and enacted a dramatic scene. These students' level of talent was as remarkable as it was varied in style. As I conveyed my congratulations at the end, I told the SKNCOE students that I was a frequent guest presenter for my university's student chapter of Engineers Without Borders and that I would certainly chastise our engineering students at the University of Colorado for not entertaining me so grandly. What also came out in conversation was that Priya was a leader of this group during her tenure at the institution, and that she had authored and directed multiple plays that they produced— one devised by the students and entirely based on women's status within society. I was also surprised to learn that Priya was not an anomaly as a theatrically active professor at this engineering college, but that she was joined in this effort by several others whom I met during our visit.

Also while in Pune, I was honored to be a guest in the home of Ravindra Kulukarini, who leads a theatre group called Natya Samskar Kala Academy of which ARTI's Arun Patwardhan is a member. There I was treated to an extraordinary performance of a dramatic monologue by my host's son, Sakshim Kulukarini, who is an accomplished and quite famous Marathi actor in television, film, and stage. Later during my visit, I was also taken to the main civic theatre in Pune, Balgandurv Rangamandir, to attend the performance of a Marathi play—*Navagadinavrajya*—by Arun's son, Kshitij Patwardhan.

All of this reiterated for me the extent to which Pune is a major center for Indian Theatre, especially Marathi Theatre. It also made me wonder if there is some connection between a propensity towards theatre and sustainable development. Both seem to require creativity and the willingness to try out a variety of possible scenarios, especially in the work of ARTI as they are not only endeavoring to develop new innovative technologies, but also generate creative ways for rural people to discover income-generating opportunities from these new technologies. It could also be that the level of artistic creativity expressed throughout Indian culture is to credit for this abundance of talent. Regardless, it seems uncanny and is worth noting that both Priya and Arun at ARTI are so experienced and accomplished in both theatre and development. This was the beginning of my appreciation of the linked characteristics of applied theatre and successful development work: a nimble responsiveness and deep engagement of all participants.

Since my work with Priya in 2011, she and I served on an ad-hoc planning committee for an all-day preconference, "Engaging Women in Clean Energy Solutions Workshop," in Denver, Colorado, on May 13, 2012, directly preceding the World Renewable Energy Forum (Farhar et al. 2012). It was during this time, when she was a guest in my home state, that we were able to share many conversations that led to my deeper understanding of her work as it relates to women's participation. All of this was supplemented by interviews conducted in January of 2013 by a former student of mine, Daniel Oxenhandler, with members of the ARTI staff. Since Daniel was traveling in India, I asked if he would conduct interviews in Pune with Dr. Priyadarshini Karve, Mr. Arun Patwardhan, President of ARTI Mr. R. D. Deshmukh, and with ARTI founder Dr. A. D. Karve. Listening to recordings of his insightful interviews filled in missing pieces of ARTI's story and greatly enhanced the writing of this chapter.

Site description

India is a country of incredible diversity and contrast in almost every way imaginable. The land within India is a diverse mix of snowcapped mountains, expansive deserts, fertile plains, and areas that receive some of the highest rainfall in the world. It is bordered in the northeast by China, Nepal, and Bangladesh, and the northwest by Pakistan, the southeast by the Bay of Bengal, and on the southwest by the Arabian Sea. The population of India is over 1.2 billion and is second only to China, which it may surpass by 2030 (National Geographic 2013).

India is home to one of the earliest urban civilizations, the Indus Valley Civilization, which ranged from 3300 to 1300 BCE. It was the first great culture to inhabit areas of the north, along the Indus River Basin (Brandon 1997, p. 64). From 1500 to 500 BCE was the Vedic period associated with the writing of the sacred Vedas, which constitute the foundation for Hinduism (Mittal & Thursby 2004) and are written in the ancient language of Sanskrit. Since the seventh century—with the introduction of Islam—India has dealt with issues of accommodation, syncretism, and opposition between Muslims and Hindus, stretching from the campaign of Muhammad bin Qasim in Sindh in 710, to the partition of an independent India and Pakistan in 1947 (Ahmad 1999). The colonization of India by Great Britain began as a business partnership through the East India Company, charted in 1600, and evolved into a rule maintained through both trade and conquest. British power spread through the greater part of the subcontinent in the early nineteenth century and by the middle of the century had gained direct or indirect control over almost all of India (James 2000). Independence was gained for India in 1947, guided by Mahatma Gandhi, at which point Pakistan was partitioned from India as a sovereign Islamic country. Currently, India is referred to as the most populous democracy in the world. Since the 1990s, India became one of the fastest-growing economies and industries, yet continues to be plagued by challenges of poverty, illiteracy, corruption, and a high birth rate. Through India's age-old caste system, a highly complex system of societal structuring and hierarchy continues to challenge efforts to lift the poorest in India out of poverty (Bayly 2001).

A vast majority of Indians are Hindu, with more than 138 million Muslims as well, giving India one of the world's largest Muslim populations (National Geographic 2013). Other religions in India include Christianity, Sikhism, Buddhism, Jainism, and Zoroastrianism. There is not an official language in India (Khan

2010), although Hindi is widely thought to be the official language, with English as the secondary language, along with several hundred regional languages. The focus of this chapter is on Maharashtra, a state in the western region of India, in which the official language is Marathi.

Local gender information

In the *Global Gender Gap Report 2010*, India, Nepal, the Islamic Republic of Iran, and Pakistan all compete for last place within the Asian regional ranking (ranked 112). Pakistan and especially India perform above average on the political empowerment of women, but lag behind in the other categories. In addition, India is the lowest ranked in the report of the BRIC economies featured in the report's index. The report states that "the persistent health, education and economic participation gaps will be detrimental to India's growth" (Hausmann et al. 2010, p. 28).

According to the 2011 Census in India, not only literacy rates, but also many other issues keep women from achieving gender equity:

> Now, if we consider female literacy rate in India, then it is lower than the male literacy rate as many parents do not allow their female children to go to schools. They get married off at a young age instead. Though child marriage has been lowered to very low levels, it still happens. Many families, especially in rural areas believe that having a male child is better than having a baby girl. So the male child gets all the benefits. Today, the female literacy levels according to the Literacy Rate 2011 census are 65.46% where the male literacy rate is over 80%. The literacy rate in India has always been a matter of concern but many NGO initiatives and government ads, campaigns and programs are being held to spread awareness amongst people about the importance of literacy. Also the government has made strict rules for female equality rights. India literacy rate has shown significant rise in the past 10 years. (Census-2011, Population Census India 2011)

Other obstacles for Indian women in achieving educational opportunities are substantial. Less than 27% of Indian women aged over 25 have had a secondary education (The Indian Express 2011). For those who attend public schools, there is gender discrimination and lack of sufficient toilet facilities for girls.

In terms of the gender violence Indian women face, statistical differences for women begin even before birth. There is a sharp increase in the number of women aborting female fetuses because they want boys or feel pressure to birth male children. The 1996 law—which banned gender-screening tests in an attempt to reduce female feticides—is considered to be a failure. Research at Toronto University's Centre for Global Health, based on the latest 2011 census and earlier population data, estimates that up to 12 million girls were aborted in India over the last 30 years (Nelson 2011). In addition, women regularly face sexual harassment and assault, and neither the police nor the judicial system are seen as adequately protecting them. As reported in a recent article in the *New York Times*, "Gang rapes have become almost routine in India, a country that some surveys suggest has one of the highest rates of sexual violence in the world. Rape complaints increased 25% between 2006 and 2011, although it is impossible to know whether this represents a real increase in crime or simply an increased willingness by victims to file charges and by the police to accept them" (Das 2013).

Local theatre history

India's theatrical history is vast and rich, and, arguably, the most diverse and prolific of anywhere in the world (Osnes 2001). We see early evidence of the existence of Sanskrit Theatre in *A Treatise on Theatre* in the *Natyasastra,* an ancient Sanskrit text attributed to Bharata Muni (dated between 200 BCE and CE 200) (Rangacharya 1999). Given the low status of women in Indian society and throughout history, it is interesting to note that in India's ancient Sanskrit drama men and women both acted, either together or in troupes of their own sex. In fact, women were thought to be better suited to enact certain sentiments, not considered appropriate for men to perform (Brandon 1997, p. 66). However, at the lead of any Sanskrit Theatre troupe was a male stage manager known as *sutradhara,* who not only directed all of the actors but also served as the stage manager and perhaps as the lead actor as well. In the centuries following, a great diversity of dance and music-based dramatic forms flourished in India. In nearly all that are classified as theatre—rather than dance—men took on the roles of female characters. During Great Britain's colonization of India, theatre was used as a vehicle for teaching the British way of life. The use of theatre by Indians to express anticolonial sentiments prompted the passing of the Dramatic Performances Act of 1879. This law was put in place to stop theatre because it inspired people to act against the colonial rulers; it is still technically in existence today (Ganguly 2010, p. 5).

Modern theatre in India differs from region to region and is most often composed in local, regional languages. From the late nineteenth century through the early twentieth century it experienced widespread growth. Amateur theatre companies have flourished in the second half of the twentieth century until current times, with over 3,000 registered amateur troupes in Calcutta alone (Brandon 1997, p. 75). The director is key to each company.

Relevant to this case study, the Marathi play *Himalayachi Saavli* (*The Shadow of the Himalayas*) written by Vassant Kanet and published in 1972, is inspired by the life of Dhondo Keshav Karve. The character of Nanasaheb Bhanu is a composite character based on Karve and other Marathi social reformers of the late nineteenth and early twentieth centuries. The play dramatizes the tension between his public life as a social reformer and his family life, which suffered from the social backlash and economic hardships his children and wife had to endure because of his activism.

In 1943, the Indian People's Theatre Association (IPTA) was formed, which was strongly connected to the Communist Party. IPTA was committed to social, political, and aesthetic concerns and began new theatre workshops and festivals devoted to women-centered issues. IPTA inspired a significant increase in plays being written by women, in particular, plays that do not seek to resolve issues, but rather involve the audience in questioning stereotypes and dealing with emotions (IPTA 2013). Many applied theatre groups have kept this style of work alive throughout India, from Jana Sanskriti (written about in Chapter 1), to the recently formed Center for Community Dialogue and Change in Bengaluru, India (Center for Community Dialogue and Change 2013).

Description of applied theatre by ARTI

Since this case study is analyzing ARTI as an organization that has used both their own staff *and* an outside facilitator for applied theatre, I will analyze examples of each approach. First, I will analyze ARTI's own use of theatre in the trainings ARTI offers rural people in India. I will also analyze the making and the use of promotional films written by ARTI staff and produced with participation from local women and the ARTI staff. In writing on these aspects of ARTI's theatre-based work, I am primarily relying upon interviews with the ARTI staff conducted by Daniel Oxenhandler in January of 2013 for this book. Supplemental to this are the actual films made by ARTI in my possession, the ARTI website, and my communication with Priya. Next I will analyze a "training of the trainers" Vocal Empowerment Workshop I led as an *outside* applied theatre facilitator for ARTI staff in 2011.

ARTI training led by ARTI staff

As previously stated in the description of ARTI's programs, ARTI has developed multiday training modules on such topics as nursery techniques, crop production on permanent raised beds, biomass burning chulhas, and fuel from light biomass. ARTI trains a wide variety of people in rural areas throughout the country. There are various types of trainings conducted and the audience of the trainings varies. Generally speaking, ARTI works with a range of communities in rural areas, seeking to disseminate knowledge around their technologies and their applications. Many trainings are organized by NGOs or other organizations seeking to provide education and opportunities to the communities. Others are independently organized by ARTI (Patwardhan 2013). Dramas and skits are utilized to provide participatory, creative opportunities for those involved in the training. During the trainings, participants (trainees) work to design their own small dramas and skits to perform on the final day of their training. These skits are meant to illustrate the concepts they've learned throughout the training—for example, the health benefits of using a smokeless cookstove.

Goals of training

There are two goals for the trainings. The first is to train trainees in how to use a given technology—through theory, practice, and film screenings. The second is to give the trainees a working knowledge of how to start businesses using the technologies, either through sales or direct use. If ARTI has determined internal indicators for measuring the success of their trainings, I was not able to obtain that information. It seems as though they rely to some extent on the theatrical skits created by trainees at the end of the training to determine if the trainees comprehended the intended objectives.

Design of training

Trainings last anywhere from 10 days for a training on Biomass Burning Chulhas and Fuel from Light Biomass, to 2 days for a training on Crop Production on Permanent Raised Beds (Appropriate Rural Technology Institute 2013). These trainings can take place at ARTI's Rural Entrepreneurship Development Center, which is a few hours' drive away from Pune in the more rural setting of Phaltan. Alternately, a group seeking training can have an ARTI trainer travel to their location. The exact design of each training is specific to whatever technology is the focus of the training, yet each includes participation and most include elements of applied theatre. The trainings are comprised of a few different participatory and interactive elements: discussion, practical engagement with the technologies/processes, and creative interventions. Every day is started with an engaging and interactive question and discussion session. The final day of training is focused specifically on interactive engagement around what has been learned: discussions, conversations, and performances (Patwardhan 2013).

Outcomes of training

According to Mr. R.D. Deshmukh, women actively engage in all parts of the trainings that ARTI conducts in different ways based on the literacy level of the women. Those with lower literacy levels will focus more on the practical side of the trainings, for example, making rice beds, mixing manure into the soil, and bagging seeds. Those who have higher literacy levels will take more interest in the theoretical side of things and attend the lectures. During discussion sessions, participants are actively encouraged to share their perspectives and thoughts. These discussions often serve to provide unique insights about the trainees' experience with the technologies. One such insight sits at the intersection of local culture and technology. While conducting trainings about the cookstove, Mr. Deshmukh (shown in Photo 4.2 with a miniature version of an ARTI cookstove) reports learning that the way in which women in certain communities wear their sari affects their use of the clean-burning cookstoves. Usually women will pick up hot dishes with the cloth from their sari. In different communities, women wear their saris with different orientations (with the final remainder of the cloth being draped over the right or left shoulder). In some circumstances the way in which a woman wears a sari can affect the way she uses the stove. Depending on the setup and the direction of the flame, a woman might have to adjust her sari in an unconventional way to best maneuver.

In regards to the importance of these discussions, Mr. Deshmukh repeated the phrase, "Users are good teachers"—a testament to the value gained from the

Photo 4.2 Mr. Deshmukh illustrating the orientation of a particular stove as it relates to the way in which a woman cooking wears her sari (using a miniature model of ARTI's clean-burning cookstove design).

participatory nature of the training and the technologies (Deshmukh 2013). Beyond discussion, there are opportunities for trainees to participate actively in the practical exploration of the technologies. One part of the training involves trainees actually getting hands-on experience with the technologies and methods for using them. Depending on the technology, the nature of this practical engagement varies.

There are also other creative interventions organized by the participants. For example, at some trainings, trainees have written songs about their experience of the technologies. In other instances, groups have spent significant time organizing skits to perform at the completion of the trainings. The trainees write, direct, and act in these skits, which explore topics and issues they've learned throughout the training. ARTI's staff simply provides support and encouragement. Describing the creativity that Mr. Deshmukh has seen at these performances, he stated that "every person is a poet" (Deshmukh 2013).

Depending on the training, the percentage of women involved varies. For example, in the Sarai Cooking System, Improved Cookstoves, nursery program, and compost-making trainings, there are a higher number of women involved. When the groups are mixed, Mr. Deshmukh says about 30–40% of those involved in such programs are women. There are some trainings conducted for women's self-help groups, in which all participants are women. Finally, some trainings— such as biogas energy and charcoal-making technologies—only see about 10% women's participation. Overall he said there are more than 300–400 entrepreneurs that ARTI has trained, of which about 30–40% were women (Deshmukh 2013).

Monitoring and evaluation

Although there is no formal information on monitoring and evaluation of applied theatre methods used by ARTI trainers during these trainings, they have maintained these practices for more than a decade, which attests to the staff's belief that they are effective methods for synthesizing lessons learned during the trainings. These theatrical expressions created by trainees also seem to serve ARTI staff in assessing if the content of the training was understandable and accessible. It was also stated that through these active and participatory training methods, ARTI staff learns about the usefulness and appropriateness of their own technologies.

ARTI films by ARTI staff

ARTI has created two promotional films for use in their training and outreach, both written and directed by ARTI staff members. Each of these films tells a story that revolves around the use of clean-burning cookstoves. Both of the films were shot on location in rural areas and some of the background people in the films were local residents. Also both films include songs in the style of mainstream Indian cinema, which were composed by ARTI staff member, Arun Patwardhan (whom I refer to as Arun). The finished films are used to invigorate interactive discussions—often in a public setting—about the technologies featured in the films. Both films are in the local language, Marathi. Even though ARTI refers to these products as films, they were shot, edited, and distributed as digitalized video recordings.

Goals of films

When the first film was made in the 1990s, the government of India was freely giving away the clean-burning cookstoves through a subsidy program, so the purpose of that film was to convince people to use the stoves. That film focused only on two models of stoves that ARTI had at that time. By 2004, ARTI had many more types of stoves, the government subsidy program had ended, and the goal of the second film was to try and convince people to purchase the clean-burning cookstoves. The purpose of the second film was to convince people that money spent on an ARTI stove was not money wasted. Another goal for the second film was to disseminate information about what cookstove options were available, and the health aspects that were associated with the use of the improved cookstoves.

Photo 4.3 A photo of a scene in the film in which ARTI staff member, Arun Patwardhan, is acting as the storyteller in a promotional film he also wrote and directed about clean-burning cookstoves.

According to Priya, the goal of the second film was to help people connect the dots and make conscious choices (P. Karve 2013). There were no formal indicators set by ARTI to measure if these goals were met by the respective films.

Design of films

The first movie was written and directed by ARTI staff member, Arun Patward-han. Professional actors performed all other parts, and a professional crew was used to shoot the video. Arun also acted in the film in the part of the storyteller (see Photo 4.3). The story line of the first film is as follows: there is a tradition of villagers coming together in the temples during the evening to hear stories by a storyteller about how to behave properly and live well. The film opens on an evening in which the storyteller tells a story about clean-burning cookstoves. In the audience, there is a woman who recently had a big fight with her husband because her stove did not light properly. Because of this, her cooking was delayed and her husband was angry. This woman asks the storyteller where to get information. Upon learning where to go, she and some friends go to meet another lady who is actually building the clean-burning cookstoves and even has a business building stoves. This lady explains how the stoves operate and how useful they are. Once the news spreads, then the whole village discusses building these stoves and how the government can help.

The second film was written by Priya and was directed by Arun. Priya's contacts with women in the local amateur theatre scene provided the actresses for the film, and a professional film crew was paid to shoot and edit the footage. The story

Photo 4.4 A photo of a scene in the ARTI film in which a daughter is scrubbing a pan with excessive black soot from a dirty-burning cookstove. Film written by Dr. Priyadarshini Karve.

line for this film follows a mother who has to go to the market. While still at home, her college-aged daughter (see Photo 4.4) complains because she has to clean the cooking utensils, which have black soot on them from the use of a traditional cookstove. Cleaning the utensils is delaying the girl from going to college, since she has to finish that work before she can depart. In frustration, the mother shouts at her daughter and leaves in a very bad mood. The mother goes to the market and meets a friend there who takes the mother to her home. There the mother sees the friend cooking on this very different-looking stove and notices that none of her cooking utensils are black. When the mother asks about this, the friend tells her about the clean-burning cookstove and how the reduction in smoke has made her life better. She takes the mother to a workshop where these stoves are being produced and sold. The mother buys the new stove and installs it. The film ends after the mother herself starts her own shop for selling the stoves. Both of the films include original songs that further the action of the story, deepen the emotional connection to the material, and are entertaining.

Outcomes of films

The first film was made with villagers near Phalton, and some of the local women even had a line of dialogue. However, the main actors were professionals, and professionals did all other production elements. The second film was made in a different village closer to Pune, and the local villagers were included in the background. Arun directed the film with a professional camera crew following his direction. In casting the film, Priya's aim was to not only involve the villagers but also to involve some socially conscious amateur actors from the more urban set-ting of Pune, to have them gain experience with the issues in the video.

The films have been used in a variety of ways. Around the time of the release of the second film, ARTI was running a commercialization program through a network of 10 grassroots NGOs that were working directly with the people in different parts of the state. Each NGO—some working specifically on women's issues—was using the film throughout its own area. ARTI worked only with NGOs that were working hand in hand with the villagers and had the trust of the people. The film was distributed primarily through NGOs for village meetings, as a starting point for this program. The idea was that the NGO would incubate an entrepreneur in the village who would sell the clean-burning cookstoves. There was funding for the NGOs to hold awareness meetings around the village and promote the entrepreneur. In those meetings, these films were used to basically attract people and get them involved. In such meetings, after the film was shown, people were asked what they thought about the story and the themes in the film. For example, they may be asked if they feel the same way as the women in the film. The films help jump-start a conversation-based approach for these participa-tory meetings.

ARTI also broadcast these films on the local cable channels, which at that time were more popular than the government-run television channels—made up mostly of news-based programming. These local cable channels affordably reached a few thousand houses. In addition, ARTI paid to have their videos shown on local buses; at that time, state transport had initiated a program where they had installed televisions in the buses to compete with private bus operators. The final way that the films were used was as a part of ARTI's own trainings. As previously noted, as one of the features of the residential multiday training programs that ARTI con-ducts, participants are told to put on a performance of their own, based on what they are learning—like how they will promote the technology through some art form. Often these skits by trainees are inspired by the films.

Monitoring and evaluation

When asked, Priya said it was very difficult to assess outcomes of the film, but that anecdotally ARTI has received feedback that the films are effective in getting people interested in issues, especially in the linkage between women's health and indoor air pollution. Priya believes that ARTI's videos help to catalyze more con-versation and raise awareness. Many grassroots NGOs amplify the use of ARTI's films by using their own people to do street plays and skits or to sing songs after the showing of the film.

Likewise, there is no data about what impact or outcomes occurred in response to the broadcasting of the videos on local cable television or in the buses. NGOs and ARTI trainers received feedback that the videos touched an emotional chord with the women. Priya notes that ARTI heard stories of women even crying in the audience of the first film, where the woman had been fighting with her husband. Because they got pulled into the emotional part of the story, Priya believes that the women were more attentive to the informational part. She adds, "But if that all translated into people actually buying the stoves and what was the contribution of these films, that is not known" (P. Karve 2013).

Even though the videos were made in Maharashtra, and for Marathi-speaking people, the films were created in villages around Phalton and Pune, a relatively small area. Priya concedes that this video may be less effective in other parts of Maharashtra, since there are cultural variations throughout the state. For example, people from different areas of the state pronounce certain words differently and use different intonations. Dialects vary, and even words are specific to only one area. Priya said that when making these films she believed that unless viewers felt a relationship with the characters in the film, they would not be as effectively moved as if they recognize themselves in the characters. The NGOs can compensate for some of the regional differences by bridging those gaps using local performance styles to relate issues in the film to the local culture. The films can be accompanied by some kind of live performance in their local dialect, using the local traditional art forms. Priya also explains:

> We are talking about an improved cookstove for which you have to pay. This is for people who could just as well be doing their cooking on a three-stone fire, which costs nothing. However low your cost is, it is still more costly than the traditional approach. A lot of convincing is necessary for people to see that this cost is for future health. It requires a totally different way of looking at cooking options—from the standpoint of health. Even when women do understand that the smoke from the traditional stoves is hurting their own health, the women themselves don't value their own health. They don't think the money is worth their future health. There are a lot of gender issues involved in this. In the face of this, you just have to keep talking about it. (P. Karve 2013)

Applied theatre can be an effective method for getting women to keep talking about their beliefs about their worth, agency, and participation.

Description of applied theatre by an outside facilitator

I was invited by Priya at ARTI to conduct a two-day "training of the trainers" workshop for vocal empowerment as an outside facilitator in March of 2011.

Goals of "Training of the Trainers" workshop

Based on communications with Priya prior to my arrival in India, the goal was to offer training for the ARTI staff (who lead the ARTI trainings) to facilitate applied theatre methods for women's participation. To this end, I led participants in learning how to lead the Vocal Empowerment Workshop that I developed as part of the *MOTHER tour*. Another goal was to "train the trainers" to support women in critically engaging with issues that they self-identified as concerns. By rehearing using their voices to act on these concerns, our goal was to facilitate women in authoring their own lives.

Given those goals, the indicators to measure if those goals had been met were as follows. One of the indicators was the participant's ability to facilitate applied theatre methods for women's participation. Therefore, on the last afternoon of the two-day "training of the trainers," Priya had 14 rural women from a self-help group come to our location to be facilitated in applied theatre methods by the participants in the workshop. Therefore, we had built into the design of our workshop an opportunity for participants to attempt facilitating various portions of the Vocal Empowerment Workshop for women. Because facilitation was shared by all participants being trained—and because I was actively overseeing the process—it was a controlled environment in many ways. However, it provided a valuable first experience of leading women in these applied theatre techniques. We were able to measure to what degree the Vocal Empowerment Workshop was providing support for the women to critically engage in using their voices by whether they were able to suggest scenarios from their lives, and be the authors of working towards solutions to the obstacles they faced. This was also measured by the feedback we received from participants at the conclusion of the workshop. To measure if the workshop conveyed shared tools for supporting women's participation for ARTI trainings, I rely on interviews of key ARTI staff members conducted a year and a half after the training took place.

Design of "Training of the Trainers" workshop

The Vocal Empowerment Workshop was the design that Priya had been exposed to at the WERC conference at which we met, so that is what she requested. In designing the training, the primary focus was on women's voices: how they feel about their voices, skills for strengthening their voices, and rehearsing ways for using their voices to act upon their concerns and author their own lives. The first day and a half of the training included 18 staff members from ARTI, with an additional three social workers from Pune, and four local women associated with self-help groups that work with ARTI. We met for two full days. Many participants in the training were semifluent or fluent in English, but we translated every part for the benefit of those who were not. Although Priya had assigned an ARTI staff woman to be the translator, others often jumped in and offered their interpretation of how to effectively translate what I was trying to convey. Priya was particularly astute at translating the theatre concepts.

We began our training by arranging the chairs into a circle in one of the large lecture rooms in the Rural Entrepreneurship Development Center. After Priya and I explained the purpose of the two-day training, and we had all introduced ourselves, I led the group in examining how they felt about their own voices. I explained that it was important for them to all deeply consider their own feelings about their voices before attempting to lead others, noting that you can only lead as far as you yourself have traveled. If participants were being trained to help women empower their voices, they needed to examine their relationship with their own voices first. Then we spoke together about the idea of voice more widely, especially in reference to women's voices. I shared some thoughts about being the facilitator for a workshop for women to empower their voices, such as the need to be bigger in one's expressive range so as to stretch the limits and allow for the expanded expression of participants. Authentic listening is a powerful way to draw out another person's voice. The facilitator should attempt to feel comfortable and confident in order to model this for participants. I also emphasized the importance of creating a safe space built on trust, so women participating would feel safe to try new things and share their experiences.

I explained how the role of a facilitator is different from that of an expert or a teacher. A facilitator sets the tone, monitors the energy, gives the prompts or leads the action, and keeps everyone on task. A facilitator's job is to help the process along by repeating back to participants what she/he thinks the participant said to check for accuracy. It is to guide the women in self-identifying their own concerns. When obstacles in the action occur, it is not the facilitator's job to give answers, but, rather, to help only in the form of questions. This method engages women in critically examining their own lives and leads them to discover their own possible solutions. A facilitator can help identify obstacles and note recurring obstacles in order to encourage a discussion about possible causes and solutions. It is also an applied theatre facilitator's job to allow for just enough discussion before insisting that issues be interrogated through theatrical action so issues, obstacles, and solutions are *acted* on, rather than just *talked* about.

After our discussion, I introduced what the three parts of the workshop would be. First we would lead women in having a physical experience of their voices as strong. Second, we would invite women to use their strong voices to communicate their concerns. And third, we would practice using those strong voices to act on each woman's concern.

In this workshop we used most of the same exercises that were described in the Design of Workshop section of Chapter 3 for relaxation, open throat, and direct contact for a strong voice. One additional exercise we did for this group was to have each person, one by one, say his or her name while doing a gesture that communicated how he or she felt at that given moment. In this workshop, when we got to the second part, using our strong voices to communicate our concerns, we had everyone in the training pair up and take turns sharing their most passionate concern with their partner in a strong voice. After everyone had done that, we stood together in a circle and each person was, in turn, invited to share his or her concern in a strong voice to the entire group, traveling around the entire circle with eye contact to make authentic contact with each person. Again, as in Guatemala with Starfish One by One, we enforced having each person do this in a strong voice, which entailed a relaxed body, open throat, and authentic contact. If someone left out one aspect, they were invited to do it again. This portion took the entire morning until our lunch break.

After lunch we reassembled for the third part of the workshop: practicing using their voices to act on their concerns expressed in part two. Here we asked for volunteers to remind us of their concern and imagine how they might use their strong voice to act on this concern. Most of the participants shared their concern, and together, we imagined how we might set up an imaginary scene to rehearse acting on this concern. We took on one concern at a time. The process we used to set up each scene often went as follows. The person would state her concern. If she could not imagine a way to act on the concern, others in the group would make suggestions. The entire group had to agree that this seemed like a realistic and culturally appropriate scenario. Next we would establish where this scene was taking place and assign various members of the group to act as the characters in this scene. If necessary, the woman who had the concern would direct this and give notes to the actors to make it more realistic, and, thus, more useful for her, such as, "You are the bossy woman in my self-help group who serves as the bookkeeper for the funds."

We established rules for those *not* in the scene, so they could comment or get involved in the action. At any time, someone watching could say, "Freeze," at which point those in the scene would stop moving and talking. The person who interrupted the action could make a comment, ask a question, or give a direction, such as, "I don't think it is realistic for her to have changed her mind so quickly," or, "Where is the source of water currently?" or, "Try and get your brother to go with you to ask for help." The role of the facilitator here is to keep the discussion that ensues from this freeze to a minimum, and get the action going again as soon as possible. Once the interruption had been dealt with someone should yell, "Unfreeze," and the action should resume. Another way to get involved in the action was to come up behind an actor in the scene, tap her or him on the shoulder, and take her or his place without interrupting the action or calling attention to the fact that a new person was now portraying this character. This is a mechanism by which a bystander can insert her point of view into the scene.

After rehearsing acting on participant concerns from 2:00 to 6:00 p.m., we sat in a circle together to reflect on this portion of the workshop and critically engage with the process and the outcomes. People were asked to revisit how they felt about their voices and share that with the entire group and then with a partner. Participants were encouraged to share questions, comments, and insights. We also practiced our closing, which was similar to the closing we used in Chapter 3. To finish the evening, there was a screening of the film *Mother: Caring for 7 Billion* for participants, and then dinner at the facility.

The next morning from 8:00 to 10:00 a.m., there was a demonstration of ARTI technologies on the center grounds for participants of the workshop, other than the ARTI staff members (who were all already familiar with these technologies.) From 10:30 a.m. to 12:30 p.m. we prepared for the "training the trainers" participants to lead a workshop that was to take place from 1:30 to 3:30 p.m. For the sake of clarity, it should be noted that four women from a local self-help group were participants in the "training of the trainer" two-day intensive training, and that there was a larger group of 14 women from local self-help groups who were invited in for the second half of the second day to be led in the Vocal Empowerment Workshop.

We began that day by deciding together who would lead each portion of the workshop, attempting to have each person be responsible for leading some aspect of the workshop of their choosing, as much as that was possible. We then practiced having each person lead all of us in that activity to prepare each for leading the women. I explained to the group that when working with groups of women who are living in poverty, I have had more success having the entire group together devise ways of using their voices to act on specific concerns rather than having the woman with the concern devise her own action. I have also found that there often tend to be clusters of common concerns among women—such as lack of sufficient funds to run a household—and that these concerns can be addressed more collectively. We shared feedback with the person leading activities as issues arose, concluding by 12:30 p.m. At 1:30 we were joined by the 14 women in the self-help group—including a 12-year-old daughter of one of the women—to have the trainers lead these women through a Vocal Empowerment Workshop, concluding at 3:30. None of these women spoke English, so the workshop was conducted entirely in Marathi. I stood next to the translator, who translated for me in a hushed voice when I asked her to, or when she felt it would be useful information. I intervened in the facilitation when it seemed it served the goals of the training, or if I thought it was necessary to assist the women participating in the workshop. By 3:30 we had completed the Vocal Empowerment Workshop, thanked the 14 women for joining us, and they departed. From 3:30 to 4:30 we all sat in a circle and discussed issues that arose from the preceding experience and shared feedback to the entire experience. The training concluded with a ceremony at which Dr. A. D. Karve and I presented certificates of completion to each participant.

Outcomes of "Training of the Trainers" workshop

On the morning of day one of the two-day training, participants shared the following about their own voices. One woman said that she sometimes fears that she will be called out when she speaks and that others will accuse her of having just made up what she is saying. A man shared that after marriage he lost his voice. Another man said that he has to sit when speaking in public, he cannot stand, and that he cannot give lectures but can only have discussions with others. Yet another man said that he lost his confidence with his voice after college. A few women commented that they were generally shy with their voices when in public or with people they did not know, but more comfortable with their voices at home. When discussing the idea of voice more widely, a woman said that when one woman uses her voice, she gives permission to other women. A man shared that when a man listens to a woman's voice he encourages her voice and validates it.

When doing the first part of the workshop in which all were led in having a physical experience of their voices as strong, the gestures that people made while saying their name to communicate how they were feeling generally extended to the limit of their reach and were decisive and strong. Though there was some laughter to dispel the nervousness associated with enacting a new task outside their comfort level, it did not appear to diminish participant's strong communication of their inner state. Even for Sangita, a local woman from a self-help group,

Photo 4.5 Sangita expressing herself with strength as she says her name and does a gesture during a "training of the trainers" workshop with an outside facilitator.

it is evident from Photo 4.5 that she is expressing herself with strength as she says her name and does a gesture.

When we began rehearsing ways for each person to use her or his voice to act on her or his concern, most often bystanders would ask questions or give suggestions during the course of a scene without yelling "freeze" first. Also, the actors would often lose their focus on the scene to engage in a spirited debate about the social issue at the core of the scene. The ARTI staff especially was a lively smart bunch of people who were enthusiastic in their discussions. My challenge as facilitator was to keep the conversations brief to keep the focus on *active* methods of enactment. There is certainly a value in a discussion that critically engages with the issues. However, the goal in applied theatre is to avoid discussion that stagnates action, and to encourage discussion that critically reflects on action once a discovery has been made through active exploration. What I find the world over, when facilitating applied theatre, is that most people are more comfortable and practiced in talking about or complaining about problems than they are in actively exploring solutions around problems. I often remind participants in my workshops that conversation is a perfectly valid method for exploring problems and solutions, but that the purpose of *this* workshop is for us to practice using applied theatre to actively explore solutions to problems. I would also ask the question, "Are we ready to unfreeze the action yet?"

Given that the workshop for ARTI was mixed gender, the unsurprising outcome of the workshop was that during the rehearsal of actions men more often than women tapped an actor on the shoulder to take her or his place. People understood that the replacing person was to act as the character whose place they just took. They easily took on even the same gender characteristics in the case of a man taking a woman's place. This, of course, often resulted in laughter and delight by the audience, which appeared to also please the actor and seemed to encourage her or his attention to playing the part as realistically as possible. It did not result in them just hamming it up to get attention for themselves, but seemed to contribute energy into the pragmatic purpose of the scene. The fact that the entire process seemed to be entertaining for everyone involved kept their heightened attention on the obstacle being explored and added to the creativity being employed to devise solutions. There was a majority of men in the workshop—the staff members of ARTI and one male social worker—and they were on their own turf, which seemed to give the men a home-town advantage in the workshop. This could be identified as a design flaw of the workshop, and this situation needed to be tempered throughout the course of the two days.

The first concern we acted on was of a woman from a self-help group, Sangita, who was concerned with how she could continue to improve upon her business of making and selling a spicy snack of puffed rice with chili powder. She wanted to increase her capacity to fulfill the increased demand for her product by buying a wagon to transport her goods and a packaging machine to plastic wrap each portion of snack with her label. In order to get the capital to do this, she would have to convince members of her self-help group to give her a loan from their shared funds to improve her business. She explained that she would need to make a pitch at one of their meetings to obtain a loan, and that she would likely need to defend the worthiness of her idea over others' requests for loans.

Together we cast the roles and enacted a scene of Sangita, portraying herself in the scene, asking for the loan with her self-help group. One woman in the scene said that she needed an operation for her leg, arguing that health was more important than a business. Another woman argued that she needed the loan in order to purchase a new wedding sari for her daughter's wedding, arguing that family obligation was more important than a business. Sangita tried her best to argue her case but seemed to be deflated by their arguments. With a sigh of resignation, she shrugged her shoulders and was unable to come up with further arguments for her cause. Priya froze the action and said that since the purpose of the self-help group was to support income-generating enterprises, Sangita should stress how her loan would lead to increased income-generation that she could use to pay back her loan. The other two loan requests would not result in increased income-generation and should, therefore, not be funded by this self-help group. Unfreezing the action, Sangita explained this new angle to the group, and they agreed that she would most likely be able to repay the loan.

Next, we rehearsed using our voices to act on a concern by Prasad, a male ARTI staff member, who was concerned about the mandatory 50% leadership by women at the village level in India. He said that all too often, a woman will get elected but that her husband will lead, even to the extent that the woman will never even go into the office, but that only her husband will. Prasad proposed rehearsing using the group's voices to try and prevent the husband from entering the office. Through discussion it was decided that it would be more powerful and effective if there were many people using their voices to prevent him from entering the building. When we rehearsed them blocking the entry of the man portraying the husband, he said in an irritated voice to the others, "We are happily married. Why are you doing this to me?" To which another replied, "Then why did I hear you beating her last night?" at which everyone laughed. Here it seemed that the laughter emerged more out of recognition of a social truth, rather than out of a feeling that domestic abuse was funny. The wife was called for, and when she came, someone asked her, "Why did you run for office if you were not going to really rule?" She said that because otherwise the position would have gone out of her family. The husband interjected, "There was an opposition candidate. Why didn't you elect her if you knew I'd take over?" After more banter back and forth like this, the scene had run its course and had stopped. I asked Prasad what he had realized from this. He said that he learned that this is a problem that needs to be solved collectively. In the discussion that ensued, it was suggested that a 'no confidence' motion could be brought up as a consequence of the woman not ruling. Resuming the scene again, participants rehearsed telling the wife who had been elected to the position that if she doesn't actually rule they will bring up a 'no confidence' motion against her, in which case her family would lose the position regardless. Since it was conferred by many in attendance that there is a provision that the community can actually do this, all agreed that this was a very convincing way to use their voices to act on this concern.

Another concern expressed by a female participant, Bharati, was that religious fundamentalism was taking over her children's school. Her way to act on this concern using her voice was to talk with the schoolteachers to ask them to stress concern for all humanity, rather than extreme views. We set a scene with her coming to talk with a teacher, who, once she expressed her concern, said that this type of thing is the parent's job to teach. Bharati responded that the teacher could tell the parents to do this at the parent/teacher's conferences. The teacher said that parents don't even come to the conferences anyway. A man took the woman's place and tried another strategy. He suggested to the teacher that they do a skit on tolerance for all humanity at the All School Day when everyone comes and the students do skits and dances. Another man froze the action and commented that the teachers are already overworked and that the students are only at school for four hours a day, but with their parents much longer, so it should be the parent's responsibility to teach them. No consensual solution emerged from this rehearsal. The woman said as a final comment that she felt it is very hard to convince people about beliefs, and that her children are going to the wrong school (referring to the fact that she felt there were fundamentalists at her children's present school). Another person said that in the previous example they tried to solve the problem as a group and that here she tried to go it alone. He suggested that maybe the reason she felt discouraged and why it didn't work was that they didn't come up with a strategy for acting on this concern together.

As a facilitator I naturally tend to want a happy ending and a solution for every concern, but I have learned that something valuable comes from sitting with the failure and frustration. The fact that she realized at the end that she was, perhaps, sending her children to the wrong school could be an insight into the most appropriate action for her to take—to send her children to a different school (providing that is even a possibility for her family). There are also some concerns for which there is not a ready or accessible solution. As facilitator, I could have asked the group before we did the scene if this was a concern for which they thought this method would likely find an answer. Even in the face of this seeming impossibility, rehearsing possible actions gives participants a more nuanced understanding of what they are up against. Some concerns, such as other people's fundamentalist beliefs, are extremely difficult to change and could need to be dealt with indirectly rather than with direct action.

At the conclusion of having all the participants rehearse using their voices to act on their concerns, we sat together in a circle and participants shared insights and feedback. In general, participants felt that this was an effective way of improving women's confidence. This demonstrates that participants closely associate women's confidence with their willingness and ability to use their voices to act on their concerns. A male ARTI staff member shared that he thought it was good for men to be involved in this kind of a training as well as women, noting that because he was included as a man, he learned of many issues facing women that he would not have otherwise been aware of, or understood to the same extent. Another comment was that because it was based on drama, it was entertaining. Others agreed that both acting out and witnessing other people acting out stories and wrestling with various solutions was highly entertaining and kept their attention.

The next morning the non-ARTI participants took a tour of the ARTI development center. Highlights included getting to witness the process ARTI had developed to increase the outdoor life of bamboo. Bamboo logs have some of the same properties as steel, but when bamboo gets wet, it is vulnerable to fungus and bugs. At ARTI they developed an inexpensive method for infusing the bamboo logs with a poison to extend its usefulness for years longer than untreated bamboo. There was also a demonstration of the Sarai Cooking System, which is a portable stainless steel device operating on the combination of principles of steam cooking and retained heat cooking. This has been hailed as one of the cleanest ways of using charcoal for household cooking. The charcoal to be used can either be ordinary wood charcoal, or charcoal left over in a wood-burning stove, or char briquettes made from agricultural waste. This stove design won the Ashden Award for renewable energy in 2002. Dr. A. D. Karve is well known for the compact biogas plant he developed that is unique in that it doesn't rely on dung to create biogas, but can produce methane (used as a fuel for cooking) using food scraps, making it appropriate for use by a modern middle-class family (Samuchit 2012).

When the complete group of "training the trainers" convened at 10:30 a.m., we discussed who would lead each part of the workshop following in the second half of the day for the 14 women from the self-help group. We had some trainees work together to lead a specific portion so that everyone would have an experience leading part of the workshop. Some aspects of the workshop are more challenging to lead than others. For example, the relaxation exercises are much more straightforward than facilitating the declaration of concerns, which includes relaxation, open throat, and direct contact. We let each person practice leading the rest of us in the given activity. What we found was that nearly everyone took far too long explaining what she or he wanted the participants to do, rather than just briefly describing the activity and then actively modeling it. Many exercises that are interactive are both intimidating and exciting for people. Most often participants need to be coaxed to do them. Here I offered the metaphor that each exercise was like jumping into a cold pool of water. The longer you have your participants standing by the edge of the water waiting to jump in, the harder it is to take the plunge. Since we only had two hours to assign roles for the entire workshop, we were not able to give too much detailed feedback or guidance, but everyone did get the chance to rehearse leading their section and receive some feedback.

At 1:30 p.m., when the 14 women from the self-help group arrived, many of them seemed slightly intimidated by the surroundings they found themselves in (which included nearly as many men as women, and was a professional environment with which many of them had little experience). The 14 women were markedly more reserved in their expressive range than the four women from self-help groups who had participated in the entire two-day "training of the trainers." My understanding is that the four women who were invited to participate in the two-day training were unofficial leaders in their community, and had likely gained more confidence from the many experiences that led them to that state.

Once we were all assembled, we welcomed the women, and I gave a brief explanation as to what we would all be doing and why. There were more than 30 of us assembled together in a tight circle that just barely was accommodated by the room we were in. We began the first part of the workshop with the exercises for having an experience of a strong voice. The facilitators of the activities seemed confident and thoughtful of the invited guest's experience, and were encouraging and praised participants when they attempted each exercise.

For the second part of the workshop—using their strong voices to communicate their concerns—a male social worker, Chayan, explained this activity and invited each woman to share her most passionate concern, one at a time. Chayan purposefully started with a person in the circle who was a part of the "training of the trainers" so that she could model declaring her concern with a relaxed body, an open throat, and with direct contact. Since some women did not understand what was being asked of them, Chayan changed the wording in Marathi closer to "what is your biggest worry," and that seemed to help. There was a wide range of responses to this exercise with one woman saying that she didn't feel that she could speak her concern with so many men in the room—at which point I interjected and asked that we move on so she was relieved from having to make a declaration. The next woman declared that she was happy and had no concern, at which point she clapped her hands with excitement. Many other women declared that they were concerned with various issues related to poverty, such as access to health care, education, and adequate resources for their household.

Chayan approached his role facilitating this portion with extreme serious-ness and an intense interest in learning from the experience. As he approached each woman, inviting her to declare her concern (or worry), he physically stood before each woman watching her to ascertain if she was maintaining relaxation, an open throat, and direct contact. Twice, I interrupted the action and suggested to Chayan to be a part of the circle standing supportively beside each participant rather than in front of each woman, intensely watching as she attempted to speak, seemingly poised to correct her with passion if she did it 'wrong.' I suggested he think of being *with* each woman rather than *over* each woman as she spoke. I also stressed that an effective way to beckon women's strong voices is through authentic interest in what they have to say and deep listening. Chayan appeared to be good-naturedly embarrassed that he was doing this in his enthusiasm to get it right, and in the discussion that followed conveyed an understanding of how more supportive methods would contribute to the goals of the workshop. As he continued, he did seem to grow in sensitivity to his approach of the women as he stood beside them, maintaining his place within the circle, and listening intently.

In the third part of the workshop—using their strong voices to rehearse acting on their concerns—since several women's concern was that they did not have enough money to run their household, it was decided by the group to rehearse a way in which the women could make more money. An ARTI staff member sug-gested having the women increase the amount of sugarcane shoots they were growing for ARTI. ARTI has a program with women's self-help groups in which the women receive sugarcane seedlings, plastic bags, and some proper soil. The women pot the seedlings in the bags with the soil, tend to these shoots for two months until they mature, and then sell the more mature seedlings back to ARTI.

Challenges arose when a male ARTI staff member, Arun, led a portion of the third part of the workshop. Facilitating this third portion is perhaps the most challenging part of the workshop, so it is completely expected that this is where we would experience the most growth for the trainees. We began acting out the sugarcane-growing scene with the women portraying themselves and a few men from ARTI explaining the program. After the competition of the scene, many of the trainees commented that this scene lacked any drama because this method had already been proven to be successful. Another person noted that nothing new was discovered by enacting this scene, which made the rehearsal of it unnecessary. It was useful for all to witness that an unknown solution to a concern should be the focus of a scene when setting it up for rehearsal. It's a bit as if the facilitator is setting up a miniplay each time she or he facilitates setting up a scene. For the scene to be useful, it has to have a clearly defined action, obstacle, and characters that can attempt a variety of tactics for achieving the desired goal. If some part of this formula is missing, the scene will lack drama and it will have nowhere to go.

However, even enacting this simple scene brought up some useful insights. Throughout the scene, Arun had led the action and seemed to draw from his experience as a theatre and film director. As noted earlier in the chapter, the traditional Indian theatre and the Western model for theatrical direction—largely adopted by Indian theatrical directors during colonialism and perpetuated after independence—tends to be structured hierarchically with often a male director as the ultimate authority. This was made evident by Arun saying "Silence" several times in order to gather the attention of the women so he could direct the action. It was also made evident when he moved chairs away from the front of the room to the sides of the room and bodily took the position at the head of the classroom to address the others, corralling them into a group facing him in a more traditional classroom-style setting. That structural change in how participants were arranged in the workshop—from a circle to a traditional classroom arrangement—changed the way that power was being shared in that setting. It seemed to take power away from the women participating and give power to Arun. In a traditional theatrical setting, this behavior would likely be the norm, but in applied theatre it was counterproductive to the goals for the workshop.

My impression was that his motivation was to instill order where he perceived chaos (many people talking at once) so that the women themselves would get the most from the workshop experience. However, it seemed to be a case of not fully understanding the extent to which the theory for applied theatre is embedded in the methods. The methods he was using, which were more authoritarian and hierarchical, do not match the theoretical foundation for applied theatre that is based in Paulo Freire's work (Freire 2000). Applied theatre is a process-oriented, messy, sometimes chaotic, but profoundly participatory method for engaging people in devising their own solutions to their concerns. It is based in Freire's idea of a dialogical education in which students critically engage with the material at hand. It is not a process in which a teacher stands above and directs the process.

I consulted with Meena, who very kindly intervened in the action. At this juncture, Meena reminded all the men involved that they had to be especially sensitive and aware of how they were using their voices and their bodies, stressing that this entire workshop was to promote gender equity and encourage women's participation. I asked her also to make the point that it was not our role to direct the women, but, rather, to *facilitate* them in rehearsing their own actions. Here we revisited the differences between leading and facilitating that was presented on the first day. Meena's presence at the workshop added a lot, especially since she was a participating member of the entire workshop, not just an observer, and because of her respected role as wife to Dr. A. D. Karve, and her long-time experience with the organization. Her wisdom and sensitivity helped resolve a few different points that were difficult to convey and required a delicate change of perception or a paradigm shift, such as the example described above. Arun was gracious in receiving the feedback and seemed to understand the profoundly different approach of applied theatre to the theatre to which he was accustomed and quite accomplished.

This is also a point on which Priya intervened and communicated some of the fundamental basics of this process-oriented work. She explained that it was not

Photo 4.6 A young participant of the Vocal Empowerment Workshop, Kirti (on the right), with her mother.

only the *outcome* of the rehearsal that mattered, but what skills and confidence the women gained by going through the *process* themselves. Priya explained that it was okay if it was a bit messy and seemed unorganized at times; those would be the times that the women themselves decided on a way to act. She advised the facilitators to just gently keep them on task and let the participants take time to figure it out. It seemed to me that Priya's experience with theatre and gender equity served her ability to explain applied theatre, even though she had no previous experience with Freire-based theatre work before this workshop.

After Arun, another woman who is a social worker, Panchasheela, took a turn leading the women in rehearsing using their voices to act on their concerns. She focused on the concern of the young 12-year-old daughter, Kirti (see Photo 4.6), who shared that her concern was that she had to fetch water daily for her family from a source that was very far away from her home. She said that doing this took a lot of time and that the water was very heavy. Working together, everyone decided they should have a community meeting to discuss this problem. Panchasheela helped recruit both men and women who wanted to portray community members. Then she asked the young girl to share her concern again for the community to discuss. Kirti was able to explain her predicament in the applied theatre setting with a soft voice. One person asked if she had a sister who could help her carry the water, to which she said, "No." Another asked if she could borrow a wagon to carry the water to make fetching it easier and, perhaps faster, but she said she did not have access to a wagon. She said that there were many people who lived where she lived for whom this was a problem, so if anyone had a wagon, they would use it for themselves. Finally someone suggested they talk with a government official to see about getting the source of water closer to where this girl lives, especially since there are many people like her without close access to clean water.

Panchasheela helped everyone reconfigure the scene, assigning one man the role of the Sarpach—the local village government head who is the focal point of contact between government officers and the village community. The girl and the other community members came into his meeting room and described the situation. The Sarpach responded that this was a problem of which he was aware, but that they did not have the funding and human power to remedy the situation. A man in the scene asked him if the city could provide the pipes to run the water to this girl's area, if the community would provide the labor. Upon considering this, the Sarpach agreed that this seemed like a reasonable solution and said he would look for the funds for the pipes.

Since a solution had been found, Panchasheela stopped the action and asked the group what they thought of this solution. Meena commented that she thought it was realistic since arrangements such as this do, indeed, happen. Others agreed. The young girl seemed to be delighted with the attention paid to her concern and overcame her initial hesitancy to use her voice in this setting throughout the course of the rehearsal.

In general, the girl seemed to be more involved and comfortable with the workshop setting than her mother, who remained somewhat reserved throughout the process. As a group, we gravitated towards rehearsing concerns that seemed to benefit most from being acted out, and the concerns of women who seemed more willing to participate. To judge willingness, we watched to see who seemed most comfortable during the exercises, willingly declared their concern, seemed engaged and active during the rehearsal process, and volunteered to participate.

After the completion of the third part of the workshop, a male ARTI staff employee, VJ, invited the women to share their feelings about what they had experienced in the workshop. One woman from the self-help group said she was reminded of her school days when they would act things out in class. Another woman from the self-help group said that she enjoyed the holiday from her daily work. A man who worked at ARTI said that he learned ways to facilitate having people interact to express their views. Another man said that it is important to guide the actions being rehearsed so that they are doable. A woman who is a social worker said that at first she felt unsure of how to do this process, but now she feels she could lead it. VJ went around the circle inviting people to share, but did not require each person to speak, which resulted in several of the women from the self-help group passing when it was their turn. Generally, people had a positive response to the workshop and seemed to enjoy this novel way of working through their concerns. To close, Sangita led everyone in making a tight circle, crossing right arm over the left, holding hands and saying, "We have strong voices," and while turning outwards saying, "and we are taking them out into the world." We thanked the women for joining us, and they departed.

Monitoring and evaluation

I have already provided my own thick description of the outcomes of the workshop design in the preceding section, which I acknowledge as coming from my own perspective but with an attempt to include multiple viewpoints. The primary way in which feedback was gathered from the 18 trainees was that in the final hour we sat in a circle to critically reflect on the applied theatre Vocal Empowerment Workshop they had been trained in facilitating. A woman who is a social worker said that during the applied theatre process, she learned how important it is to listen and to take the correct steps to get the desired results. I assume that what she meant by listening is listening to the women themselves. We discussed many benefits of deep listening, such as to validate each woman's voice and to support her in using her voice to declare her concerns. By taking the correct steps I assume she was referring to the three parts of the workshop: having a physical experience of the voices as strong, using that strong voice to declare concerns, and rehearsing ways to use that strong voice to act on a concern. In terms of acting effectively on concerns, she said she learned that there is power in numbers, referring to the many times during the rehearsal of concerns in which community members worked together to successfully address a problem. She also said that she could see the importance of guiding the actions so that they are doable. By this I think she was referring to the time we rehearsed a woman using her voice to eradicate religious fundamentalism at her children's school. Conventional wisdom from nearly every culture tells us that this is extremely difficult, if not impossible, to do.

Arun said that he liked that this training was organized with prepared notes, but that it was active and had everyone on their feet. He appreciated that it was not a boring lecture, like most trainings. This point was reiterated by many of the others in their feedback, that they really appreciated how entertaining the training was and how much they enjoyed having their own concerns become the focus. Many participants added that they felt much more engaged for a longer period than usual because they were participating in so many different ways: vocally, physically, critically, and even emotionally. A man who is an ARTI staff member said he felt that learning this methodology was useful as he has been a trainer for two years with ARTI. He feels he can work some of this into his trainings to make it more active and to get people really participating. Panchasheela, a female social worker, said that she runs many public meetings, but that something was always missing. Now she knew what it was: active participation and engagement by those in the meeting.

The men all agreed that they were glad to have been included in a Vocal Empowerment Workshop for women, citing that it made them more sensitive to issues specific to women and taught methods for including women's voices. This point was not further explored in our discussion, but in hindsight, I wish I had dug deeper into this issue. I would like to know what the women in our group felt about the presence of so many men. I would have liked to ask them for suggestions on how to balance the masculine and feminine presence in the group. Based on this experience, when I design the workshop again, I will encourage my host to consider several mechanisms to balance this, such as having the workshop for the 14 women from the self-help group take place at a location comfortable for the women, ensuring there are more women than men in the room, and providing gender sensitivity training for the men, prior to the workshop.

Overall impact assessment

In terms of the long-term impact of the promotional films made by ARTI, Priya offered additional information in January of 2013 regarding distribution of the films and a change in approach for future ARTI film projects. Priya noted that now people have much better access to CD players and computers, even in rural houses. Because of this, ARTI currently distributes CDs of their films when they participate in exhibitions and meetings, since the cost of making mass copies of the films on CD is quite low. A digitalized version of the films is also on the ARTI website so people can download it and show it. Priya noted that even in the rural areas, the Internet access is pretty good. Priya believes that for future promotional film projects, Web-based distribution would be most effective in terms of reach and cost. Even small villages have Internet cafes, and students are being taught how to use computers in school. Priya feels that this makes getting information out to people much easier (P. Karve 2013).

Another long-term impact of ARTI's promotional films is that since the making of these films—both in rural settings in the previous years—Priya has since changed in her fundamental approach to how she would use theatrical representation to promote the use of clean energy technologies. ARTI is no longer marketing its technologies only to rural people. ARTI focuses on developing biomass-based energy cooking devices that provide a fairly good quality of energy with minimal pollution. Given the high cost of fuel in both urban and rural areas of India, ARTI now has an increase of users in urban areas. Priya believes that this use of clean energy technologies in urban settings is what is needed to convince people in rural areas to adopt the use of ARTI's technologies. Priya states, "If rural people can see these devices being used in urban areas, they are willing to take them on" (P. Karve 2013). Her view is that as long as one is marketing a product specifically for rural people, it will take a lot to convince rural people this is not something second-rate being pushed on them. Priya cites the reason for this as being recent increases in access to television programming in rural areas.

> Now everyone is seeing how people live in urban areas through watching television and that is what rural people aspire to; it is how they want to live. Rural people will not spend their money on something unless they see urban people using it. So this is a radical change in approach, away from trying to blend in with the many rural cultural contexts. In all ARTI marketing now,

such as with the Sarai cooking system, it was a conscious choice to show it as being used in a typical urban household. There is another company, which did a fairly widespread marketing campaign for improved cookstoves. In all their films they have shown very rich, well-to-do families, women wearing fancy saris, although the product is made originally for rural people. If rural people are looking to urban lifestyles, then we need to bring the change to urban lifestyles. (P. Karve 2013)

It is unlikely that future films will represent traditional theatrical forms—like ARTI's first film in which Arun portrays a traditional storyteller. Future films are likely to portray a more homogenized urban representation of people using the technologies, one based on urban sensibilities and tastes.

Based on interviews with key ARTI staff members a year and a half after the "training of the trainers," the impact of the training seemed to be primarily an increased use of interactive techniques, physical movement, and expression by ARTI staff during ARTI trainings. Arun said he uses various exercises and activities that he learned in the training when he leads ARTI trainings, as well as in his own personal drama work (Patwardhan 2013).

When Priya was asked what she thought about the long-term impact of the "training of the trainers," she said:

I found this as an interesting idea to help women voice their concerns, which is something I had not seen happening before. When NGO meetings are conversation-based, the topics of conversation are always chosen by the NGO and do not come from the audience. This way the concerns come from the women and then they get acted upon, and that I found was a fascinating way of working on this, an effective way to find out what people are thinking about. (P. Karve 2013)

This information from interviews conducted with Arun and Priya a year after the training, points to two primary impacts of the training. First, it provided practical exercises and activities for ARTI trainers to use during their trainings. Second, it provided the beginnings of a conceptual shift that put women first in identifying concerns addressed in a gathering. It conveyed a methodology for supporting women in self-identifying their own sustainable development concerns, and it provided a method for facilitating the women in discovering ways they could use their strong voices to act on those concerns. Finally, the entire method encourages critical engagement and reflection on the action by all involved, not just by a hierarchical director or expert.

Overall lessons learned and recommendations

In regard to ARTI's use of films to promote clean-energy technologies, Priya's current approach is to focus just on aspirational aspects of the product (it looks urban) rather than the actual health and environmental benefits. Although there will likely be many benefits to this approach of focusing on urban tastes, one cost may be that rural viewers of the film will no longer see themselves represented in the film to the same extent as before. Also, they will likely be viewing this film in their homes—on a CD player or computer alone, or with only a few other people—instead of at community gatherings at which many people can discuss the film together after viewing. In light of these two changes, it could be advantageous for ARTI to find ways to preserve the vibrancy experienced in watching these films in communal settings that support active, conversation-based participation, critical engagement, and reflection. Methods for critically engaging viewers of the films in their own home could also be explored.

Priya said that she has been talking with her colleagues working in environmental conservation about the possibility of creating a soap opera that can show the characters using appropriate technologies. Priya said, "The story line could be anything, but the lifestyle that is depicted could be the sustainable urban lifestyle. If that soap opera becomes popular, then the lifestyle will become aspirational. We may not even utter a single word about environmental considerations" (P. Karve 2013). Priya notes that other commercial advertisements have used exactly the same kind of strategy, in which they don't refer to the properties of the product, but rather to a lifestyle associated with the product. This last point by Priya sets up a natural segue into the next chapter, which focuses on the use of soap-opera-style programming to communicate behavior change messages. Perhaps ARTI could have their products be used by urban characters in Population Media Center's *Humraahi,* a soap opera in India that explores family planning (Population Media Center 2013a).

Implementing some form of monitoring and evaluation for ARTI's use of applied theatre in their trainings and in their films would likely help sustain the use of applied theatre methods as it would verify the likely effectiveness of these efforts. Working with an outside consultant on how to devise such methods could assist in attracting continued outside funding for such efforts. Since they have the talent and the aptitude within their organization, it would be advantageous to capitalize on that unique coming together of artistic talent and technological expertise—all within one organization.

In general, it's messier when men are included in applied theatre intended to support women's participation in sustainable development. There are challenges and it is more work, but the results are often worth it. Certainly, it needs to be tempered, and the costs versus the benefits carefully weighed for each situation, but it should not be discounted. When beckoning women's public voices out, it can sometimes simply be too intimidating for some women to experiment with personal expression while in the presence of men. Then, certainly, it is appropriate to have only women be involved. When a woman experiences being expressive with men present—even if it's more challenging to create that opportunity—the benefits seem to be greater, because she has overcome a more difficult barrier to her expression and has gained the validation of both sexes in her society. This is a timely subject, evidenced by the fact that the journal *Gender & Development* devoted their entire March 2013 issue on working with men on gender equity

(Gender & Development 2013). Indeed, it was astounding how many men were attracted to participate in the workshops I led throughout Phaltan and Pune for the empowerment of women's voices. Although participation was expected of ARTI employees, participation by men in the other workshops I led in Pune was completely voluntary. Future efforts would likely benefit from improved preparation for the men to lead the activities within the workshop in a more gender-sensitive manner. There are many resources that already exist to support gender sensitivity training, and that could be adjusted for appropriate use within the design for this Vocal Empowerment Workshop (Aksornkool 2002; Asian Project Management Support Programme 2012).

Future applied theatre trainings with ARTI could work more closely with the trainers to devise specific ways in which applied theatre methods could encourage more participation by women in a gender-sensitive manner. At the end of our training, several of the male trainers for ARTI said that they would like to include aspects of this kind of work into their trainings. One recommendation to emerge from this case study would be to inquire if these trainers would like to collaborate with an applied theatre practitioner in doing this. An appropriate next step could be for an applied theatre expert to work directly with trainers to collaboratively design more participatory training methods, even taking the time to apply these methods during actual trainings, so as to continue improving upon the methods. Including discussions on the theoretical foundation for applied theatre could make this work even more grounded and purposeful.

A lesson that emerges from this case study is that most people tend towards lecturing rather than doing when given the chance to facilitate an applied theatre activity. When thrust into a new position—such as facilitating applied theatre—it seems as though people naturally draw upon familiar models of leadership that often perpetuate what Freire would identify as the old "banking system" of education that is hierarchical in nature. It is likely the system in which most of the participants were schooled. One of the jobs, when training the trainers for facilitating applied theatre work, is to begin the process of unlearning. Here a teacher could be likened to a facilitator in applied theatre. It is necessary to unlearn notions of what someone facilitating an activity can, and should, be. This person does not need to be someone who knows the answers, is the expert, or sets the agenda. It can be someone who truly stands beside another and leads through questions that move everyone towards action. One easy mechanism for training the trainers in these ideas and values could be to not allow facilitators to speak on the social issue upon which the activity is focused (as an expert or with the answers), but to only question participants to further them in their understanding of the issue. This could help facilitators—especially in the beginning—to relearn how to facilitate an activity in a manner that encourages active dialogue. This dialogue between participants puts them in the position of being the experts on and authors of their own lives.

Another lesson learned from this case study is that it can be advantageous to include the elders within an organization who are champions for gender equity and women's participation. Here I am referring to Meena Karve's participation throughout the entire two-day intensive, and Dr. A.D. Karve's presence during many parts of it, and in handing out the certificates of completion at the training's closing ceremony. The founder of ARTI and his wife were uniquely able to tie the value of women's participation back to the organization's program objectives. Their presence added validation for the use of applied theatre for women's participation and encouraged participants to engage in it as fully as possible. In this case, Meena was instrumental, explaining important and delicate aspects of gender equity at key junctures during the training. Perhaps, even more importantly, she modeled what she was professing through her participation.

Conclusion

ARTI is an exceptional research and development technology institute for many reasons, not least of which is their successful use of theatre to further their sustainable development aims. Not only is ARTI's staff exceptionally adept, willing, and successful at using theatre for women's participation, but also the institute itself exists in a country with a rich history of theatrical expression. Even though ARTI was applying theatre as a tool for the participation of women in their sustainable development aims, it is interesting to note that they were not (to my knowledge) aware of the theoretical foundation for what is referred to as applied theatre in this book, and in the field of applied theatre at large. Primarily they were not aware of the theoretical work of Paulo Freire and Augusto Boal. The result of this is that they had not fully deconstructed some of the hierarchical and patriarchal methods inherent in traditional Indian and Western theatre forms that can keep women from participating as fully as possible. It is really a conceptual shift that acknowledges the women as authors of their own solutions through a process of critical engagement that is *facilitated* rather than *directed.* Clearly ARTI has made amazing progress including women in their trainings since its founding. It is, indeed, incredible that a scientific research and development institute has been so creatively and consistently using theatre as a participatory tool for their technical trainings and their promotional films. What this case study demonstrates— especially when key ARTI staff members grew in understanding of the difference between facilitation and direction—is that understanding the theory of applied theatre can unleash an even more effective and appropriate approach to theatre for women's participation.

5 Population Media Center

Family planning and reproductive health in Ethiopia

Today we interviewed three different Islamic leaders from the outlying areas in Ethiopia about Population Media Center's trainings on female genital mutilation. One Mullah said that they used to not talk about things regarding sexuality, but that now they see that it needs to be talked about for women to have respect, good treatment and decency.

Journal, July 2010 Osnes

Population Media Center (PMC) is an international NGO using entertainment-education (EE) programming to improve the health and well-being of people and our planet. The organization aims to: educate people about the benefits of small families; encourage the use of effective family planning methods; elevate women's status; prevent exploitation of children; and promote avoidance of HIV/AIDS. PMC programs also address other high-priority issues of specific relevance to each of the 18 countries in which they are situated. The reach of PMC's work extends beyond the boundaries of those select nations through PMC's interregional trainings and the many tools they have generated that are widely respected and used throughout the world.

The mission of PMC is: to work with mass media and other organizations worldwide; to bring about stabilization of human population numbers at a level that can be sustained by the world's natural resources; to lessen the harmful impact of expanding levels of humanity on the earth's environment; and to help large numbers of disadvantaged people live better and move out of poverty. PMC uses a unique methodology of social change communications known as the Sabido Methodology. This strategy involves creating long-running serialized melodramas—written and produced in participating countries in local languages—in order to create characters that gradually evolve into positive role models for the audience, inspiring changes in social norms and behaviors with regard to the issues being addressed.

PMC's Vice President for International Programs, Kriss Barker, shared a briefing with me that contained the following important explanation of the relationship between the work of PMC and issues relevant to women's lives.

EE has been particularly effective in improving women's lives. This is primarily due to the fact that women's issues (such as reproductive health, cultural practices surrounding pregnancy and childbirth, women's status, and violence against women) are often very sensitive issues about which there is often little overt discussion in more traditional societies. Thus, EE programs such as radio or television serial dramas, provide a forum for presentation of these issues in a way that does not directly attack or censure local beliefs or practices, and can motivate discussions about these issues between spouses, parents and their children, or even among family members, neighbours or friends. Research has shown that such discussion is an important mechanism for behaviour change. (Barker 2012, p. 1)

Although the work of PMC is in countries across the globe, this chapter will focus specifically on their programming within the country of Ethiopia (Population Media Center 2012a) where they first started and where they have had impressive results in terms of behavior change. As stated in a PMC newsletter, "PMC-Ethiopia as been a role model for all PMC programs around the world, both in the continuity of effort over many years and in the comprehensive approach taken in our work there" (Population Media Center 2010, p. 4).

Background

The International Conference on Population and Development (ICPD) that occurred in Cairo, Sept. 5–13, 1994, codified views long advocated by women's health activists the world over, which recognize the rights of all people to reproductive health, calling special attention to women's empowerment (Haberland & Measham 2002, p. 1). This conference and the resulting ICPD Program of Action marked a turning point for those working on the issue of population—resulting in the prioritization of reproductive health and women's rights. Specific to theatre and media, from the *Report of the International Conference on Population and Development,* one recommendation is, "effective information, education and communication activities include a range of communication channels, from the most intimate levels of interpersonal communication to formal school curricula, from traditional folk arts to modern mass entertainment, and from seminars for local community leaders to coverage of global issues by the national and international news media. Multichannel approaches are usually more effective than any single communication channel" (UNFPA 1995, p. 78).

The fact that PMC was founded in 1998, just four years after the ICPD, reflects its response to the ICPD call for action. William Ryerson founded PMC with the intention of carrying out comprehensive broadcast media programs in developing countries, designed to encourage adoption of small family norms, use of family planning, and elevation of women's status. The organization works to stabilize human population numbers at a level that can be supported sustainably by the world's natural resources, and to lessen the harmful impact of humanity on the Earth's environment. From 1986 through 1998, Ryerson was the executive vice president for Population Communications International, which worked in Latin America, Africa, and Asia in the development of effective mass media communications dealing with personal decision making about family size and family planning.

PMC's program in Ethiopia began in 1999 when Ryerson traveled to Ethiopia's capital, Addis Ababa, to meet with Dr. Negussie Teffera, who was then the director of the government's National Office of Population and the person responsible for developing Ethiopia's population policy and overseeing its implementation. Dr. Negussie (as he is widely known) advised PMC on how to proceed with implementing a communication intervention within the country. The ambitious goals of the entire team brought together by PMC included: reducing the ideal family size; increasing the ideal age of marriage and childbearing; enhancing understanding of the relative safety of contraceptives compared to early and repeated childbearing; overcoming fears of infidelity resulting from use of family planning; increased belief in appropriateness of determining for oneself the number of children one would have (as opposed to that being determined by a divine being); enhancing public acceptance of employment for women outside the home; promoting education for girls; and promoting gender equity and elevation of female status (W. Ryerson & Negussie 2004, p. 180).

The Sabido Methodology of behavior change communications—used by PMC—was developed in Mexico by Miguel Sabido when he was vice president of the Mexican network Televisa. The strategy is based upon the theories of Stanford University psychologist Albert Bandura (described in greater depth in Chapter 2). Sabido's work is described in a book by Heidi Noel Nariman entitled *Soap Operas for Social Change* (1993). Additional detail is provided in *Soap Operas for Social Change to Prevent HIV/AIDS: A Training Guide for Journalists and Media Personnel*, edited by PMC Vice President for International Programs Kriss Barker and Miguel Sabido, published in 2005 with support from the United Nations Population Fund (UNFPA) (2005).

Issues of population are inherently tied to women's issues, since women are the ones birthing the children. If we want to address the issue of population, we need to concern ourselves with the many issues surrounding women's reproductive lives. The decisions made by or for women of reproductive age will decide the future of our planet. These decisions will decide if population stabilizes, or continues to rise—putting more pressure on our already limited resources, increasing poverty rates, and further burdening our environment. As reiterated in a *National Geographic* article "Population 7 Billion: How Your World Will Change": "Around the world, the childbearing decisions of young women will determine whether global population stabilizes or not" (Olson 2011, p. 38).

Stating that population stabilization depends on decisions made by or for women of childbearing age raises the questions: What choices are available? Who is making them? For what reasons? It also brings into question: Who has the right to be making these decisions? As stated, PMC began its work after The International Conference on Population and Development in Cairo in 1994. The ICPD Program of Action defines reproductive health as a "state of complete physical, mental and social well being in all matters relating to the reproductive system and to its functions and processes" (UNFPA 1995, p. 40). This implies that people have the capability to reproduce and the freedom to decide if, when, and how often to do so.

Important to this approach is helping women empower themselves by improving access to education, health care, and employment. One of the outcomes from the Cairo conference was this reframing of reproductive health in terms of reproductive *rights*. This has shifted the focus of issues related to population onto women and their reproductive rights within their given societies.

Giving women rights over their own bodies and allowing them to plan for their desired family size not only changes women's lives, but also improves the well-being of an entire community. "At the household level, lower fertility has also been found associated with better health and schooling outcomes, and lower poverty" (Das Gupta, Bongaarts, & Cleland 2011, p. 2) as well as "reduced maternal mortality and morbidity, increased women's labor force participation" (Das Gupta et al. 2011, p. 15).

Programs

In each country in which it works, PMC builds a collaborative process between radio and/or television broadcasters, appropriate government ministries, and non-governmental organizations, to design and implement a comprehensive media strategy for addressing family and reproductive health issues. Because of the known effectiveness of entertainment-education serial dramas in changing attitudes and behaviors, such programs are generally the centerpiece of the strategy. Other forms that are used to strengthen the messages include live theatre, published books, video games, and training and capacity building programs. PMC uses a Whole Society Strategy, which involves using several media formats to send mutually reinforcing messages that deal with deeply held beliefs about women's roles, about the desirability of children, about relations between men and women, and about taboos. Selected key elements of the Whole Society Strategy include: "(1) segmentation research to identify audience segments and the media formats consumed by each; (2) research to identify media formats that can leverage other media to stimulate cross-segment reinforcement . . . and (5) collaboration with government and NGO activities through partnerships" (W. Ryerson & Negussie 2004, pp. 178–179).

In designing all of these programs, PMC works with stakeholders to identify the various cultural issues and prevailing attitudes affecting decision making about sexual risk behaviors within the country. They also analyze barriers and opportunities for effective use of the mass media for promoting reproductive health. Finally, they develop an action plan that incorporates as much of the broadcast media as possible in a concerted campaign designed to promote sexual and reproductive health.

To date, PMC has produced seven radio serial dramas in Ethiopia. The initial two radio dramas—*Yeken Kignit* (*Looking Over One's Daily Life*) and *Dhimbibba* (*Getting the Best Out of Life*)—were aired June 2002 through November 2004. Both programs focused on the issues central to reproductive health, family planning, HIV/AIDS, and the elevation of women's status, as well as the themes of marriage by abduction, the education of girls, and spousal communication about issues of reproduction. During this time, approximately *half of the population* of Ethiopia listened to at least one of PMC's radio dramas. This equates to approximately 40 million listeners (Population Media Center 2012b).

In 2005, PMC produced a talk radio and panel discussion program *Alegnta* that was aimed at youth. During the program young people called in with questions and concerns regarding social and health issues, and a panel—which included other young people, adults, professionals, and teachers—discussed the topic brought up by the caller. The aim was to stimulate dialogue on these issues and disseminate accurate information. Topics covered included: adolescent sexuality, addiction in youths, the development of life skills, building self-confidence, developing communication skills, and developing successful interpersonal relationships (Population Media Center 2012b).

Within Ethiopia, PMC has published numerous literary works over the past 11 years. The object of these publications is to raise awareness about reproductive health, family planning, HIV/AIDS, and Harmful Traditional Practices (HTP). It is hoped these works of art will encourage attitudes and behaviors that help Ethiopians protect themselves from health-related hazards. These publications included collections of short fictional and true stories in *Alegnta*, a magazine for youth, leaflets, and posters. These are given away free of charge and distributed through libraries, governmental agencies, UN agencies, professional associations, schools, and other relevant organizations (Yasin 2010).

PMC is responsible for the production of a full-length play entitled *Ysak Jember* (*Laughter at Dusk*) that was launched in September of 2003 and was attended by the former President of Ethiopia, Dr. Negasso Gidada. It was staged in the capital for four months and then performed in 14 other cities within Ethiopia. Stage dramas are relatively inexpensive and are seen as credible by the traditional elements of society. They can also attract attention and stimulate thinking—if situations are effectively dramatized—and reinforce the radio messages (W. Ryerson & Negussie 2004, p. 186).

One of the cornerstones of the activities of PMC is their training and capacity-building programs. In Ethiopia, PMC organized more than 40 capacity-building training programs from 2003 to 2010 in which more than 1,494 participants—65% male and 35% female—haven taken part. Journalists, media managers, and practitioners, together with writers and theatrical art specialists, are given priority attention, due to their crucial role in increasing public awareness about important health-related issues. People in media and the arts have the opportunity to help people to understand the concepts of health and social issues, and can be powerful agents of change when activated. Training is also provided for youth so that they may gain experiences to identify as positive social change agents. PMC also conducts training programs for women to help them empower themselves and to encourage them to participate actively in the elimination of the practice of female genital mutilation (FGM) and all forms of discrimination against women. There are also trainings for religious leaders (see Photo 5.1), community elders, and

Photo 5.1 An Ethiopian Muslim Mullah being interviewed about Population Media Center's training on female genital mutilation.

female circumcisers to develop positive behavior towards the eradication of FGM. Training is also provided to law enforcement professionals.

Participants from a training session for religious leaders communicated that they all knew that FGM was somehow bad, but never knew the extent of the harm it had in terms of the psychological, physical, and sexual life of women in their society. They had no idea of the severity of the injury to reproductive health. The training offered a comprehensive and consolidated knowledge and helped them to examine their scriptures in greater depth. Sheik Nadir Seid Nur, Vice Chairman of the Somali region Council of Islamic Affairs, stated, "The training was exceptionally good, comprehensive and unforgettable. It made us see and feel the pain and the multifaceted suffering our sisters and daughters have been subjected to" (Moges 2010, p. 55). Another comment was shared by Woizero Aiysh Mohammed, head of the Afar Region Women's Affairs Bureau, "In Afar there are good traditional practices that should be appreciated and preserved. For example we have no street children, and no prostitutes, owing to our traditions of mutual assistance that derives from the clan based social organization. . . . We also have a number of harmful traditional practices of which FGM is the most gruesome. So we need to sieve the bad from the good and strengthen the latter while abandoning the former" (Moges 2010, p. 55).

PMC is also conducting a program with support from UN Women, which is designed to address violence against women in Ethiopia. The project's objective is to provide information related to both violence against women and female empowerment through a multimedia communication and capacity-building program. PMC has conducted five capacity-building workshops to address these issues.

Not specific to just Ethiopia, but related to the focus on addressing violence against women, is the multilingual *BREAKAWAY* video game and the *BREAKAWAY* Facilitator's Guide that was created through a collaboration between PMC, the Emergent Media Center at Champlain College, and United Nations Fund for Population Awareness. Launched in 2010, it has been played online in over 180 countries. *BREAKAWAY* is an episodic electronic football game (soccer in the United States) that utilizes entertainment-education strategies to combat violence against women and girls, bullying, and gender inequality. The game is geared towards boys aged 8–15 and encourages a change in gender norms around the world. The Facilitator's Guide provides the educator or coach with the specific tools to delve deeper into the issues addressed in the video game, where players must make critical decisions throughout the story related to gender equality, violence against women and girls, bullying, and more (Population Media Center 2013b).

Stance on gender

The two leaders of PMC's work in Ethiopia, PMC president William Ryerson and director of PMC-Ethiopia Dr. Negussie Teffera, write that, "In Africa, it is difficult to address the adoption of family planning or HIV/AIDS prevention without simultaneously addressing the status of women" (2004, p. 185). PMC realizes that improving the status of women worldwide is the most effective and humane strategy for stabilizing population. PMC works with leaders and governments within a culture to identify the many factors that keep women's status low—often including Harmful Traditional Practices (HTP). In Ethiopia the leading HTPs addressed by PMC are female genital mutilation, marriage by abduction, and early marriage. PMC designed a media strategy to disseminate accurate health information surrounding these multiple factors and practices. PMC's fifth radio drama, *Sibrat* (*Trauma*), is taking on issues relevant for women in Ethiopia, such as female genital mutilation (FGM), reproductive health, HIV/AIDS, and early marriage and childbearing. A listener from Harar in Ethiopia writes about former traditional attitudes surrounding FGM that were changed by listening to the drama:

> Formerly I used to believe that unless a girl is circumcised, she becomes addicted to breaking utensils, tends to be insubordinate defying the authority of her would-be husband, and will prove to be sexually frigid and cheap. Now I have understood from the drama that all these beliefs are false. I telephoned my mother and told her to listen to the drama. At the time, my mother was preparing herself to witness the circumcision of my sisters. I explained to her how inhumane and repugnant the practice was. Since I was successful in making her follow the drama closely, she completely abandoned the idea and my two sisters were spared from the pain that they were about to undergo. (Population Media Center 2009a, p. 1)

PMC's messaging extends beyond just HTPs and includes other issues surrounding reproductive health and women's rights.

Photo 5.2 A young rural Ethiopian girl.

At the heart of all of PMC's programming is a passionate commitment to improving the lives of women worldwide (see Photo 5.2), as expressed in this letter from William Ryerson on their website:

> The cost in human suffering that results from excessive childbearing is staggering:
>
> - 600,000 women and girls die worldwide every year from pregnancy and childbirth—a figure equal to U.S. deaths in World War I, World War II, the Korean War and Vietnam combined. Most of these women are in their teens and early twenties, forced by their societies into bearing children at a young age and far too frequently.
> - 140,000 women bleed to death each year during childbirth. Tragically, many die within reach of medical facilities because their relatives refuse to allow them to be treated by male doctors.
> - 75,000 women die each year trying to end their pregnancies. The U.N. estimates that worldwide, 50,000 women and girls try to induce abortions on themselves each day (18.3 million per year). Many of those who survive face life-long, disabling pain.
> - Approximately 100,000 women die each year from infection, and another 40,000 women die from the agony of prolonged labor. And those are only the fatalities. UNICEF's statistics show that for every woman who dies, 30 survive with gruesome injuries and disabilities. That's more than 17 million women per year.

Add to that the exhausting burden of repeated pregnancies and births, and you have a global picture of suffering on the part of women that demands global response. What is infuriating is that these deaths and tragic injuries are almost entirely preventable. Since these figures were compiled, however, U.S. support for preventive family planning information and services has been slashed. Given the worldwide shortage of funds for such programs, the very cost-effective mass media strategy used by Population Media Center makes more sense than ever. (B. Ryerson 2012)

Sustainable development aims

Given the expansive scope of PMC's mission, their sustainable development aims cut across nearly every sector of development. Using the Millennium Development Goals (MDGs) as one way to divide various areas of specialization within sustainable development, the work of PMC could easily be seen as positively impacting all eight goals (United Nations Millennium Development Goals 2000). PMC's aim to bring about stabilization of human population numbers at a level that can be sustained by the world's natural resources will contribute to food security, fresh water preservation, energy access, and beyond. PMC's aim, to lessen the harmful impact of expanding humanity on the earth's environment, will help preserve forests and other natural environments as well as lessen rates of pollution. As stated in the paper, *Population, Poverty and Sustainable Development,* "The most feasible way to reduce mankind's ecological footprint may be to further reduce the number of feet being born" (Das Gupta et al. 2011, p. 16). Finally, PMC's aim to help large numbers of disadvantaged people live better and move out of poverty contributes to the improvement of women's lives—since women disproportionately constitute the poorest in the world.

Ultimately, all countries will need to address population growth, because of limits to energy, fresh water, ecosystem services, forests, and agricultural production. As I heard stated by a participant at Rio+20, "Either we reduce our numbers willingly, or nature will do it brutally." The plan for addressing population by PMC—which centers on the empowerment of women—certainly seems more desirable as a proactive measure than waiting around for rampant overuse of resources and destruction of the natural world to run its course.

Funding

To produce their programs, PMC partners worldwide with bi- and multilateral agencies, philanthropic organizations, national governments, socially responsible corporations, and committed individuals. Their most significant, long-term relationships are with the UNFPA, the Packard Foundation, UNICEF, Save the Children, and the Oak Foundation. A strong alignment between the missions of PMC and various agencies of the United Nations has led to more than half of PMC's programs receiving support from UN agencies. Primary corporate support comes from the Bayer Corporation and Colgate-Palmolive (Population Media Center 2012b).

Description of how I worked with this organization

My association with PMC and the issue of population originated with my involvement in the documentary film *Mother: Caring for 7 Billion* (Fauchere 2011). I was approached by the producer of the film, Joyce Johnson, to serve as the "human thread" in the film because of my role as cofounder of Mothers Acting Up, a movement to mobilize mothers to act on behalf of the world's children (Mothers Acting Up 2011). They decided to include my personal story in the film as well, once they found out that I was the youngest in a Catholic family of 10 children, but with my husband, JP, had only two biological children and one through adoption. PMC was the organizational sponsor for the film and allowed the film company, Tiroir A Films, to fundraise for the project through their nonprofit organization. Because PMC in Ethiopia is such a success story in terms of programming that effectively impacted population, it served as one of the central stories in the film.

I traveled to Ethiopia in July of 2010 with the filmmaker, Christophe Fauchere. This visit was planned to correspond with the 10th Anniversary celebration for PMC-Ethiopia. During this time, I was able to work with the director of PMC in Ethiopia Dr. Negussie Teffera, the Ethiopian PMC staff, PMC founder William Ryerson, Communication Director Katie Elmore, and Vice President for International Programs Kriss Barker. I conducted my Vocal Empowerment Workshop in Ethiopia for PMC in Addis Ababa for use as possible footage in the film—which given the thorough description in preceding chapters, I will not detail here. During the course of filming other footage, I was able to visit the studio while a PMC radio drama was being recorded (see Photo 5.3). The program being recorded was *Mieraf (New Beginning)*, Population Media Center's sixth radio serial drama in Ethiopia that was launched in June 2010 and ran through June 2011.

Photo 5.3 Ethiopian actors performing during a studio recording of Population Media Center's sixth radio serial drama *Mieraf (New Beginning)*.

I was able to attend part of a PMC training for Ethiopian script writers, where Kriss Barker and Kimani Njogu were leading a training for writing in the Sabido Methodology. At that same session, I attended a presentation on transmedia storytelling (Phillips 2012) by Katie Elmore. Though this approach had not yet been adopted by PMC in Ethiopia, it was currently being introduced with enthusiastic support by Ryerson.

I conducted interviews for the film with Islamic leaders from the Afar and Somali regions of Ethiopia about the issues of female genital mutilation, and the training they received on this issue from PMC. It was incredibly moving to learn through the translator that these men had such sincere regret for their part in perpetuating this Harmful Traditional Practice for so long. For Ethiopian Christians, FGM is a cultural practice, but for Ethiopian Muslims it is a religious ceremony. As part of PMC's Whole Society Strategy, they brought in highly respected Imams from the Middle East who taught the local Mullahs that the practice of FGM has no basis in the Koran or any other part of Islam. They went on to convey that FGM was a sin against God and that anyone who did it would be cursed. These Ethiopian Mullahs then taught the local women who did these procedures what they had learned. One Mullah said that at first people thought he was crazy for believing this, but that now people are starting to teach each other that FGM is not a good practice. The Mullahs we interviewed expressed deep remorse, and said that about 60% of the people in their areas have stopped.

I also led a focus group of young women of childbearing age—who were listeners of PMC radio dramas—to learn of the impact of the dramas on their lives. Although all of the women had stories, it is the story of Zinet Muhammed (see Photo 5.4) that stood out. She said that in her family there are 14 children, and

Photo 5.4 Focus group of young Ethiopian women of childbearing age, who are all listeners of PMC's radio dramas, including Zinet Muhammed (center).

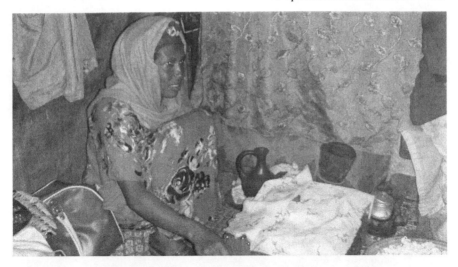

Photo 5.5 Zinet Muhammed's mother who has given birth to 14 children.

that this was her father's second marriage and that he had many children with his first wife. Conditions were bad, such that her family could only afford to eat one meal a day. When she was young, her father wanted to marry her off to a much older rich man, but she refused and ran away to her aunt's house and stayed for over a year. She said that the character Ababa from the radio drama inspired her to make this choice. While she was away, Zinet's younger sister died of AIDS, leaving behind a three-month-old daughter, Wasila, who likewise tested positive for HIV. Throughout all of this time, Zinet continued with her schooling while holding down a job at a local AIDS prevention organization and helping to support her family. She moved back home after her sister's death and has since been like a surrogate mother to her little niece. Zinet also convinced her mother (see Photo 5.5) to seek out birth control, because of what she learned from the drama. When she went to the hospital with her mother, the doctor refused to give her the pill without her husband's permission. Zinet cried and begged the doctor saying that they didn't have anything to live on.

The doctor said okay and the mother took the pills secretly. Zinet convinced her father to listen to the dramas too, and afterwards he believed that the pill could stop a pregnancy and that having fewer children was better. He said that his wish for his children was for them to have two children each. Zinet has formed many listening groups in her own community to get more people to learn from PMC's radio dramas. As Zinet said, "Ababa helps people more than herself. I'm a lot like her" (Muhammed 2010). After learning of her compelling story from the focus group, we arranged to travel to her village to visit with her family. There we met her mother, father, and her many siblings (see Photo 5.6) who all expressed admiration and gratitude for Zinet's presence in their lives. Zinet's inspirational story truly is the emotional core of the film *Mother: Caring for 7 Billion*.

Photo 5.6 Zinet, her niece Wasila, and her father in their home in the village.

Site description

Ethiopia is located in the horn of Africa, with Eritrea to the north, Djibouti and Somalia to the east, Sudan to the west, and Kenya to the south. Though completely landlocked, it is a major source of the Nile River. The major ethnic groups are: Amhara, Tigre, Gurage, Adere, Oromo, Sidama, Afar, Saho, Somali, Konso, and the Sudanic peoples of western Ethiopia. It is a nation whose rich history dates back over three thousand years. Scientists assert that Ethiopia is one of the oldest sites of human existence (Hopkin 2005).

In the fourth century, Ethiopia officially became Christian and since that time, the Ethiopian Orthodox Church has influenced the history, politics, and culture of Ethiopia. Ethiopia and the bordering Eritrea have historically been predominantly Orthodox Christians, surrounded by Muslim nations since the spread of Islam. A determining cultural factor for at least thirteen hundred years in the region—including current-day Eritrea and Ethiopia—is that "as Semetic-Hamatic peoples, they also have languages, scripts and culture which are profoundly different from those of the Arab, Bantu or Nilotic people who surround them, some of whom were until very recently in relationship of vassalage to the Amhara leadership of the Ethiopian empire" (Plastow 1998, p. 99). Ethiopia is also unique among most African nations in that it has a history of self-rule dating back to nearly 1000 BCE.

Ethiopia's victory against Italy's militaristic attempt in 1895–1896 to colonize them distinguishes Ethiopia as the only African nation that successfully resisted European colonization, which is a great source of pride within the country. However, Ethiopia's position between the two Italian colonies Eritrea and Somalia made it enticing land for Italy to attempt to conquer. Early in the 1930s Benito Mussolini's Fascist regime sought to claim Ethiopian territory again to unite its African colonies and make up for past defeats. Ethiopia was invaded and occupied by fascist Italy 1935–1936 but was liberated during World War II by the Allied powers.

Haile Selassie (1892–1975) was the Emperor of Ethiopia from 1930 to 1974. He is heir to a dynasty that traced its roots back to the tradition of King Solomon and Queen Makeda (otherwise known as the Queen of Sheba). Ethiopia's monarchy traces its roots back to 200 BCE (Hayford 1969, p. xxv) and persisted until the end of Haile Selassie's rule in 1974. The Soviet-backed Derg, or Coordinating Committee of the Armed Forces, Police, and Territorial Army, which later changed its name to the Provisional Military Administrative Council, deposed Selassie in 1974 and then ruled until 1987. Shortly after, land, banks, and companies were nationalized, and Ethiopia was declared a socialist state. This communist–led governing body imprisoned and executed thousands of its opponents without a trial during its rule (Waal 1991). Following national elections, the provisional Military Administrative Council was abolished in 1987. The Ethiopian People's Revolutionary Democratic Front (EPRDF) came to power in 1991 after defeating the military dictatorship of Mengistu's Derg (Pausewang, Tronvoll, & Aalen 2002). Meles Zenawi of the EPRDF continued to rule through 1997, attempting to establish Ethiopia as a democracy (Gebeyehu & Edemariam 1997, p. 115). The many famines that have occurred in Ethiopia are well known. For many in the Global North, when the subject of famines arises, Ethiopia is the first country that comes to mind. Historically, the fundamental cause of "acute" and "chronic" malnutrition (short-term and long-term starvation) and the many famines throughout the history of Ethiopia, was poor governance, not drought (Mariam 2012).

With a population of 87.1 million people, Ethiopia has a fertility rate of 5.3 children born per woman. Surprisingly, access to contraceptive methods is not the main problem; it isn't access but misinformation. Misconceptions about contracting HIV/AIDS as well as a lack of desire to reduce family size continue to be formidable stumbling blocks for stabilizing population and preventing the spread of HIV/AIDS (Population Media Center 2013a).

Most Ethiopians are currently either Orthodox (Coptic) Christians or Muslims, with a small minority of Roman Catholics, Pentecostals, and people of the Jewish faith. Although all of the many Ethiopian languages enjoy official state recognition, Amharic is the "working language" of the federal government, and along with Oromo, it is one of the two most widely spoken languages in the country. English is also a language of the state, and the language of university education.

Local gender information

According to author Paulos Milkias, "More than 85 percent of Ethiopia's women reside in rural areas, where peasant families are engaged primarily in subsistence farming. Peasant women are integrated into the rural economy, though their worth is rarely recognized, and the labor they engage in is crushing over a lifetime" (2011, p. 222). Women endure the physical hardship of carrying loads of firewood and water jugs over long distances. They have far fewer opportunities for advancement than men of equal economic and social status, in terms of education, employment, or personal advancement. The work of women is not valued as productive labor because it does not often result in cash, but is rather housework, care work, or farm labor. Women who migrate to urban areas because of armed conflict or other factors have great difficulty attaining work because of high unemployment rates in urban areas and because of their lack of skills. Many are forced to resort to prostitution to survive. Ethiopian families are dominated by the males in the family, with the wife and daughters taking subservient roles.

Women's health in Ethiopia is undermined by a combination of social, cultural, and economic factors that lead to their low status in society. Especially in rural areas, traditional value systems have imposed, and continue to impose, heavy burdens on Ethiopian women. Bearing children at a young age due to early marriage often leads to a condition known as fistula, a medical condition in which a tear occurs between the vagina and the rectum. It is said that 100,000 women in Ethiopia suffer from untreated fistula, with an average of 9,000 developing this condition every year (Milkias 2011, p. 227).

One medical procedure that is commonly practiced—irrespective of religion or economic status—is female genital mutilation or female circumcision, a procedure by which some of a woman's external genital tissues, such as the clitoral hood, the clitoris or labia, are removed (Ethiopia, Women's Affairs Office 2004). According to a study performed by the Population Reference Bureau, Ethiopia has a prevalence rate of female genital mutilation of 81% among women ages 35 to 39, and 62% among women ages 15–19 (Population Reference Bureau 2010, p. 3). This smaller percentage among younger women—though still over half of all the women in Ethiopia—shows that the practice is less prevalent than it once was. While I was in Ethiopia, I was told of an instance in which a teen-aged girl's parents gained awareness that this practice was not needed for her health or mental stability, and informed their daughter that they were not going to have it done to her. The girl pleaded with her parents for it to be done so she would fit in among her peers and be attractive to men. Her parents conceded by having the public ceremony *as if* she had been circumcised, but did not actually have the procedure done. This story illustrates how entrenched traditions can become, and insidiously perpetuated. Older women in the community—who rarely have had access to medical training—most often perform this practice, and the procedure can lead to many complications, contributing to difficulties and pain during intercourse and childbirth.

Most women marry very young and have no say in who they marry. The average age for marriage for girls in Ethiopia is 15.6 years, but in some cases girls are married as young as 9 years old (Population Reference Bureau 2010, p. 3). Abduction is a legitimate and common way of procuring a bride in southern Ethiopia. The practice has been going on so long that its origins as a social practice are unknown. The usual procedure is to kidnap a girl, hide her, and then eventually rape her. Then, based on her having lost her virginity or becoming pregnant, the man can claim her as his bride. According to surveys conducted in 2003 by the National Committee on Traditional Practices in Ethiopia (NCTPE), the prevalence of marriage by abduction is 80% in Oromiya Region, and as high as 92% in

Southern Nations, with a national average of 69%. (IRIN: Humanitarian News and Analysis 2007). Rape is not considered a serious crime in Ethiopia, although the prevalence of sexual violence has a dire impact among women (Falola & Heaton 2010). Because women in Ethiopia have so little control over their lives and their sexuality, they are not able to avoid many of the risks that leave them disproportionately vulnerable to becoming victims of HIV/AIDS (Merso 2008).

Fear of being abducted into marriage can cause many families to keep their girls home from school once they near or reach puberty. In poor families, the girls are often taken out of school to be married off young or to work at home. Additionally, since girls are generally seen as less valuable than boys, their education is not often a high priority. For every 100 boys enrolled in secondary education, there are approximately only 77 girls enrolled. The number of female dropouts is especially high in the transition from primary to secondary school. In 2009, only 41% of girls completed their primary education and only 30% enrolled in secondary education. This leads to the extremely low literacy rate of 18% for Ethiopian women over the age of 15 (UNESCO 2012).

Local theatre history

There have been very few script-based Ethiopian plays in any language other than Amharic. When considering theatre in Ethiopia, it is important to remember that Ethiopia was never colonized, so its theatrical history differs significantly from other African nations. That is not to say that Ethiopia was not influenced by the colonization occurring all around them, and by educational models from colonizing countries. However, there is not the same colonial control over language and culture that occurred in other places throughout the continent and find expression in such works as *Decolonizing the Mind* by Ngugin wa Thiong'o (1986). In Ethiopia there is, though, the same separation between indigenous forms of theatre—which rely heavily on dance and music—and Western-style drama that is most often the spoken performance of a written script.

Dialogue-based drama was introduced to Ethiopia in 1912 by an Ethiopian aristocrat, Tekle Hawariat Tekle-Mariam, who wrote the first Ethiopian play, *Yawrewoch Komediya* (*Comedy of the Animals*). Common to the African continent, the traditional music and dance-based indigenous forms of theatre were carried on by the more rural populations, and the elite in urban areas took up the dialogue-based drama. Before the 1990s, dialogue-based drama was both written and performed in Amharic, which is the language of the ruling ethnic group, representing only 20–25% of the population (Plastow 1998, p. 100). The first genuinely popular play written in Amharic is Yoftahe Negusse's *Afajeshion* (*You Got Me Caught*), which was written while the emperor was in exile in the late 1930s, and questioned the way in which he had handled the war.

The Ethiopian National Theatre, formerly known as the Haile Selassie I Theatre, is in the very center of the capital, Addis Ababa. Early playwrights in Ethiopia tended to be members of nobility and were highly educated, while actors were more varied and often of lower classes—coming from performers of *azmari,* or minstrels. Female *azmari* were especially looked down upon by society for being assumed to be loose women. By the 1960s, the National Theatre began to produce plays with more social relevancy and sophistication. With the Marxist Revolution of 1974, plays became more political. Various forms of agit-prop and popular theatre were used in Ethiopia from the mid-1970s through the mid-1980s to allow people to participate in the national debate about how their country should develop and to involve people in making choices about their future (Plastow 1998, p. 101). These efforts were largely linked with resistance movements influenced by Marxist thinking.

In 1979, a Theatre Arts Department was established at the University of Addis Ababa, which has provided trained actors, directors, and writers for Ethiopian theatre ever since (Gebeyehu & Edemariam 1997, p. 116). In 1984, the Ethiopian government established the Rural Arts Program, which aimed to send trained personnel in the fine arts, literature, music, and drama to each of Ethiopia's then 14 regions, with the aim of encouraging the formation of amateur arts groups (Plastow 1998, p. 105). In 1983, the government established a committee to oversee which plays were produced, resulting in some censorship and the banning of plays. This has changed since 1991 and now there is more theatrical work presented in languages other than Amharic, and work that takes on the many social challenges Ethiopia faces.

As far as views of women who participate in theatre, Jane Plastow writes in her introduction to *African Theatre Women* that "a theatre lecturer at the University of Addis Ababa in Ethiopia told me that he would never go out with an actress, they could not be trusted not to go off with other men" 2002, p. xii). Plastow goes on to note, when the first modern stage plays were performed, men played women's roles (2002, p. xii). The stigma of being an actress seems alive and well in Ethiopia as it is historically around the world.

One play that deals with social issues impacting women—that has been published in English—is *Snatch and Run* or *Marriage by Abduction* by Menghestu Lemma. This play tells the story of a group of childhood and school-day friends who plan to abduct a young wife for one of them in the traditional manner (Lemma 1970; 2009). It is telling about this subject that it is a comedy. Menghestu's second play published by Arada Books is *Marriage of Unequals*, in which Baharu, an educated young man of the modern Ethiopian elite, plans to marry a simple uneducated country girl.

Description of applied theatre

This case study will examine the radio drama *Yeken Kignit* (*Looking Over One's Daily Life*), which was one of the first dramas created by PMC-Ethiopia. It aired on Radio Ethiopia from June 2002 to November 2004 in Amharic. Each episode was 20 minutes long, and there were two episodes per week. The broadcast of these episodes was also repeated. The multiple storylines in the drama addressed HIV/AIDS, family planning, education of girls, and spousal communication (Salem et al. 2008, p. 6). At the same time PMC-Ethiopia broadcast *Yeken Kignit*, there began the 140 episodes of a second program called *Dhimbibba* (*Getting the Best Out of Life*), which addressed a wide range of issues and was produced in another widely spoken language, Oromiffa. It is useful to note that when monitoring and evaluating the impact of these programs, results are sometimes conflated between the two distinct programs, since they were developed and broadcast simultaneously. In 2009, PMC rebroadcasted the 257 episodes of *Yeken Kignit* throughout the southern region of Ethiopia. This came at the request of the Ethiopian government and was funded by the Ethiopian Southern Peoples and Nationalities Regional Government, with additional support from the Packard Foundation (Population Media Center 2009b).

Goals of the radio drama

The goal of the radio drama *Yeken Kignit* was to address the issues of family planning and reproductive health, HIV/AIDS, and women's empowerment through Fikirte, the primary female character. The overall program objective for *Yeken Kignit* was to promote family planning use for birth spacing and limiting, and to improve the reproductive health of men and women in Ethiopia. Communication and behavioral objectives were for the audience to improve their knowledge, attitudes, and practices about contraceptives; increase their HIV/AIDs awareness, attitudes, and behaviors; and impact perceptions of women's status and related factors that influence reproductive health and family planning (Salem et al. 2008, p. 6).

The many indicators for measuring to what extent the program reached its goals were knowledge, attitude, and behavior change clustered in the following categories: HIV/AIDS prevention, use of family planning, reproductive health, education of female children, and gender equity.

Design of the radio drama

The design of the research-based radio serial drama *Yeken Kignit* followed these steps. Before making a plan, PMC conducted a consensus-building workshop with several government agencies, scriptwriters, theatre artists, donor governments, foundations, local nongovernmental organizations, business leaders, and reproductive health researchers and professionals. This preliminary work was to begin developing a strategy for focusing the program's mission and to assure that objectives and messages were appropriate for Ethiopia. A literature review was conducted to identify research and information gaps, explore the effectiveness and capacity of other implementing agencies, understand the status of social-content radio serial dramas in the country, and determine whether any audience research had already been conducted (Teffera 2008, p. 36). This was followed by an assessment of media in Ethiopia to determine what format and stations reached what audiences. Ideal broadcast times were also researched, in order to reach the largest audience.

The formative research that was conducted included research into previous health communications within Ethiopia, identification of audience subgroups, and interviews with technical experts (Salem et al. 2008, p. 6). This included assessing the target audience's knowledge, attitudes, and behaviors regarding key issues to be addressed in the drama—such as HIV/AIDS and family planning. Socioeconomic and cultural aspects of the target audience were also explored as part of this formative research.

PMC recruited coordinators for this program with experience in radio broadcasting and theatre. They also sought out scriptwriters familiar with the many issues surrounding family planning and HIV/AIDS. Once the production team was assembled, its members, along with selected stakeholders, participated in a five-week training workshop on designing an educational and also highly entertaining radio serial drama. It should be noted that the writers of this drama were all Ethiopian. At this capacity-building training, PMC researchers shared findings from their research among the target audience. Producers and scriptwriters used this information to guide them in developing the key characters. A technical advisory committee was also established, composed of scriptwriters, radio program producers, a creative arts adviser, a senior research officer, a gender expert, a communication expert, and a representative from the Ministry of Health (in order to check the accuracy of the material presented) (Teffera 2008, p. 36). They also helped keep the balance between the script being entertaining and educational.

Before writing the dramas, the story line was developed and discussed to establish character profiles and the settings for the action. These choices were made based on the issues identified in the formative research. The plots for each scene were also discussed and developed as well as exciting cliff-hangers for the end of each episode. The design for writing the radio drama *Yeken Kignit* according to the Sabido Methodology was as follows. There were three scenes per episode with bridge music and sometimes a narrator speaking in between scenes. Within the entire radio drama, there were three story lines and settings. Of the nine main characters, three were transitional, three positive, and three negative—with extensive interactions and complex relationships between them all. It was important that members of the target audience recognized parts of themselves in the characters who served as role models. Characters were realistic, but simultaneously a little bit larger than life. This adjustment was made carefully; if a character was too large, no one believed it, but if a character was too normal, no one tuned in. The positive and the negative characters in the drama remained what they were from beginning to end. It was the transitional character's journeys that were key for the audience.

The story was designed to reflect the key concerns of the audience in an environment they recognized. The dialogue was written to sound like the natural speech of the local people within the target audience. Since one radio drama reached both rural and urban populations, both styles of speech were represented via different characters and settings. Various emotional pitches were explored so as to not exhaust or bore the audience. Humor was sprinkled in to sustain interest and relieve the heaviness of many of the social issues being addressed. Careful attention was paid to detail in both references within the dialogue and with sound effects. Finally, a suitable epilogue was written for each episode.

The creative team created four pilot episodes initially, and pretested them with focus groups comprised of members of the intended audience. They used standard pretesting tools to test for relevancy of the various story lines, suitability of the language, and reception of the characters as compelling and believable. Once that feedback was shared with the creative team and the advisory committee, adjustments were made by the scriptwriters, who then continued writing the rest of the program.

While *Yeken Kignit* was being broadcast, there were other mechanisms built in for audiences to provide feedback. To monitor the program, there were three waves of focus groups that were conducted, listening groups from whom PMC collected listening diaries, and listener letters that were analyzed for feedback. Finally, an independent research firm measured the impact of the entire program by conducting a postintervention survey.

Outcomes of the radio drama

Initial steps towards the creation of the radio drama were informed by the consensus-building workshop and the literature review conducted by PMC. The outcome of the media assessment conducted by PMC identified radio as the most favored channel for communication for the program. In the two and half years of broadcasting, a total of 257 episodes of the Amharic *Yeken Kignit* and 140 episodes of the Oromiffa *Dhimbiba* were produced and broadcast over Radio Ethiopia, with repeat broadcasts over FM and Ethiopia Radio National Service, respectively. It was determined that Radio Ethiopia should air the premiere of the drama since it reaches a majority of Ethiopia's population. In Ethiopia, as in many other African countries, the government essentially controls broadcasting. This fact makes collaborating with governmental agencies on the creation of the radio dramas essential for effective dissemination of the programming. Television reaches a much smaller portion of the population in Ethiopia (W. Ryerson & Negussie 2004, p. 181) and its programming is much more expensive to produce than radio programming.

Problems identified by the formative research included: high levels of unmet need for family planning, negative attitudes and misrepresentations about contraceptive methods, lack of spousal and parent-child communication about HIV/AIDS, lack of knowledge about modes of HIV transmission and prevention, and high levels of stigma and discrimination against people with HIV and AIDS (Salem et al. 2008, p. 6).

An impressive army of experienced experts was involved in the five-week capacity-building workshop that was provided by PMC for Ethiopian scriptwriters and playwrights, acquainting them with the Sabido Methodology for entertainment-education, in preparation for their first PMC radio dramas to be written in Ethiopia. Trainers included:

> Miguel Sabido; Tom Kazungu, the first person in Africa and the first person in radio to use the Sabido Methodology in a radio program that he produced in Kenya; Rose Haji, the producer of the Tanzanian radio drama that was studied for its effects on family planning use and AIDS avoidance in the 1990s; Ramadhan Swalehe, who led the research center in Tanzania that gathered the survey data; Virginia Carter, former head of drama for Norman Lear's "All in the Family," "Maude," and "The Jeffersons"; and David Poindexter, a 30-year veteran of promoting entertainment-education programs worldwide (W. Ryerson & Negussie 2004, p. 184).

Once the production team had undergone the five-week training workshop, they took the information given to them by researchers and developed the key characters in the drama. Fikirte was the primary positive character. Throughout the course of the drama, she talks to her friends and family about the benefits of family planning and encourages her stepfather to send her sister to school. The production team also developed Damte, the primary negative character, who has multiple sex partners and traffics drugs. A transitional character, Wubalem, received advice from Fikirte to use contraceptives to avoid getting pregnant so soon after her fistula surgery, and while her family's financial security is unstable. With Fikirte's help, Wubalem is able to convince her husband to space their children by using contraceptives for a period of time (Salem et al. 2008, p. 7). It is important for the audience to feel as though they can identify with the characters, such that audience members might say, "I know that character; he or she is just like my neighbor." Likewise the circumstances of the characters must also seem familiar to audience members who should be able to say, "That happened to my brother" (W. Ryerson & Negussie 2004, p. 183).

Excerpts from audiotapes of the 34 focus group discussions that were conducted by a local agency, Birhan Research, were useful for the writers and producers to get a sense of how individuals sound when they talk about certain subjects (W. Ryerson & Negussie 2004, p. 183). Birhan Research was also commissioned to design an interview questionnaire—adjusting it for various regions of Ethiopia—which they used to conduct a total of 1,020 personal interviews with a sample of people from different regions, urban and rural, and men and women of different ages and marital status from the target audience for the dramas. Information about people's attitudes, behaviors, and knowledge about issues to be covered in the dramas was collected. PMC views this formative research as very participatory, as they interviewed people around the country, and listened to their input and their way of describing the issues. This aspect is identified by PMC as a "bottom up" aspect of their work.

The producers and scriptwriters visited rural villages in order to get a sense of life in those settings, to record village sounds, to learn what topics people discuss, and to obtain a sense of what the clinics and other health/social services are like

Photo 5.7 Women waiting at a Family Clinic in Ethiopia.

Photo 5.8 Senior scriptwriter for Population Media Center, Mesfin Getachew.

(see Photo 5.7). They even recorded sound effects from the villages, such as cows mooing or children playing on the streets, to have in the background of the dramas. They also gathered Ethiopian proverbs that reflect negative attitudes towards women and children, which were used by scriptwriters as a source of material in the radio dramas (W. Ryerson & Negussie 2004, p. 184).

Senior scriptwriter for PMC, Mesfin Getachew (in Photo 5.8), remembers that when he first attended a PMC training on the Sabido Methodology, he had to learn how to write collectively rather than as an individual artist. He also commented on the characterizing feature of the Sabido method that makes use of three character traits: positive, negative, and transitional. About this Mesfin wrote:

> What particularly baffled us is the strict requirement by Sabido methodology that the positive characters should be absolutely positive and that the negative character should be absolutely negative. We raised serious doubts against the methodology wondering how on earth one can be absolutely positive or absolutely negative. As we continued our training, our instructions gave us elaborate explanations and finally managed to dispel from our minds all the suspicions we had entertained earlier. They told us that if our drama messages have to be correctly put across to the audience, it is first of all necessary to create positive and negative role models. They explained that if the drama is to bring about the required change, the positive character must infallibly be positive. It was further explained that if such a character makes mistakes, this would mislead the audience into making incorrect conclusions. Similarly, if the negative character is not absolutely negative in nature, the audience would be tempted to dismiss the messages as unreliable and unacceptable. It is on the basis of such thorough explanations that we finally managed to cast away all our doubts about the feasibility of Sabido methodology, especially after we proceeded to practical work. (2010, p. 13)

Since so much of the drama deals with family planning and medical issues, a technical committee made up of health professionals reviewed the scripts for technical accuracy. An advisory committee—made up of scriptwriters, producers, gender and health experts, communication experts, and local theatre artists—was created during the formative research phase. This committee guided the development of the program content and planned to ensure that health and family planning services for issues brought up by the drama were in operation and ready for an increase in clients in all listening areas, due to the radio drama.

PMC senior scriptwriter, Mesfin Getachew, writes of his method for playwriting—before his work with PMC, "I gathered some pieces of information and then went ahead with writing my drama, according to my own imagination. . . . Previously, I never imagined that moving from place to place and talking to members of the target audience would be of any use. My perception about this matter was completely changed after I started engaging in such a study prior to writing the drama" (2010, p. 13). Mesfin explains how the fieldwork accomplished with his collaborators proved to be completely different from what they had imagined at the outset. He writes, "The practical reality in the field completely changed our previous approach. We felt that all those drama scripts we used to write without research studies were baseless" (2010, p. 14).

The scriptwriting team created character profiles so that there would be consistency in the way each character was portrayed. The writers reported that once strong characters were created, they tended to lead the creation of the story. The script writing team also plotted out the story line, based on issues before they started writing. Suspense was maintained from one episode to the next by often ending with a cliff-hanger.

All of the preliminary workshop and process-oriented collaborations resulted in the following plot for *Yeken Kignit*. The central positive character in the drama is a young woman named Fikirte who grows up in a poor, rural home until she is sent to live with her grandfather, who sends her to school. Fikirte likes school and her new life. She works hard to please her grandfather. However, her life takes a turn for the worse when her grandfather dies, and a negative male character, Damte, attempts to take over the grandfather's house to use it as a bar and brothel. Since Fikirte's objection to this plan is the only obstacle for Damte, he proceeds with many attempts to slander her name and good reputation with both Fikirte's boyfriend and others. Fikirte refuses to sleep with her boyfriend and delays their marriage because she wants to gain economic stability before having children and marrying. Damte tells Fikirte's half-sister, Lamrot, lies about Fikirte, in an attempt to get her kicked out of the family house. Damte gets Lamrot addicted to drugs and alcohol and gets her pregnant. In response, Lamrot nearly bleeds to death from an attempted abortion and ends up in the hospital where it is discovered she is also HIV positive. Fikirte's steadfast loyalty and honesty prevail, and all involved in the story discover that Damte is evil and that his accusations against Fikirte were all false. As a climatic last effort, Damte sends someone to stab Fikirte to death, but she survives and ends up in the hospital. While she sleeps, Damte comes to her hospital room to shoot her but is sighted by a police officer and shot.

Through all the trials and obstacles overcome by Fikirte, she is able to empower herself and to help others around her. She helps many friends and family members while educating them about family planning, reproductive health, the importance of education as it relates to economic stability, protecting oneself against rape, the sex-trade industry and other forms of gender violence, and issues around HIV/AIDS.

Another story line revolves around Anguach and Demlew, a loving young couple with a bright future. Demlew's mother, who doesn't like Anguach, begins to meddle and pushes a neighbor to seduce Demlew. He succumbs, sleeps with the neighbor, and gets infected with HIV. Anguach is devastated, but forgives him, and cares for him until he dies. Although she is terrified that she might be HIV positive, Anguach gets tested and finds out that she is negative. Anguach eventually marries again and finds happiness. This storyline deals specifically with the need for early detection and prevention of HIV (Population Media Center 2009b).

Monitoring and evaluation

PMC Ethiopia Country Representative, Dr. Negussie Teffera (in Photo 5.9), writes in the preface to the Birhan report, "Past experiences in population communication endeavors have shown that behavior change is the bottom line for both the use of family planning and the prevention of the spread of HIV/AIDS. That is why PMC gave a research-based radio serial drama approach a special consideration. Dramas of this kind are culturally and linguistically sensitive to people's needs and demands, and appeal to their audiences by portraying real life situations. They help to create a positive attitude and to encourage the adoption of behaviors of those characters that play exemplary roles" (Birhan Research and Development Consultancy 2005, p. x).

Photo 5.9 Population Media Center Ethiopia Country Director, Dr. Negussie Teffera (left) with PMC Founder and Director, William Ryerson (right).

As a part of PMC's monitoring and evaluation of their dramas—before production and transmission of the serial dramas—PMC's senior management technical committee analyzed the script in relation to the content of the message, the clarity and simplicity of the language, logical sequence, and entertainment value of the serial drama. In May 2002, before the broadcast launch, Birhan Research conducted a quantitative baseline survey to establish benchmark information and indicators against which the progress and impact of the radio program could be measured and evaluated. The baseline and endline surveys that formed the evaluation of the program in Ethiopia actually covered both radio serial dramas *Yeken Kignit* in Amharic and *Dhimbibba* in Oromiffa. This chapter only focuses on the results of the Amharic-language program, *Yeken Kignit*. In Amhara regions, both urban and rural residents were surveyed; the entire number surveyed included 1,200 households from 24 rural areas and 16 urban areas. The baseline study was conducted during May 2002. Key results showed:

- Radio listening: 36% of men and 50% of women had never listened to the radio.
- Family planning: Nearly 9 out of 10 women and men interviewed reported to have heard of at least one family planning method, but only 12% of women were currently using a family planning method.
- Spousal communication about family planning: two-thirds of married women and nearly 60% of married men reported that they have never discussed family planning with their spouse.
- HIV/AIDS: 91% of women and 94% of men had heard about HIV/AIDS, but risk perception associated with HIV/AIDS was very low, and only 7% of respondents had ever had a test for HIV. (Birhan Research and Development Consultancy 2005)

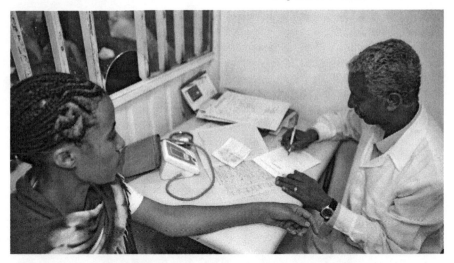

Photo 5.10 An Ethiopian woman being seen at a Family Clinic in Ethiopia.

Early feedback from the four pilot episodes and programs indicated that the audience felt the key negative character, Damte, was portrayed too much as a devil, and that Fikirte was too pious and unrealistically angelic. Therefore, scriptwriters toned down both characters to make them more believable and credible for the audience (Salem et al. 2008, p. 7). After other recommended adjustments were made, Radio Ethiopia broadcast 257 episodes of PMC's radio drama *Yeken Kignit*—twice a week in the evening and afternoons between June 2002 and November 2004.

In addition to the pre- and postbroadcast surveys of listeners and nonlisteners, focus groups, and listener letters, PMC asked 48 health service agencies to participate in gathering information on why people seek reproductive health services. Data included the number of clients (see Photo 5.10) seeking services before, during, and after the radio dramas were broadcast.

Open-ended questions were asked as to why individuals sought health services, and whether a client listened to one of the radio serial dramas (W. Ryerson & Negussie 2004, p. 189). A quantitative study was conducted in December 2004, immediately following the broadcast of the final episode of *Yeken Kignit*. The sample design for who was surveyed that was used in the final evaluation—or endline—was the same as the one used in the baseline. As previously stated, the indicators for measuring to what extent the program reached its goals were knowledge, attitude, and behavior change, clustered in the following categories: HIV/AIDS prevention, use of family planning, reproductive health, education of female children, and gender equity.

In terms of HIV/AIDS prevention, male listeners sought HIV tests at four times the rate of nonlisteners, and female listeners at three times the rate of nonlisteners. There was an increase in the belief that women can negotiate the use of condoms by 15% by women and 26% by men. There was a reduction among listeners of both genders in the stigma against people affected by HIV/AIDS (Population Media Center 2009b).

In terms of family planning, demand for contraceptives increased 157% during the period of the broadcast of *Yeken Kignit*.

> Half the entire population of Ethiopia reported being regular listeners to PMC's programs (which includes *Yeken Kignit* and *Dhimbibba*). Listeners were five times more likely than non-listeners to know three or more family planning methods. Among married women in the Amhara region who were listeners, there was a 55 percentage point increase in those who had ever used family planning methods, while among non-listeners, the change was only 24 percentage points. A similar increase occurred among male listeners in the Amhara region. Spousal communication about family planning issues among married women climbed from 33% to 66%. (Population Media Center 2009b)

In terms of reproductive health, 63% of new clients seeking reproductive health services at 48 different service centers in Ethiopia reported that they were listening to one of PMC's serial dramas. Eighteen percent of these new clients named one of PMC's programs by name as the primary motivating factor for seeking services. Of new clients who cited radio programs as a motivation for seeking services, 96% said that they were motivated by one of PMC's programs (Birhan Research and Development Consultancy 2005).

In regard to the education of female children, the percentage of men who recognized the importance of educating girls increased 51.7 percentage points, and the percentage of women who recognized the importance of educating girls increased 20.8 percentage points. For gender equity, there was a 37.4 percentage point increase among men and a 13.1 percentage point increase among women in the belief that women are fit to hold public office. About the belief that women should be able to marry a man of their choosing, there was an increase of 11.8 percentage points by men and 18.5 percentage points by women. There was a 30% increase among men and a 48% increase among women in the belief that female circumcision should be discontinued (Population Media Center 2009b).

Clearly, in just two and a half years of nationwide broadcasting of the serial drama *Yeken Kignit*, the program achieved dramatic change, as evident from these primarily quantitative results. The results indicate that there were more dramatic changes in issues and topics that have been recently introduced to Ethiopian society—such as HIV/AIDS and modern forms of family planning—than in deeply entrenched Ethiopian values and attitudes about women, their place, and the amount of agency they should have in marriage.

The outpouring of emotion in Ethiopia in response to PMC's programs has been profuse, evident from more than 15,000 letters sent to the PMC's office in Addis Ababa by listeners. One letter from a listener in Addis Ababa, Haimanot Hailu, expresses gratitude for the program.

> *Yeken Kignit* has become instrumental in improving communication in our family. The drama has helped us to develop a new culture of speaking out and

of listening to others. First, every member of the family listens to the drama. Then, we take part in a discussion every night. On this occasion, I invite my family members to give their opinions on various issues. Formerly, they used to tell me to mind my own business. You may be surprised to know that this is not the case any more. Today, thanks to *Yeken Kignit,* I have found an audience. I was careful and reserved when I talked in the past about reproductive health, family planning and other issues. Now I am free and I talk without any inhibitions. Not only me, but also my mother feels the same, because she has become the main teacher. In general, there is much change in my family. (Assefa 2006, p. 12)

PMC reports that the many letters they have received in regard to their radio programs are like the letter above; writers thank PMC for providing positive role models who dramatize stories relevant to their lives.

Impact assessment

PMCs radio drama *Yeken Kignit* has made substantial shifts in attitudes and behaviors around issues of HIV/AIDS, family planning, reproductive health, gender equity, and girls' education in Ethiopia. Population indicators available for Ethiopia that are relevant to this study are from 1994 (when the population was 53.5 million and the growth rate was 2.9%), and 2007 (when the population was 73.8 million and the growth rate was 2.6%) (Central Statistical Agency Ethiopia and ICF International 2011, p. 3). Given the impact PMC's programming made on attitudes and behaviors around family planning, it is likely that PMC's programming should be credited for the decrease in growth rate. The example of PMC's success with this drama has been disseminated through conference presentations internationally and through publications (Barker 2012; Singhal et al. 2003; Teffera 2008). Ethiopia's news media have run more than one hundred stories on the soap opera phenomenon PMC has created. Its success also resulted in subsequent PMC radio dramas in Ethiopia, such as *Menta Menged* (*The Crossroads*), *Maleda* (*Dawn*), and *Sibrat* (*Trauma*).

Even the prominent Ethiopian actress who played the role of Fikerte, Haregewoin Assefa (in Photo 5.11), was impacted by her participation in this radio drama. Since the radio drama took over a year to be fully broadcast and has been run multiple times, she is well known for playing the part of Fikerte. Of her experience she said:

By playing this role, I had, on top of all other things, learned to be patient and to convert myself into a good person. By being a good person, you lose nothing. In fact, the benefits accruing from it will be very rewarding. Entertaining a good idea at all times and thinking positively make you always victorious. I have learned from Fikirte that such ideas will enable you to become a winner. Being a good person will give you peace of mind and strengthen the relations you have with other people. (Population Media Center 2006, p. 16)

Photo 5.11 The Ethiopian actress, Haregewoin Assefa, who played the role of Fikerte in the Population Media Center radio drama *Yeken Kignit*.

Assefa complained of being taken for Fikirte by people when she was out in public, and of receiving phone calls by radio listeners who wanted to ask her advice on problems in their lives. This seems to demonstrate that many listeners had a difficult time discerning between the fictional drama and reality. This blurring of the line between reality and fiction could be seen to confirm the success of PMC's goal to have the characters in the drama feel like the neighbors and family members of listeners.

Lessons learned and recommendations

A clear lesson learned from this case study is that the use of both formative and summative research was key to *Yeken Kignit's* success. PMC's monitoring and evaluation is extremely sophisticated when compared to most applied theatre. Though many other applied theatre organizations do research in the making of their work—such as Sistren Song and Stepping Stones (Allison 1986; Welbourn 1995)—not many invest such a large percent of their overall budget in monitoring and evaluation of the impact of their work as PMC, nor do most allocate funds to hire an outside research firm to conduct unbiased research. Because they do, PMC can provide evidence of the reach and impact of their programming, which significantly contributes to the sustainability of their efforts.

Early pioneer of entertainment-education David Poindexter writes that "to achieve such massive behavior change, a methodology that informs and motivates mainly by stimulating interpersonal communication among peers is needed. Many development program leaders rely on exposure to messages to reach their objectives. However, these messages seldom lead to the magnitude of changed behavior that is required to solve a social problem" (2004, p. 36). The fact that PMC's attitude and behavior change messages are embedded in entertaining dramas makes the issues within these dramas come alive. They are something to talk about with peers, to deliberate over and analyze, especially since the issues these compelling characters are facing are relevant to the listener's lives. Positive characters model peer communication and critical engagement with issues, as they discuss these issues with other characters within the dramas. Peer communication and critical engagement are further encouraged through PMC's listener groups, talk radio shows, and focus groups.

The final recommendations from the Birham report on the drama are based on the findings of the postintervention survey. They include:

- In view of the relatively short time of the program duration and that a longer duration would allow greater achievement, the program should be repeated. Even if encouraging results were achieved, much remains to be done to address deep-rooted reproductive health problems, and thereby, to achieve the desired behavioural change.
- Taking into consideration the efficiency and effectiveness of the PMC program, we recommend that attempts should be made to replicate it in other areas of the country.
- It is important that the PMC approach be popularized in the country by any means; that is, means should be sought whereby other governmental or nongovernmental organizations engaged in similar tasks learn from the lessons learned from the PMC project and adopt its approach in their own activities.
- Means should be sought to enhance possession or access to radio (especially in rural areas) and to develop the culture of critical listening and thinking. (Birhan Research and Development Consultancy 2005, pp. ix–x)

PMC responded to these recommendations by both continuing and expanding the reach of their programming in Ethiopia to other areas. Also, as noted previously, *Yeken Kignit* was rebroadcast in 2009. PMC-Ethiopia has gone on to create several more radio dramas including *Menta Menged* (*The Crossroads*), *Maleda* (*Dawn*), and *Sibrat* (*Trauma*). Listening groups for all of these dramas are one way that PMC has encouraged a culture of critical listening and thinking. In these groups, listeners are asked to keep diaries of their critical reflections, which are then shared with the writers of the dramas and PMC's monitoring and evaluation team. Following the Birhan report in 2005, PMC produced and broadcast a series of programs using formats specifically designed to encourage listeners to interact actively with the content of the program through call-in and discussions. From 2005 to 2010, PMC produced a radio talk show, *Alegnta* (*Security*), which encouraged listeners to phone in and talk about issues surrounding harmful traditional practices. Two regional dramas, *Igaddaa* (*We Do Not Want It Anymore*) in Somali, and *Naedetaa* (*Let's Stop*) in Afar, also addressed these issues, and used a magazine-style format made up of short dramas, interviews, storytelling, and narration.

Beyond considering women as recipients of these radio dramas—and the subsequent critical listening, collective assessment, and discussion—I recommend increased participation by women of the target audience in deciding upon the messages being communicated and in the design and execution of the dramas. As previously noted in Chapter 1, participation denotes taking part in an endeavor and having a share in the outcome. William Ryerson and Negussie Teffera write of their lessons learned from this drama: "All relevant leaders in the host country for an E-E project should be involved early and consistently in the process of conceiving, designing, implementing, and evaluating an E-E intervention" (2004, p. 189). Given the focus of this book, my recommendation is to include among "relevant leaders" as many women as possible from the target audience in that early process of conceiving, designing, implementing, and evaluating, so as to put women first in a development planning process that primarily focuses on women's issues. I acknowledge that women are consulted through the research process in multiple ways, which does allow for some level of participation. Also, the talk radio shows allow women to author their own views and be heard, which could be seen as a much higher level of participation. Still, I recommend that women be supported in moving into more proactive roles that allow for greater amounts of women's authorship and leadership in the programming. I believe this additional inclusion would result in an even greater level of empowerment and agency for girls and women, and an increase in the rate of positive cultural change.

The typology of participation from *Participatory Learning in Action* offers a classification of seven levels of participation that is useful when describing and gauging levels of participation.

1. Passive Participation: People participate by being told what is going to happen or has already happened. It is a unilateral announcement by an administration or project management without listening to people's responses. The information being shared belongs only to external professionals.

2. Participation in Information Giving: People participate by answering questions posed by extractive researchers using questionnaire survey or similar approaches. People do not have the opportunity to influence proceedings, as the findings of the research are neither shared nor checked for accuracy.

3. Participation by Consultation: People participate by being consulted, and external people listen to views. These external professionals define both problems and solutions, and may modify these in the light of people's responses. Such a consultative process does not concede any share in decision-making, and professionals are under no obligation to take on board people's views.

4. Participation for Material Incentives: People participate by providing resources, for example labour, in return for food, cash, or other material incentives. Much on-farm research falls in this category, as farmers provide the fields but are not involved in the experimentation or the process of learning. It is very common to see this called participation, yet people have no stake in prolonging activities when the incentives end.

5. Functional Participation: People participate by forming groups to meet predetermined objectives related to the project, which can involve the development

or promotion of externally initiated social organization. Such involvement does not tend to be as early stages of project cycles or planning, but rather, after major decisions have been made. These institutions tend to be dependent on external initiators and facilitators, but may become self-dependent.

6. Interactive Participation: People participate in joint analysis, which leads to action plans and the formation of new local institutions or the strengthening of existing ones. It tends to involve interdisciplinary methodologies that seek multiple perspectives and make use of systematic and structured learning processes. These groups take control over local decisions, and so people have a stake in maintaining structures or practices.

7. Self-Mobilisation: People participate by taking initiatives independent of external institutions to change systems. They develop contacts with external institutions for resources and technical advice they need, but retain control over how resources are used. Such self-initiated mobilization and collective action may or may not challenge existing inequitable distributions of wealth and power. (Pretty et al. 1995, p. 61)

PMC's use of formative research seems to offer women in the target audience involvement at participation level three, given the above classifications. My understanding of the listening groups maintained by PMC seems to offer women a level five, and perhaps, some aspect of six. The PMC-produced radio talk show *Alegnta* (*Security*), which encouraged listeners to phone in and talk about issues surrounding Harmful Traditional Practices, seems to engage women closer to level six.

It seems likely that some adjustments would need to be made to include women without training in this field, or women without formal education, to be able to participate in higher levels. It also seems likely that participatory applied theatre methods could serve this inclusion and contribute towards local capacity building among women. This could likely render the process more relevant and empowering for the women.

There is evidence that more participatory methods are already under way. Two leaders in the field of EE, Arvind Singhal and Everett Rogers, write:

> In the future, E-E interventions are likely to see more integration with participatory communication approaches. . . . The work of Brazilian theatre director Augusto Boal, who founded the Theatre of the Oppressed (TO) movement, is particularly relevant here. TO's techniques, based on Paulo Freire's principles of dialogue, interaction, problem-posing, reflection, and conscientization, are designed to activate spectators ("spect-actors") to take control of situations, rather than to passively allow actions to happen to them. (2004, p. 18)

Indeed, PMC is already adopting more participatory methods in their subsequent programming, though not in Ethiopia. In Jamaica, PMC conducted a qualitative participatory assessment study of youth listeners to the Jamaican radio serial drama *Outta Road*, a program targeting Jamaican adolescents with the purpose of getting them to adopt healthy behaviors and reduce the risk of violence, early sex, and use of illegal drugs. The research design consisted of conducting focus group discussions, individual interviews, and sketching exercises with adolescent boys and girls from Ruseas and Green Island high schools in Hanover Parish, Jamaica. The participatory research included a sketching exercise that allowed participants to represent visually how the program impacted their lives. The advantage to using this method is that it allows audience members to participate by making a visual representation of how the program may have influenced them. A PMC report of this participatory evaluation process states that "this technique has been advocated by Paulo Freire, an educator from Brazil who believes that assessments of educational programs would benefit from more participatory methods including using sketching and photographs to represent the reality of participants' lives" (Connolly, Elmore, & Stein 2008, p. 4). Although this example is based on the theoretical work of Freire and represents progress in terms of participation by intended audience for PMC's programming, this is still an example of participation as a recipient of programming, rather than participation in the creation and design of the actual program.

By the very nature of the large-scale reach of many EE programs, these methods are not as participatory for women as some of the smaller-scale methods explored in this book. One of the questions that emerges is: Are there situations in which large-scale methods are more appropriate? Are there social situations—such as population growth that drives a country into abject poverty or the rapid spread of a disease such as HIV/AIDS—that are similar to a house on fire, in which the ethical response is to just carry people out of the building to save their lives? Is participation a luxury that cannot ethically be afforded in those instances? In relation to this, Paulo Freire writes:

> Attempting to liberate the oppressed without their reflective participation in the act of liberation is to treat them as objects which must be saved from a burning building; it is to lead them into the populist pitfall and transform them into masses which can be manipulated. (Connolly et al. 2008, p. 4)

This is emphatically *not* to say that large-scale methods do not involve and critically engage women to some extent; they do. I am simply asserting that smaller-scale methods with more direct participation on the part of women often have a higher degree of engagement and allow for more agency, subjectivity, and authorship on the part of the women themselves. The critical awareness that results from fuller participation can leave those who critically participate less vulnerable to manipulation by outside forces. Does the EE methodology leave its audience open for other—perhaps less well intended—large-scale messaging? Certainly this same methodology could be used to gather popular support for something like Uganda's antihomosexual legislation (BBC 2012), with or without the blessings of Miguel Sabido. When developing any tool there is the risk it will be used for a purpose other than for what it was intended, and this misapplication could cause human harm. The fact that a hammer could be used as a weapon does not make a hammer bad. However, it does cause the designer of any tool—especially such a powerful one as the Sabido Methodology—to, as much as is possible, make all efforts to ensure the tool is used by, for, and on an informed populace who can be aware of its power, proper use, and risks.

When choosing what type of applied theatre programming is appropriate for a given crisis or social problem, perhaps it becomes a question of what degree of participation by women can be afforded, given the social situation. Applied theatre practitioner Sheila Preston writes that "whether an applied theatre practice allows for the more radical possibilities of participation within a project depends on the ideological intentions of the project (and the interests being served in it), the scope of the work and the openness for the creative strategies offered" (2008, p. 129). I understand the urgency of this issue of population stabilization and HIV/AIDS. I also acknowledge the amount of human suffering brought on by the poverty that results in overpopulation and the spread of HIV/AIDS—especially in Ethiopia. In spite of, or even *because* of that urgency, the necessity of inclusion of women at every stage of development is still vital for the actual transformation of any society and its ultimate sustainability. I ask these questions so as to hopefully enrich our conversation and collective exploration of the costs and benefits of different scales of reach within applied theatre programming. Given the potential and critical contributions of work such as PMC, I am interested in the development of sophisticated criteria that we are fortunate enough to need now: Who benefits—financially or in other ways—from EE programming? Who has identified the needs the program addresses? What is transparent and what is opaque in this process? I believe PMC could be instrumental in articulating this criteria, so that the world—as we face increasingly serious challenges—can reap the benefit of such powerful work, while staying alert to potential misuses.

Upon reflection, the difference between EE and most other forms of applied theatre (for which Freire's work is its theoretical foundation) is that EE's end goal is behavior change, whereas the end goal of applied theatre work is conscientization first, and secondly, whatever behavior change evolves from that. I imagine not all applied theatre practitioners would articulate this as I have, but it seems nearly all would include the necessity of consciousness-raising as a part of the end goal. Social change without the significant critical engagement of those who are oppressed cannot be said to be work modeled on Freire's core values. The extent to which EE programming works towards behavior change *and* towards conscientization could be a measure of how much it should also be classified as applied theatre.

It seems useful to examine methods for determining and disseminating messages in order to clean out any colonial attitudes that may be involved in crafting the messaging. When conducting a phone interview with Jane Plastow, who specializes in theatre for development in Ethiopia and other surrounding countries in Africa (Plastow 1996; Plastow 2004; Boon & Plastow 2004; Plastow & Boon 1998), she expressed uneasiness with the certainness of much EE programming— especially that originates from the United States. She promotes the strategy of creating messages for applied theatre work with the people themselves. Likewise, she states that asking questions is preferable to asserting messages. She stated that many governments in the world prefer asserting messages because it doesn't make people think, just act in a desired manner. Her opinion of EE style programming is that is a blunt and dogmatic tool, not a delicate exploratory instrument (Plastow 2013). It should be noted that she was not familiar with PMC-Ethiopia in particular, and that her comments were directed towards EE work in general.

In an article entitled "Participation," applied theatre author Majid Rahnema entitled her last section "Beyond Participation" (2008, p. 145). I am intrigued with this idea in relation to the inner, intimate landscape of women in regard to the issues surrounding population, as championed by PMC. What I witnessed and understood from the focus group I led in Ethiopia for PMC, and from interviews with many people, was that these dramas were one of the first communications of *any kind* these women had encountered that discussed issues of extreme importance to them, in a manner that felt relevant and not only comfortable, but entertaining. My impression from these interviews was that their very personal relationships with the radio drama characters unleashed an inner freedom that allowed these women to think for themselves against the prevailing cultural traditions. The fact that many of the issues addressed are taboo to discuss in private or public—and are rooted in patriarchal views of women—compounds their sense of freedom. Applied theatre author Majid Rahnema writes, "Inner freedom gives life to outer freedom and makes both possible and meaningful" (2008, p. 146).

The emotional component—which is so successfully addressed by PMC's radio dramas—adds meaning and even beauty to people's lives in Ethiopia. Work toward systemic change can sometimes neglect this vital aspect. It could even be that those drawing from the revolutionary theoretical writing of Boal—who advocates for Brecht's model of alienation (Boal 1985, pp. 83–115) that discourages audience from getting swept away by the emotional content of a scene so as to keep them critically engaged with the issues—could do well to consider the way emotional connections can also spur something resembling critical reflection. Rahnema notes, "While outer freedom is often a great blessing, and a necessity to protect people from violence and abuse, it remains hollow and subject to decay, in the absence of inner freedom" (Rahnema 2008, p. 146). Further research might explore this contrast of melodrama and epic theatre for each form's effectiveness in unleashing inner freedom—perhaps even specifically for women—and how that freedom could be related to the release from internalized oppression.

Conclusion

PMC has made incredible strides for women's rights in Ethiopia by significantly reducing such cultural practices as FGM and marriage by abduction. They have delivered lifesaving messages about HIV/AIDS transmission and have reduced the stigma of the disease for those living with it. They have relieved stress on families and our environment by teaching about modern family planning methods and encouraging open communication within the family. These are not small achievements. Before meeting PMC and learning about their form of education-entertainment, I did not know that entertainment was capable of societal change on such a vast scale. Researching it further and consulting with Jane Plastow, an expert on theatre for development in Ethiopia, I grew to understand the costs and benefits of such an expansive reach. I personally feel great admiration, respect, and affection for William Ryerson, Dr. Negussie Teffera, and the entire PMC-Ethiopia staff. I bear the testimony of those intimate meetings with real women whose lives have been radically changed for the better because of PMC's efforts. Monitoring and evaluation by an external research firm verifies the profound, broad-scale impact made by the radio dramas by PMC-Ethiopia. Viewing EE from a feminist applied theatre lens makes evident opportunities for increased participation by women as relevant leaders in conceptualizing, designing, and executing radio programming that has such an extensive reach. Continuing efforts towards participatory communication methods could more fully engage women to increase the extent to which the programming of PMC is created *with* rather than *for* women and will likely improve upon what is already an outstanding and profoundly effective example of applied theatre.

6 Conclusion—sustaining women's participation through applied theatre

Navajo Women's Energy Project on the Navajo Nation

On the Navajo Nation, 12 women ranging in age from 11 to 86, one speaking only Navajo, others Navajo and English, met to lay the groundwork for a Navajo Women's Energy Project. With my Navajo partner Adrian Manygoats, we had designed an all-day session to go deep in our consideration of the many issues surrounding energy. I have a long-term commitment to working on this project through the University of Colorado Outreach in collaboration with Eagle Energy (Eagle Energy 2013). Through various applied theatre activities, the women told the story of energy on the Navajo Nation that has already been told—the story of energy that includes coal mining, uranium extraction, high cancer rates, and contaminated water tables. This is the story that has been written largely without women's participation. We imagined a new story of energy written by women: one in which women had influence in how tribal money is invested in clean energy for a more sustainable future. As a bridge from the old story to the new, we thought of specific actions that our group could do, and then we rehearsed those actions together so as to identify likely obstacles and work towards solutions together. By the end of the day, we had a plan for action and our next two meetings scheduled. Not only that, but applied theatre made this process highly engaging, unifying, and even aesthetically stirring.

For one activity, we used a simple muslin shadow screen behind which was a solar-powered light. When a woman stood between the screen and the light (see Photo 6.1), her profile was illuminated in shadow on the screen. Each woman was asked to step behind the screen and say what she thought the ancestors would want to tell us to guide us in this journey towards a sustainable energy future. People shared the following messages:

Remember how we used to live without modern conveniences.
Think about the consequences of your actions.
We are better than this.
Work with the earth, not against the earth.
We've forgotten how to live in harmony and reverence.

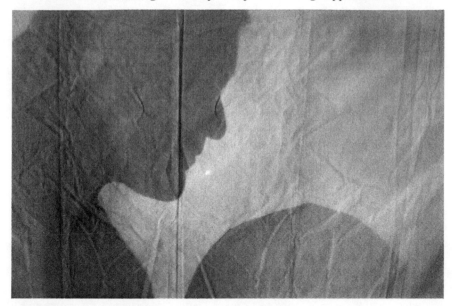

Photo 6.1 A participant in the Navajo Women's Energy Project speaks in shadow on behalf of her ancestors.

Don't take more than you need.
We need to incorporate the spirit people in this journey.
We are the Earth.
Have you forgotten who you are? Where you come from? Who your creators are? (Manygoats & Osnes 2013)

The theatricality of the shadow play was remarkably beautiful and really seemed to bring the spirit of the ancestors into the room. Responses from the Navajo elders participating were particularly positive in regard to this exercise. One elder woman, a tribal leader, expressed gratitude that the ancestors had been included in the design of the day.

I share this example at the conclusion, because while writing this book I have concurrently been working on this new project, the Navajo Women's Energy Project. I am moved by how the ideas I've encountered through writing this book have invigorated and deepened my work. I am renewed in my belief that applied theatre is not only a uniquely effective and appropriate tool for including women in their own sustainable development, it is an exciting, emotionally rich, often beautiful, nuanced and delicate tool for reaching into deep crevasses of history, feelings, connections, and possibilities. The day I spent with these women on the Navajo Nation was exceptional. Applied theatre allowed us to cover an incredible amount of ground with the participation of a diverse group—in terms of age, language, and education levels. Because of the unique attributes of applied theatre, Caroline, an elder matriarch who only speaks Navajo and has attended very little school, was able to contribute her knowledge and experience since no formal education is necessary for participation. The younger Navajo women, who are university students, were also engaged and challenged by this process. With the use of applied theatre there is a complex language of action being employed at a sophisticated level. The process calls upon the intelligence that can be gained from many different ways of living. Using applied theatre in a diverse population helps to 'even the playing field' and dismantle societal hierarchies that often disadvantage women living in poverty.

Lessons learned

As Alice Welbourn of Stepping Stones (see Chapter 1) advises, no one program or methodology should be relied upon to provide all the answers, but that communities should consider using a range of existing materials available (2002, p. 58). Likewise, applied theatre should be thought of as one of many tools or methods that can be drawn upon to address challenges that impede women's participation. As is seen in the case study on PMC-Ethiopia, their holistic, wraparound services approach was instrumental to their success. Applied theatre is most effectively used as one aspect of a more comprehensively envisioned plan for women's participation.

Applied theatre can be compared with other tools, such as a hammer; it is pretty simple to use and can do many things. It can pound things in, and when used like a lever, can pull things out or apart. Most people doing any kind of handy work seem to own a hammer and know how to use it. Granted, in the hands of a carpenter, it can do more with greater efficiency, ease, and beauty. Yet a hammer is a highly accessible tool even in the hands of a beginning woodworker. Like this, applied theatre can be used quite simply with positive results, and, when led by a trained and adept facilitator, can produce amazingly specific moments of transformation.

Each country's theatrical history and culture will influence the impact of the applied theatre conducted there, and will determine the amount of effort required to achieve an impact. History and culture are factors that influence how willing and adept participants are, and how they benefit from the experience. In India, for example, the staff of ARTI was already active and adept in theatrical expression. India has a rich theatrical climate that supports the theatrical expression of participants, with minimal investment or effort from an outside facilitator. In Guatemala, Starfish One by One is working in a country in which the theatrical history is sparser. Even the Starfish staff member, Vilma—who is the primary champion of using applied theatre for Starfish's Vocal Empowerment Program—describes herself as struggling to be expressive in many circumstances. She stated that she will benefit from coaching and training to be able to successfully facilitate applied theatre for her organization. By this I do not intend to suggest that applied theatre should not be done in countries with sparse theatre history and culture. It is simply to note that applied theatre programs in those countries will likely require larger investments of time, resources, and effort.

It is stated and intimated numerous times throughout this book that women living in poverty have important contributions to make towards solving our shared challenges associated with sustainable development, such as their gendered knowledge, resilience, perspective, and insights. However, sometimes an outside agent or intervention is necessary to help women living in poverty step out of their poverty trap, in order to be in a position to participate in their own sustainable development. As with any trap, a poverty trap is something from which one cannot escape, given one's own position (Bowles et al. 2006). Often times, poverty is passed down from one generation to the next through a complex multitude of factors. The process by which parents living in poverty pass on their poverty and disadvantage occurs primarily during their children's early years of life (Morán 2004). For this reason, many organizations that are successful in facilitating the participation of women often start with young women so as to address those factors that would otherwise impair a women's ability to participate in her own community's development.

Common characteristics

By reviewing the applied theatre programs examined in this book, some common characteristics emerge among organizations that successfully utilize applied theatre for women's participation. Primarily, there is most often a focus on gender and a commitment to gender equity from the core of the organization. At the root of many organizations that focus on women, there is a very strong personal story by the founder that connects them to a lifelong commitment to this work. Connie Ning, who is cofounder of Starfish One by One, told me of a time when she was visiting a hospital in Vietnam, early on in her humanitarian work. In a hallway, she passed a stretcher on which was laid a woman with open sores, as a result of advanced and untreated cancer. She remembers stopping to offer whatever comfort she could give this woman. When their eyes locked, in that moment of connection, the division between this woman and herself dissolved. She experienced this woman's suffering as her own. She cites that moment as a galvanizing occurrence that feeds her continued commitment to gender equity. With the Appropriate Rural Technology Institute in India, Dr. A.D. Karve, and his daughter Dr. Priyadarshini Karve, were influenced by the work of their forefathers, who were progressive reformists for women's rights. In this case it seems to be an immersion in a forward-thinking culture within Pune and the Karve family, their friends, and visitors, that influenced a commitment to gender equity. In an interview with William Ryerson, founder of the Population Media Center, he conveyed a story from his childhood that impacted his commitment to gender.

> In my childhood, I remember thinking that keeping higher education just for men was a terrible waste of half the population's ability. My own mother, who was valedictorian of her high school class, was not sent to college because she was a girl. Her family's funds were limited so her brother got to go instead. She worked as a housewife all her life with only small interruptions. In my

own family, emphasis on good grades was very clearly focused on the males in the family. My father had a post college degree; my mother had no degree. I remember family discussions about giving girls equal access, and my father would say that the problem with investing in girls is they get pregnant and drop out of the work force to raise children. I understood how people reached that conclusion, but never could accept the concept that because of parenthood girls were less deserving of education. (W. Ryerson 2012)

Here we find an individual commitment to gender equity emerging in part from the educational potential that went unrealized for a mother.

We notice that founders of organizations don't need to be women to have this strong personal connection to gender equity, nor did the formative story have to happen to them, such as it did for Alice Welbourn, who created *Stepping Stones*. In 1992 Welbourn discovered that she was HIV-positive and subsequently created a training package that would help protect others from acquiring HIV. We also see the familial commitment to gender equity that passes through generations, from Connie Ning to her son Travis Ning, who now is executive director of Starfish (see Chapter 3), and from Dr. Dhondo Keshav Karve all the way to his great-granddaughter, Priyadarshini Karve who is now project coordinator for the Appropriate Rural Technology Institute, specifically focused on energy technologies that improve women's lives (see Chapter 4). Here we see gender equity as a family value, getting passed on through the generations.

Dr. Ines Smyth, senior gender advisor of Oxfam (Oxfam 2013), identifies one of the characteristics of larger organizations that successfully integrate gender, as a commitment to gender equity at the high organizational levels of leadership. In contrast, many people working and focusing on gender in large organizations—where there is a separate arm for work with a gender equity focus—can feel that their efforts are not supported, valued, or fully understood by the core leadership of the larger organization. Because of this, they can feel limited in their ability to maintain the long-term focus required to effect lasting change. They can also lack sufficient support for gender-focused programming (Smyth 2012).

A characteristic that is common among organizations that effectively and efficiently increase women's participation is that they target as young a population of women as possible for their applied theatre programming. PMC-Ethiopia was able to achieve outstanding results by especially targeting young women of childbearing years, and secondly, their parents or other elders who will likely influence their attitude and behaviors. Starfish One by One reaches out to girls in Guatemala to break down age-old patterns of oppression for indigenous Mayan women. Even in the case study on the Appropriate Rural Technology Institute in India, the young girl in the workshop of the self-help group was more confident and willing to rehearse her concern than her mother, and many of the other older women. The lives of young women are often not yet locked into states from which it is difficult to withdraw or in conditions that are impossible to reverse. They are sometimes not as rigidly bound by the choices they have made or by the choices made for them. I am sensitive while writing this to the still worthy and valid needs of the millions of

Photo 6.2 A mother (far right) holds her daughter while participating in an applied theatre workshop as part of the *MOTHER tour* in Penang, Malaysia.

older women who are locked into lives of poverty and oppression who may wish for access to applied theatre to begin to imagine a better future. In response, I suggest including a multigenerational approach to applied theatre whenever possible, so that the applied theatre attention on the young may be enriched and informed by the participation, wisdom, and experience of older women.

One characteristic that did not emerge from the primary case studies for this book, but has consistently been a factor in other work I have done, is in regard to children. For mothers to participate, children's presence needs to be accepted in the public places where participation would occur (see Photo 6.2). In this regard, what are often referred to as "developing nations" are usually ahead of "developed nations." In these countries there is often minimal segregation by age in public gatherings and, even though children may not be expected to talk or contribute, their presence is considered acceptable. Public gatherings in developed countries are often less tolerant of the presence of children. This, in turn, lessens mothers' ability to participate. Progressive efforts were made by Stepping Stones, which created a children's peer group to allow women to participate in the program in the Pacific Islands (FSPIMedia 2011). In workshops I have facilitated for communities around the world, children have been welcome and are easily incorporated into the action and often entertained by it. Beyond that, mothers are modeling women's participation for their children. When working with Mothers Acting Up, one of our value statements was that when children act up with their mothers, we simultaneously train the next generation of global citizens. As a mother myself, I often travel with my children when facilitating applied theatre in communities. My perception is that as an outsider, I have been more readily accepted by women

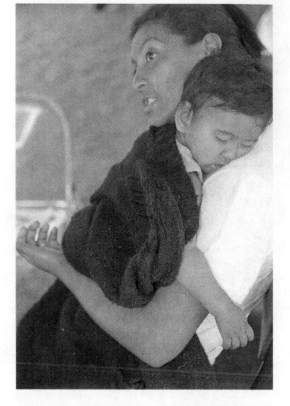

Photo 6.3 A woman in Nicaragua participating in a "training of the trainers" Vocal Empowerment Workshop while also holding her sleeping daughter.

in communities *because* of our shared experience of mothering. It has also, quite frankly, been a necessity for my participation in applied theatre. In my experience, mothers are uniquely able to maintain concentration while also nurturing a child (see Photo 6.3), and tend to have a high tolerance for what others may perceive to be chaos.

Organizations that successfully use applied theatre methods tend to have at least one person within the organization who champions applied theatre methods for reaching program objectives. Often this is a person who has some kind of affinity and aptitude for theatre, or is drawn to it. This is often the person who keeps bringing it up at organizational meetings when making decisions on how to achieve program objectives. It is ideal for that person to have access to training over a long period of time, such that methods can be attempted and then more training can improve upon those methods. It is also important for the leaders of the organization to support this person's efforts, so that it is not a constant struggle for her or him to champion applied theatre. This often assumes that organizational leaders have had exposure to applied theatre, and have some understanding of its process and potential. In an organization like PMC that solely uses theatrical methods, the above considerations are less relevant.

A characteristic of organizations that use applied theatre either extensively or exclusively—such as PMC (see Chapter 5), and to a lesser extent CARE International (CARE 2013)—is that they invest a sizable portion of the program budget into monitoring and evaluation to demonstrate verifiable results to funders, partners, and institutional administration. CARE and PMC are both large multinational organizations. For smaller organizations, dedicating funds to monitoring and evaluation of applied theatre is more of a challenge, but, nonetheless, should be prioritized for the sustainability of such efforts. In addition, effort should be made to make this evaluation a process that involves women's authentic participation and increases their feeling of empowerment (Narayan 1993).

Organizations that successfully use applied theatre tend to share similar qualities and values with applied theatre. Organizations may even share a similar theoretical foundation with applied theatre, such as Starfish One by One (see Chapter 3) with popular education and Paulo Freire. One of the primary qualities of applied theatre is improvisation, which assumes a willingness to take risks by straying from the dominant narrative. With the Appropriate Rural Technology Institute in India (see Chapter 4), we witness staff members who are willing to experience forms of applied theatre to involve women more fully in their program objectives. This is certainly both a risk and a new narrative for a research and development institute comprised primarily of scientists and engineers. Because applied theatre methods necessarily assume shared authorship, organizations that are open to its participatory methods are very likely to respect the people with whom they work, view of them as agents of change, and collaborate with them in authoring a better future. For such organizations, when working with women living in poverty, critical engagement is valued over mere instruction. Because of these qualities, organizations that successfully use applied theatre tend to be healthy, flexible, and able to improvise and adapt to various challenges. They tend to be creative and open to new perspectives and ideas.

Effective strategies

We need a different paradigm for sustainable development based on being responsive in an improvisational manner, and informed by multiple knowledges. A general plan of action that makes efficient use of available resources to achieve the goal of women's participation through applied theatre should include the following considerations:

• Every tactic or approach being taken in a project should be reimagined to discover how it could be adjusted to be more authentically participatory and contribute towards participants' empowering themselves. Dr. Tom Barton is a prominent researcher, evaluator, author, social/community development specialist, medical anthropologist, and physician within the field of sustainable development. In his home office in Uganda, a quote that hangs on the wall reads, "Does this process help users generate information to solve problems they have identified, using methods that increase their capacity to solve similar problems in the future?" (Narayan 1993). This type of a strategy is consistent with the theoretical work of Paulo Freire that stresses working *with* rather than *for* the people (Freire 2000).

• Be responsive to women's preferences, needs, and opinions. To be capable of nimble responses, sustainable development plans should be free from constraints that demand adherence to a plan or approach that does not suit the preferences, needs, and opinions of the community itself. Clearly this would require a change in how funding and planning usually occurs for development projects. It also requires a fundamental shift from believing that experts in the field of development know what is best and should be the ones devising solutions to local challenges. It requires acknowledging the expertise of the people living in local communities to be the experts of their own lives. ARTI in India is a successful example of this approach. They work among the rural people, for whom they design technologies, testing them among the people to see if they truly get adopted and used.

• Embrace a paradigm shift in how we envision development occurring. We think of development as serious business, which it is. A lot is at stake. People have very real needs that require solutions. Funders and governments invest real money into development and expect a solid plan with known objectives and likely outcomes. When we envision what a serious development meeting would look like, we certainly do not imagine the inclusion of children who may cry or fuss. We do not envision laughter. We imagine a structure for this meeting that is set, not improvised or open to suggestion, and is based on knowledge published and disseminated among development professionals. At such meetings, people largely remain seated in their chairs throughout. The room is arranged with the experts at the head of the room addressing those who are politely receiving their words. We would expect it to be expert-led and not overly participatory. If there is feedback, it occurs in an orderly way at times decided by the experts. What history tells us is that the above model all too often fails because it is not sufficiently inclusive, responsive, or locally informed.

Imagine now a very serious meeting for development that tolerates the inclusion of children so that mothers can participate. Community members take part in determining the agenda and objectives for the meeting through participatory activities that include the entire person—intellect, body, emotions, and beliefs (see Photo 6.4). Chairs are arranged in a circle and often people are on their feet moving their bodies or acting out possible development scenarios that draw forth strong emotional responses. The meeting is informed by knowledge from multiple sources and from multiple perspectives. Hierarchies among people at this meeting are intentionally dismantled to create a more even playing field.

At times this meeting is noisy and could appear to be chaotic as people passionately discuss various approaches or solutions (see Photo 6.5). People have fun and often share laughter when recognizing social truths newly revealed through the action. This is a meeting specifically designed to draw forth the ingenuity, creativity,

Photo 6.4 A development meeting that includes the use of applied theatre for the Appropriate Rural Technology Institute in India.

Photo 6.5 A woman in India enjoying her involvement in an applied theatre meeting for sustainable development amid seeming chaos.

intelligence, and agency of community members, for whom the development is being planned. It is a model that is inclusive, responsive, and locally informed.

Inherent in the design of applied theatre are qualities that can help usher in a more successful form of sustainable development. Applied theatre as a strategy is like a plan without a plan. It is a mechanism for deep listening. It is a method without an agenda. It is a container to be filled with content by the participants. It is a mobilizer for this content. It can be used to interrogate, rehearse, and improve plans for action before precious resources are invested. It can build enthusiasm, strengthen resolve, and gather consensus. It leads participants in imagining a more just model for society and can portray how that new model could usher in a more equitable and just world. Key design elements of applied theatre include: being improvisational; nonhierarchical; facilitated—not led; working *with* a community not *for* a community; and finally, capable of incorporating a variety of knowledges. Women living in poverty are well adapted to carry some of these essential characteristics forward into development projects through applied theatre. They have the least to lose in terms of real or perceived power and privilege, so are likely willing to engage in an improvisational method that destabilizes current power structures that determine privilege. Applied theatre is particularly relevant to women's participation because women—especially women living in poverty—are the adult sector of the population least able to participate in the current model of development. If women are not able to participate, the world is robbed of their insight, input, and perspective. Women are the majority of people who are subsistence surviving due to multiple factors such as climate change and political instability. They have a learned resilience from that life experience, a skill set to cope with those challenges, and knowledge that is vastly different than the usual contributors to the development conversation. This is not to say that women's contribution is necessarily superior, just that currently our world doesn't sufficiently benefit from it. Given that we as a world community are up against pretty serious challenges, we need all the knowledge available and the widest variety of skills possible.

When creating theatre with women—either in a form that will be recorded or is live—one approach is to have the people who are the intended recipients of the work see themselves and their lives represented on the stage. This contributes to audiences feeling as though the content of the performance is relevant to their lives. Another approach introduced by Priyadarshini Karve with ARTI in India was to have the drama feature the lifestyles to which the intended audience *aspires*. This approach was in response to the increased access to television and Internet by those living in poverty in rural areas. Rural populations aspire to the urban lifestyles they see represented in the programming. Thus, Karve wanted to create films next that show ARTI's clean-burning cookstoves being used in well-to-do urban homes. Though this will likely create a desire for the cookstoves, it will also likely create the desire to emulate many aspects of this life—some of which run contrary to sustainable development aims, desires that result in higher energy and resource consumption. However, Karve's idea is in many ways the antidote to this problem in that she wants to portray urban people using fuel-efficient ways of cooking.

When involving women in applied theatre, their time should be respected, especially when working with women living in poverty who often experience time-poverty. Participation in applied theatre can be a welcome respite from the drudgery of labor and should be offered to women when feasible. Sometimes, as with Jana Sanskriti, women encounter negative consequences as a result of participating in applied theatre (see Chapter 1). Women, nonetheless, should be able to weigh the costs and benefits of participation themselves and should not be overlooked out of a protective impulse. That said, make all attempts to mitigate and lessen likely negative consequences by making the project as culturally appropriate as possible, and listening to the women themselves to determine what that is. Since time for everyone is a precious commodity, respect participant's time and use it well. Prepare extensively and give them some valuable benefits in exchange for the investment of their time. Provide the chance for fun, but make it fun with substance. Account for women's likely need to bring children with them and plan accordingly. Beyond that, consider ways children can be involved such that they too are trained to see women and themselves as potential agents of change.

Another strategy that is useful when using applied theatre for women's participation is to address the need for mutual support and encouragement among women, in order to sustain their participation. Women's more empowered behavior is not always congratulated by their societies, families, or mates. Support from a community of women all sharing in this process of transformation can strengthen women's resolve to continue stepping into their new roles as agents of change in their communities. Applied theatre exercises that help to build community and increase trust can be used to support and encourage new behavior. For a "training of the trainers" workshop I led in Nicaragua, I used the following trust exercise. I asked groups of five to all stand close together with one person in the middle of the circle with her arms crossed against her chest and her eyes closed. I asked the center person to let herself continually fall off balance, relying on the rest of the group to keep her from falling.

> The outcome of the trust exercise, in which one person in the support group was literally supported by the others as she continually fell off balance, was that participants identified how important it was to be responsible as part of a support group in helping each other. Many of the women said that they were happy to have experienced both roles—the supporter and the person being supported. Another participant added that the person being supported had a responsibility too: to not put too much of her weight on the group and cause undue stress on the group. Another woman noted that when someone is missing in the group that it is harder on the others and makes the others feel more vulnerable. (Osnes 2012, p. 54)

This example demonstrates that even a simple trust exercise can yield a nuanced understanding of the importance of support and trust among women working together. Another example of building support among women can be found in Chapter 3, in which the Starfish One by One students learned methods to overcome giggling that stood as an obstacle to others trying out new empowered behaviors.

Useful approaches and tactics

The tactics for executing the strategy described above can be achieved through a seemingly endless number of applied theatre approaches and tactics. Besides those mentioned throughout this book, others can be found in these sources listed below. This list is in no way exhaustive, but does provide an idea of the types of resources available. Also note that that existing exercises described in these works can be adjusted and evolved to suit different situations and needs.

- *Augusto Boal's Games for Actors and Non-Actors* (2002) is a classic text that sets out the principles and practice of Boal's revolutionary method for engaging both actors and nonactors.
- Viola Spolin's book *Improvisation for the Theater: A Handbook of Teaching and Directing Techniques* (1999), though not written with applied theatre in mind, includes more than 200 improvisational exercises that can be used with all levels and ages of performers.
- *Theatre for Community Conflict and Dialogue: The Hope Is Vital Training Manual* (1998) by Michael Rohd is a manual that provides a clear look at the process and specifics involved in the Hope Is Vital interactive theatre techniques, beginning with warm-up exercises and bridging activities, to improvisational scene work, during which students can replace characters in the stories.
- *Theatre for Conflict Resolution: In the Classroom and Beyond* (2003) by Patricia Sternberg outlines a variety of playmaking activities and theatre games designed to teach students alternative solutions to conflict resolution.
- *Geese Theatre Handbook: Drama with Offenders and People at Risk* (2002) by Clarke Baim and Sally Brookes explains how drama can be used with offenders and similar target groups in therapy groups.
- *Interactive and Improvisational Drama: Varieties of Applied Theatre and Performance* (2007) by Adam Blatner provides useful information about psychodramatic methods for approaching applied theatre.
- *Local Acts: Community-Based Performance in the United States* (2005) by Jan Cohen-Cruz tracks the development of community-based performance as a mix of art, theatre, dance, politics, experimentation, and ritual, community-based performance that is often a collaborative effort of professional artists and local residents. It can be used for community organizing, cultural self-representation, and education.
- More general in its approach, Mat Schwarzman's *Beginner's Guide to Community-Based Arts* (2005) is a guidebook demonstrating the enormous power of art in grass-roots social change.

Recommendations for further research

One area that is touched upon by this book that deserves further research is participatory methods of monitoring and evaluation of applied theatre. The field of applied theatre in general has need of more verifiable methods for participatory

Photo 6.6 Participants of the Navajo Women's Energy Project marking their responses to baseline questions on a circular grid marked on the floor.

monitoring and evaluation. Beyond that, methods specifically designed to facilitate women's participation in monitoring and evaluation are needed. Women can share in the power and agency of the development work being done by participation in monitoring and evaluating their own progress towards their own decided goals. In this manner women can be the ones to author views and statements over their own development. At the Navajo Women's Energy Project referenced at the beginning of this chapter, I tried a new method for women to communally establish a baseline for the day's objectives. I marked three concentric circles using blue masking tape on the floor in the space in which we were meeting (see Photo 6.6). Based on their response to each of the six questions I asked, I invited participants to place themselves somewhere in the space based on their response, with the center being "very much so" and the outside circle being "not at all." The questions were derived from the goals expressed by the Navajo organizers. The questions were:

How well do you feel you know the people in this room?
How comfortable do you feel using your voice to share your personal concerns?
How comfortable do you feel using your voice to share your community concerns?
How well do you understand the project we will begin today?
How interested are you in changing the current story of energy?
How involved do you want to be in this project?

I had assigned a numeric value to each position on the pattern and took photos of the women after each question so as to record their responses for the common record.

At the end of the day, we repeated this entire process with the same questions, to evaluate the extent to which our objectives were achieved. Besides generating quantitative data, this participatory method had the added benefit of letting the women themselves come to know immediately how the rest of the community felt in regard to the objectives for the event—both at the beginning of day and at its completion. I preferred concentric circles over linear markings on the floor that may have set up some sort of hierarchy among the women, given that one of our objectives was to engender a sense of community. This process also got participants on their feet and into the space we would be using for the day. Deepa Narayan states that "in the end, the only way to become both knowledgeable in, and comfortable with, participatory evaluation is by actually doing it. There is no formula, nor can there be a blueprint or manual. By definition, participatory evaluation is a dynamic field" (Narayan 1993, p. xi). Our experience was that by just trying it, we not only were able to gather some data with which to evaluate the effectiveness of our methods, but we started to understand how we could create even more ways to monitor our efforts in a participatory manner.

For example, I began to realize how applied theatre exercises themselves could be used to monitor and evaluate progress made towards objectives. One of the objectives for the applied theatre workshop for girls in the Starfish One by One program is to increase the range of physical expression. To evaluate if this has been achieved by the workshop over time, a facilitator could lead an exercise in the beginning of a session to measure the range and then again at the end to measure any increase. A simple relaxation exercise could be used in which the arms swing up with an inhalation of breath, and swing down with an exhalation of breath. Someone in the group could take a photograph of the full extension or the apex of the swing up at the beginning of the workshop, and again near its completion. Any increase in range of motion could be assessed and noted.

Another area that could benefit from further research is the increased intersection between applied theatre and education-entertainment (EE). In this book I position EE as a form of applied theatre, but what emerged from the case study on PMC is that because the theoretical foundation of EE is *not* based on the theoretical values of Paulo Freire, EE tended to result in lower levels of participation for women living in poverty. Chapter 5 of this book notes that leaders in the field of EE, Arvind Singhal and Everett Rogers, anticipate that future EE interventions will likely see more integration with participatory communication approaches, specifically mentioning the work of both Augusto Boal and Paulo Freire (Singhal & Rogers 2004, p. 18). Indeed, PMC has already begun using more participatory evaluation methods. What is ripe for research and experimentation is the combining of applied theatre methods with EE programming—in all aspects of planning, implementation, and evaluation. The verifiable success of EE in bringing about large-scale behavior change could be combined with applied theatre to incorporate more authentic participation by women, such that both EE and applied theatre would benefit from the merger of approaches. It would be useful to determine if the strength of each can be maintained in this merger or if the combining of the two diminishes those strengths, and if so, in what ways.

Further research into a consideration between the value of live applied theatre and the expansive reach of mediatized forms specific to applied theatre could be useful. Understanding the economic and social costs and benefits of live versus recorded or mediatized forms of theatre and drama could help organizations choose how to approach using applied theatre to achieve their objectives. When interviewing PMC founder William Ryerson, he stated that the difference between the two really gets down to the cost per behavior change (Ryerson 2012). This line of thought could be one point of departure for comparing the two. Also—as is the case with ARTI in India—methods for combining the showing of films in conjunction with some local live performance could be further explored as a method for making mediatized forms of applied theatre more relevant for the group of people viewing it. Looking at trends for drama being consumed at home through devices newly accessible—even to those living in poverty—could be studied to determine the likely impact of this trend on live forms of theatre and reception of applied theatre. Though this cultural shift is often perceived as a threat to live theatre, perhaps there are ways to work with this trend to maximize reach and depth of applied theatre through creative means. Through examples such as Soul City, PMC, and The Whitehouse Project, we see television programming expanding society's collective imagination of what is possible and acceptable for women's participation, at a scale that can make a substantial impact. Balancing these explorations should also be research into the value of live connection between humans and what uniquely can result in those conditions. Human copresence may be the most arresting thing able to impact lasting behavior change. Furthermore, there may be qualities to live performance that render it difficult for oppressive forces to co-opt.

In closing

My belief is that applied theatre can help bring about a revolution, a forcible overthrow of the existing social order that will usher in a more equitable system that welcomes the participation of both men and women. Not a violent force, but, rather, a creative one, that is patient, inclusive, fun, messy, improvisational, caring, alive, and—once unleashed to the majority—unstoppable. One result will be a fundamental change in our way of thinking about women and the value of their participation in meeting the collective challenges we face as one human family on Earth.

The obstacles to sustainable development can seem too mighty to ever topple when one considers challenges such as rising population on earth, climate change, the ever-widening gap between the very rich and the very poor, desertification of once fertile land, and continual violence and unrest. The best strategy I can think of in the face of the seemingly impossible odds is to persistently and positively keep telling another story of how it *could be:* how it *could be* more equitable, how it *could* include everyone—men and women whether rich or poor—and how responsibility and privilege *could be* more equitably shared for the improvement of everyone's lives. That story is not self-evident. It is not a story being told by most governments, advertisers, corporations, or by manufacturers benefitting from society's unbridled consumption. This new story needn't demonize industry or some "other" as the source of all inequity and societal woes. This story could acknowledge our complicity and participation in much of this, and could figure out how we could transition to a new story.

I believe applied theatre is an accessible, dynamic, and adaptable tool for telling these new stories and involving a multitude of people in the telling—especially women living in poverty. It also provides an active forum for negotiating various aspects and details of these imagined realities, complete with their inevitable conflicts and challenges. It gives us practice for resolving differences and a creative process for exploring as-of-yet unimagined solutions. By welcoming the participation of women as storytellers of these sustainable futures, new perspectives can enrich our collective imagining and bring about a vibrant and glorious revolution that will benefit us all.

Bibliography

AASHE, 2013. Association for the Advancement of Sustainability in Higher Education. News, Resources, Events, and Assessment Tools for the Campus Sustainability Community. Available at: http://www.aashe.org/ [Accessed March 15, 2013].

Abbi, R., Christian, P., Gujral, S., & Gopaldas, T., 1991. The impact of maternal work status on the nutrition and health status of children. *Greenstone.org.* Available at: http://www.greenstone.org/greenstone3/nzdl;jsessionid=30E1179E23E49C5BB070489CBA1A9078?a=d&d=HASHb4e3a7f2f52d449ebd792c.4.pp&c=mhl&sib=1&dt=&ec=&et=&p.a=b&p.s=ClassifierBrowse&p.sa=.html [Accessed September 1, 2012].

Ahmad, the late A., 1999. *Studies in Islamic culture in the Indian environment,* New York, NY: Oxford University Press.

Aksornkool, N., 2002. *Gender sensitivity: A training manual for sensitizing educational managers, curriculum and material developers and media professionals to gender concerns,* C. Joerger & E. Taylor, eds., Paris: UNESCO. Available at: http://unesdoc.unesco.org/images/0012/001281/128166eb.pdf.

Allison, H., 1986. *Sistren song: Popular theatre in Jamaica,* London: War on Want.

Anderegg, W.R.L., Prall, J., Harold, J., & Schneider S. 2010. Expert credibility in climate change. *Proceedings of the National Academy of Sciences,* 107(27), pp. 12107–12109.

Appropriate Rural Technology Institute, 2012a. About Us. *Appropriate Rural Technology Institute.* Available at: http://www.arti-india.org/index.php?option=com_content&view=article&id=13&Itemid=29 [Accessed December 18, 2012].

Appropriate Rural Technology Institute, 2012b. Training. Available at: http://www.arti-india.org/index.php?option=com_content&view=article&id=66&Itemid=70 [Accessed January 2, 2013].

Appropriate Rural Technology Institute, 2013. Training modules. Available at: http://www.arti-india.org/index.php?option=com_content&view=article&id=49&Itemid=89 [Accessed February 18, 2013].

Armstrong, A.E., & Juhl, K., 2007. *Radical acts: Theatre and feminist pedagogies of change,* San Francisco: Aunt Lute Books.

Asian Project Management Support Programme, 2012. Guidelines for gender sensitivity in training and coaching programmes, APMAS Knowledge Network. Available at: http://apmasnetwork.org/tools/genderguidelines [Accessed January 1, 2013].

Assefa, M., 2006. From *Yeken Kignit* to *Menta Menged. Media and Communication for Social Development,* pp. 12–14.

Baim, C., & Brookes, S., 2002. *Geese Theatre handbook: Drama with offenders and people at risk,* Hook: Waterside Press.

Balfour, M., 2004. *Theatre in prison theory and practice*, Portland, OR: Intellect. Available at: http://search.ebscohost.com/login.aspx?direct=true&scope=site&db=nlebk&db=nlabk&AN=08330 [Accessed October 9, 2012].

Bandura, A., 1976. *Social learning theory* (1st ed.), London: Pearson.

Banerjee, A. V., & Duflo, E., 2011. *Poor economics: A radical rethinking of the way to fight global poverty*, New York: PublicAffairs.

Banham, M., Gibbs, J., & Osofisan, F., 2002. *African theatre: Women*, Oxford: Currey.

Barker, K., 2012. *Entertainment-education: Improving women's lives through the power of the media*, Shelburne, VT: Population Media Center.

Barker, K., & Sabido, M. eds., 2005. *Soap operas for social change to prevent HIV/AIDS: A training guide for journalists and media personnel*, New York: United Nations Population Fund (UNFPA).

Barratt, B., 2008. *Human rights and foreign aid: For love or money?* New York: Routledge, Chapman and Hall.

Bayly, S., 2001. *Caste, society and politics in India from the eighteenth century to the modern age* (1st ed.), Cambridge, UK: Cambridge University Press.

BBC, 2012. Uganda "set to pass anti-gay law." *BBC*. Available at: http://www.bbc.co.uk/news/world-africa-20318436 [Accessed January 31, 2013].

Beasley, C., 1999. *What is feminism?* London: SAGE. Available at: http://public.eblib.com/EBLPublic/PublicView.do?ptiID=689479 [Accessed October 18, 2012].

Beauvoir, S. de, 1953. *The second sex*, New York: Knopf.

Beetham, G., & Demetriades, J., 2007. Feminist research methodologies and development: Overview and practical application. *Gender and Development*, 15(2), pp. 199–216.

Bentley, E., ed., 1990. *The theory of the modern stage: An introduction to modern theatre and drama*, New York: Penguin Books.

Bharucha, R., 2000. *The politics of cultural practice: Thinking through theatre in an age of globalization* (1st ed.), Indianapolis, IN: Wesleyan.

Bhattacharjee, P., 2000. Stepping Stones—a participatory tool to integrate gender into HIV/AIDS work. *Development in Practice*, 10(5), pp. 691–694.

Birhan Research and Development Consultancy, 2005. *Effect of the radio serial dramas on reproductive health—KAP: Key findings from the evaluation*, Addis Ababa: Population Media Center.

Bisping, J., 2012. *Using Augusto Boal-based theatre for development methods to mediate the introduction of fuel-efficient cook stoves in Chajul, Guatemala: Provoking action through an ethical intervention*, Ann Arbor, MI: ProQuest, UMI Dissertation Publishing.

Black, M., 2007. *The no-nonsense guide to international development*, Oxford: New Internationalist.

Blatner, A., 2007. *Interactive and improvisational drama: Varieties of applied theatre and performance*, Bloomington, IN: iUniverse, Inc.

Boal, A., 1985. *Theatre of the oppressed*, New York: Theatre Communications Group.

Boal, A., 2002. *Games for actors and non-actors*, New York: Routledge.

Boon, R., & Plastow, J., 2004. *Theatre and empowerment: Community drama on the world stage*, Cambridge: Cambridge University Press.

Bossel, H., & Balaton Group, 1999. *Indicators for sustainable development: Theory, method, applications*, Winnipeg, MB: International Institute for Sustainable Development.

Bowles, S., Durlauf, S. N., & Hoff, K. eds., 2006. *Poverty Traps*, Princeton, NJ: Princeton University Press.

Brainard, L., Jones, A., & Purvis, N. eds., 2009. *Climate change and global poverty: A billion lives in the balance?* Washington, DC: Brookings Institution Press.

Brandon, J. R. ed., 1997. *The Cambridge Guide to Asian Theatre*, Cambridge, UK: Cambridge University Press.

Bruce, N., Perez-Padilla, R., & Albalak, R., 2000. Indoor air pollution in developing countries: A major environmental and public health challenge. *Bulletin of the World Health Organization.* Available at: http://www.who.int/bulletin/archives/78(9)1078.pdf [Accessed August 26, 2013].

Bryson, V., 2003. *Feminist political theory: An introduction*, New York: Palgrave Macmillan.

Budlender, D., 2008. *The statistical evidence on care and non-care work across six countries*, United Nations Research Institute for Social Development. Available at: http://www.unrisd.org/unrisd/website/document.nsf/ab82a6805797760f80256b4f005da1ab/f9fec4ea774573e7c1257560003a96b2/$FILE/BudlenderREV.pdf [Accessed July 10, 2012].

Budlender, D., & United Nations Development Fund for Women, 2004. *Why should we care about unpaid care work?* Harare, Zimbabwe: UNIFEM, Regional Office for Southern Africa and the Indian Ocean States.

Butler, J., 2006. *Gender trouble: Feminism and the subversion of identity* (1st ed.), London; New York: Routledge.

CARE, 2013. Pakistan: Kanwal's Story. Available at: http://www.care-international.org/Featured-Articles/kanwals-story.html [Accessed March 4, 2013].

Carroll, J., Anderson, M., & Cameron, D., 2006. *Real players: Drama, technology and education*, London: Trentham Books.

Case, S.-E., 1988. *Feminism and theatre* (1st ed.), New York: Routledge.

CEES, 2013. Center for Energy and Environmental Security, Energy Justice. Available at: http://www.colorado.edu/law/energy-justice-other-third [Accessed August 16, 2013].

Census-2011, Population Census India, 2011. Literacy Rate for India. Available at: http://www.census2011.co.in/literacy.php [Accessed February 24, 2013].

Central Intelligence Agency (United States), 2013. The World Factbook. Available at: https://www.cia.gov/library/publications/the-world-factbook/geos/countrytemplate_gt.html [Accessed August 19, 2013].

Central Statistical Agency Ethiopia and ICF International, 2011. *Ethiopia demographic and health survey*, Addis Ababa, Ethiopia: Central Statistical Agency Ethiopia and ICF International.

Centre for Community Dialogue and Change, 2013. CCDC home page. Theatre of the oppressed organization based in Bengaluru, India Available at: https://sites.google.com/a/ccdc.in/web/ [Accessed February 24, 2013].

Chambers, R., 1995. *Rural Development: Putting the last first* (1st ed.), Upper Saddle River, NJ: Prentice Hall.

Chambers, R., 2002. *Participatory workshops: A sourcebook of 21 sets of ideas and activities*, Sterling, VA: Earthscan.

Christie, I., Warburton, D., & Real World Coalition, 2001. *From here to sustainability: Politics in the real world*, London: Earthscan.

Chvasta, M., 2005. Remembering praxis: Performance in the digital age. *Text and Performance Quarterly*, 25(2), pp. 156–170.

Climate Wise Women, 2013. Climate Wise Women, Connecting the Global to Local. Available at: http://climatewisewomen.org/ [Accessed February 10, 2013].

Cohen-Cruz, J., 2005. *Local acts: Community-based performance in the United States*, New Brunswick, NJ: Rutgers University Press.

Connolly, S., Elmore, K., & Stein, W., 2008. *Qualitative assessment of Outta Road, an entertainment-education radio soap opera for Jamaican adolescents*, Shelburne, VT: Population Media Center.

Cowen, M., & Shenton, R. W., 1998. Agrarian doctrines of development. *The Journal of Peasant Studies*, 25(2), pp. 49–76.

Da Costa, D., 2008. "Spoiled Sons" and "Sincere Daughters": Schooling, security, and empowerment in rural West Bengal, India. *Signs: Journal of Women in Culture and Society*, 33(2), pp. 283–308.

Damasceno, L., Weiss, J. A., & Frischmann, D., 1993. *Latin American popular theatre: The first five centuries*, Albuquerque, NM: University of New Mexico Press.

Das, S., 2013. India News—Breaking World India News. *The New York Times*. Available at: http://topics.nytimes.com/top/news/international/countriesandterritories/india/index.html [Accessed February 24, 2013].

Das Gupta, M., Bongaarts, J., & Cleland, J., 2011. *Population, poverty, and sustainable development*, The World Bank. Available at: http://elibrary.worldbank.org/content/workingpaper/10.1596/1813–9450–5719 [Accessed August 16, 2013].

Dempsey, J., 2009. Intelligent optimist: Stephane Gue, co-founder of Proyecto Payaso, OdeWire. *Odewire*. Available at: http://odewire.com/58682/intelligent-optimist-stephane-gue-co-founder-of-proyecto-payaso.html [Accessed November 29, 2012].

Deshmukh, R. D., 2013. Interview with R. D. Deshmukh of ARTI.

Devaki, J., & Elson, D., 2012. *Harvesting feminist knowledge for public policy*, Thousand Oaks, CA: Sage.

Diamond, D., 2007. *Theatre for Living: The art and science of community-based dialogue*, Bloomington, IN: Trafford.

Doucet, A., 2006. *Do men mother?: Fathering, care, and domestic responsibility*, Toronto: University of Toronto Press, Scholarly Publishing Division.

Duffy, P., & Vettraino, E., 2010. *Youth and theatre of the oppressed*, New York: Palgrave Macmillan.

Eagle Energy, 2013. Navajo Solar. Available at: http://elephantenergy.org/Navajo_Solar.html [Accessed February 27, 2013].

Easterly, W., 2006. *The white man's burden: Why the West's efforts to aid the rest have done so much ill and so little good*, New York: Penguin.

Egonwa, O., 2011. *The humanities and human capital development*, Abraka, [Nigeria]: The Humanities, Delta State University Abraka.

Eisler, R. T., 2008. *The real wealth of nations: Creating a caring economics*, San Francisco: Berrett-Koehler.

Emert, T., & Friedland, E., 2011. *"Come closer": Critical perspectives on theatre of the oppressed*, New York: Peter Lang.

Encyclopedia Britannica, 2012. Dhondo Keshav Karve (Indian social reformer)—Britannica Online Encyclopedia. *Encyclopedia Britannica*. Available at: http://www.britannica.com/EBchecked/topic/312797/Dhondo-Keshav-Karve [Accessed December 19, 2012].

Epskamp, C. P., 2006. *Theatre for development: An introduction to context, applications and training*, London: Zed Books.

Esteva, G., 2010. Development. In W. Sachs, ed., *The development dictionary: A guide to knowledge as power*, New York: Zed Books.

Estrella, M., Gaventa, J., & University of Sussex. Institute of Development Studies, 1998. *Who counts reality? Participatory monitoring and evaluation: A literature review*, Brighton: Institute of Development Studies at the University of Sussex.

Ethiopia. Women's Affairs Office, 2004. *Enabling communities to abandon harmful traditional practices [i.e. practices]: With special reference to female genital mutilation, early marriage, marriage by abduction and perinatal harmful traditional practices*, Addis Ababa: UNICEF/Ethiopia.

Evans, A., & Steven, D., 2012. Sustainable Development Goals–a useful outcome from Rio+ 20? New York University, Centre on International Cooperation, New York. http://www. globaldashboard. org/wp-content/uploads/SDGs-briefing1. pdf. Available at: http://www. cic.nyu.edu/scarcity/docs/evans_steven_rio_2.pdf [Accessed November 1, 2012].

Falola, T., & Heaton, M. M. (eds.), 2010. *Endangered bodies: Women, children, and health in Africa*, Lawrenceville, NJ: Africa World Press.

Farhar, B., Osnes, B., Karve, P., To, L. & Speer, N., 2012. Engaging Women in Clean Energy Solutions Workshop at the World Renewable Energy Forum (WREF2012). *Gender & Development*, 20(3), pp. 616–617.

Farnworth, C., 2007. Achieving respondent-led research in Madagascar. *Gender and Development*, 15(2), pp. 271–285.

Farr, K., 2005. *Sex trafficking: The global market in women and children*, New York: Worth.

Fauchere, C., 2011. *Mother: Caring for 7 billion*, Available at: www.motherthefilm.com [Accessed August 16, 2013].

Fenske, M., 2004. The aesthetic of the unfinished: Ethics and performance. *Text and Performance Quarterly*, 24(1), pp. 1–19.

Flayer, A., 2009. Evaluation. Personal email communication.

Flores, Y., 2000. *The Drama of Gender*, Wor(L)Ds of Change, Vol. 38, New York: Peter Lang.

Fortson, C., 2003. Women's rights vital for developing world. *Yale Daily News*. Available at: http://yaledailynews.com/blog/2003/02/14/womens-rights-vital-for-developing-world/ [Accessed August 16, 2013].

Franke-Ruta, G., 2013. The White House Project Shutters Its Doors. *The Atlantic*. Available at: http://www.theatlantic.com/politics/archive/2013/01/the-white-house-project-shutters-its-doors/272576/ [Accessed August 18, 2013].

Freire, P., 2000. *Pedagogy of the oppressed*, New York: Continuum.

FSPIMedia, 2011a. *Community Solutions—Stepping Stones pt. 1*. Available at: http://www.youtube.com/watch?v=bP3rcVnXUCs [Accessed September 23, 2012].

FSPIMedia, 2011b. *Community Solutions—Stepping Stones pt. 2*. Available at: http://www.youtube.com/watch?v=EcaeeB9gj0c [Accessed September 23, 2012].

Ganguly, S., 2010. *Jana Sanskriti: Forum theatre and democracy in India* (1st ed.), New York: Routledge.

Gebeyehu, T., & Edemariam, A., 1997. Ethiopia. In D. Rubin (ed.), *The world encyclopedia of contemporary theatre*. Vol. 3, *Africa*. London: Routledge, pp. 113–129.

Gender & Development, 2013. Home page. Available at: http://www.genderanddevelopment. org/ [Accessed January 1, 2013].

Getachew, M., 2010. PMC and I. *Media Communication for Social and Behavior Change*, pp. 12–14.

Gilligan, C., 1982. *In a different voice: Psychological theory and women's development*, Cambridge, MA: Harvard University Press.

Global Alliance for Clean Cookstoves, 2013.The Cookstove Story. Available at: http://www.cleancookstoves.org/ [Accessed January 3, 2013].

Granderson, J., Sandhu, J., Vasquez, D., Ramirez, E., & Smith K., 2009. Fuel use and design analysis of improved woodburning cookstoves in the Guatemalan Highlands. *Biomass and Bioenergy*, 33(2), pp. 306–315.

Grandin, G., Levenson, D. T., & Oglesby, E. (eds.), 2011. *The Guatemala reader: History, culture, politics*, Durham, NC: Duke University Press.

Green, S. L., 2004. Sistren Theatre Collective: Struggling to remain radical in an era of globalization. *Theatre Topics*, 14(2), pp. 473–495.

Haberland, N., & Measham, D. M. (eds.), 2002. *Responding to Cairo: Case studies of changing practice in reproductive health and family planning*, New York: Population Council.

Hadjipateras, A., 2006. *Joining hands: Integrating gender and HIV/AIDS: Report of an ACORD project using stepping stones in Angola, Tanzania, and Uganda*, Kampala, Uganda: ACORD.

Haggbloom, S. J., 2002. The 100 most eminent psychologists of the 20th century. *Review of General Psychology*, 6(2), pp. 139–152.

Hausmann, R., Tyson, L., & Zahidi S., 2010. *The global gender gap report 2010*, Geneva, Switzerland: World Economic Forum. Available at: http://www.weforum.org/reports/global-gender-gap-report-2010?ol=1 [Accessed November 27, 2012].

Hayford, J. E. C., 1969. *Ethiopia unbound: Studies in race emancipation* (2nd ed.), New York: Routledge.

Heilbrun, C. G., 2008. *Writing a woman's life* (reprint), New York: Norton.

Heron, T., Toppin, D., & Finikin, L., 2009. Sistren in parliament: Addressing abortion and women's rights through popular theatre. *Journal of the Association of Caribbean Women Writers and Scholars*, 11, pp. 45–60.

Hesse-Biber, S. N., & Yaiser, M. L., 2004. *Feminist perspectives on social research*, New York: Oxford University Press.

Hochfeld, T., & Bassadlien, S. R., 2007. Participation, values, and implementation: Three research challenges in developing gender-sensitive indicators. *Gender & Development*, 15(2), pp. 217–230.

hooks, bell, 2000. *Feminism is for everybody: Passionate politics*, Cambridge, MA: South End Press.

hooks, bell, 2008. Choosing the margin as a space of radical openness. In T. Prentki & S. Preston (eds.), *The applied theatre reader*, New York: Routledge, pp. 80–85.

Hopkin, M., 2005. Ethiopia is top choice for cradle of Homo sapiens. *Nature News*. Available at: http://www.nature.com/news/2005/050214/full/news050214–10.html [Accessed January 12, 2013].

Hudson-Weems, C., 2004. *Africana womanism: Reclaiming ourselves.*, Bedford Pub.

Inside the Greenhouse, 2013. An initiative at the University of Colorado to promote creative climate communication. Available at: http://www.insidethegreenhouse.net/ [Accessed February 25, 2013].

Integrated Regional Information Networks & United Nations. Office for the Coordination of Humanitarian Affairs, 2007. *The shame of war: Sexual violence against women and girls in conflict*, Kenya: OCHA/IRIN.

International Institute for Environment and Development. Sustainable Agriculture Programme, 1998. *Participatory monitoring and evaluation*, London: Sustainable Agriculture Programme, International Institute for Environment and Development.

Indian People Theatre Association (IPTA), 2013. Mumbai. Available at: http://www.iptamumbai.org/festival.html [Accessed February 24, 2013].

IRIN: Humanitarian News and Analysis, 2007. Youth in crisis: Coming of age in the 21st century. *IRINnews*. Available at: http://www.irinnews.org/IndepthMain.aspx?InDepthID=28&ReportID=69993 [Accessed January 19, 2013].

Jackson, T., 2009. *Prosperity without growth: Economics for a finite planet*, Sterling, VA: Earthscan.

James, L., 2000. *Raj: The making and unmaking of British India* (1st ed.), New York: St. Martin's.

Jana Sanskriti, 2013a. Centre for Theatre of the Oppressed home page. Available at: http://www.janasanskriti.org/index.html [Accessed February 10, 2013].

Jana Sanskriti, 2013b. JANASANSKRITI: Sarama. Available at: http://www.janasanskriti.org/publication.html# [Accessed February 10, 2013].

Jewkes, R., Wood, K., & Duvvury, N, 2010. "I woke up after I joined Stepping Stones": Meanings of an HIV behavioural intervention in rural South African young people's lives. *Health Education Research*, 25(6), pp. 1074–1084.

Johnsson-Latham, G., & Miljövårdsberedningen, 2007. *A study on gender equality as a prerequisite for sustainable development*, Stockholm: Environment Advisory Council, Ministry of Environment.

Jung, C.G., 1981. *The archetypes and the collective unconscious* (2nd ed.), Princeton, NJ: Princeton University Press.

Kabyemela, J.T., 2012. *Theatre for women empowerment and development: Experience of politics in rural Tanzania*, Saarbrücken, Germany: LAP Lambert Academic.

Kamlongera, C., 1986. *Theatre for development in Africa: With case studies from Malawi and Zambia*, Bonn: Zentralstelle für Erziehung Wissenschaft und Dokumentation.

Karve, A.D., 2013. Interview with A.D. Karve.

Karve, D.K., 1936. *Looking back*, Poona (now Pune): Hindu Widows' Home Association.

Karve, I., 1960. *Hindu society*, Poona: Deschmukh.

Karve, P., 2013. Interview with Priyadarshini Karve.

Kemp, R., Parto, S., & Gibson, R.B., 2005. Governance for sustainable development: moving from theory to practice. *IJSD International Journal of Sustainable Development*, 8(1/2), pp. 12–30.

Kerr, D., 1995. *African popular theatre: From pre-colonial times to the present day*, London; Portsmouth, NH: Heinemann.

Khan, Saeed, 2010. There's no national language in India: Gujarat High Court. *The Times of India*. Available at: http://articles.timesofindia.indiatimes.com/2010–01–25/india/28148512_1_national-language-official-language-hindi [Accessed February 24, 2013].

King, E.M., & Hill, M.A., 1998. *Women's education in developing countries: Barriers, benefits, and policies*, Baltimore: Published for the World Bank [by] the Johns Hopkins University Press. Available at: http://search.ebscohost.com/login.aspx?direct=true&scope=site&db=nlebk&db=nlabk&AN=33281 [Accessed August 29, 2012].

Kolawole, M., 1997. *Womanism and African consciousness*, Trenton, NJ: Africa World Press.

Kristof, N.D., & WuDunn, S., 2009. *Half the sky: Turning oppression into opportunity for women worldwide*, New York: Knopf.

Kuppers, P., 2007. *Community performance: An introduction*, New York: Routledge.

Kusek, J., Z. & Rist, R.C., 2004. *Ten steps to a results-based monitoring and evaluation system: A handbook for development practitioners*, Washington, DC: World Bank Publications.

Latifee, H.I., 2003. Microcredit and poverty reduction. In *International Conference on Poverty Reduction through Microcredit. Taksim-Istambul*. Available at: http://web01.grameen.com/grameen/gtrust/Microcredit%20and%20Poverty%20Reduction%20June%202003%20in%20TurkeyF.pdf [Accessed July 10, 2012].

Lefevre, T., & Nikiforova, N., 2004. *Tools for behavior change communication for HIV/AIDS: An annotated bibliography*, Arlington, VA: Family Health International, Institute for HIV/AIDS.

Lemma, M., 2009. *Marriage by abduction, marriage of unequals: Two comedies*, Addis Ababa: Arada Books Ethiopia.

Lemma, M., 1970. *Snatch and run or marriage by abduction, a play by Menghestu Lemma* (4th ed.), Addis Ababa: Ethiopia Observer.

Lerner, G., 1987. *The creation of patriarchy*, New York: Oxford University Press.

Limitless Horizons Ixil, 2013. Limitless Horizons Ixil | Different Worlds Working Toward One Horizon. Available at: http://www.limitlesshorizonsixil.org/ [Accessed February 10, 2013].

Lunch, C., & Lunch, N., 2006. *Insights into participatory video*, Oxford, UK: Insightshare.

Luthra, R., 2003. Recovering women's voice: Communicative empowerment of women of the south. In P. J. Kalbfleisch, ed., *Communication Yearbook 27*, Mahwah, NJ: Lawrence Erlbaum, pp. 45–65.

MacLean, P. D., 1974. *A triune concept of the brain and behaviour* (1st ed.), Toronto: University of Toronto Press.

Manygoats, A., & Osnes, B., 2013. *Navajo Women's Energy Project: Report of first meeting*, unpublished report.

Mariam, A., 2012. Ethiopia: An early warning for a famine in 2013—al mariam. Open Salon. Available at: http://open.salon.com/blog/almariam/2012/10/07/ethiopia_an_early_warning_for_a_famine_in_2013 [Accessed January 12, 2013].

Mattel, 2013. Vote Barbie for president: Stickers & printables, girls' activities & leadership tips. Barbie I Can Be. Available at: http://icanbe.barbie.com/en_us/dolls/president.html [Accessed March 6, 2013].

Mayo, P., 1999. *Gramsci, Freire, and adult education: Possibilities for transformative action*, London: Zed Books.

McCarthy, C., 2010. *The Cambridge introduction to Edward Said* (3rd ed.), New York: Cambridge University Press.

McCarthy, J., & Galvao, K., 2004. *Enacting participatory development theatre-based techniques*, Sterling, VA: Earthscan. Available at: http://search.ebscohost.com/login.aspx?direct=true&scope=site&db=nlebk&db=nlabk&AN=126121 [Accessed October 9, 2012].

Merso, F., 2008. *Women & girls and HIV/AIDS in Ethiopia*, UNFPA. Available at: http://ethiopia.unfpa.org/drive/WomenandGirlsandHIV-AIDSinEthiopia.pdf.

Mies, M., & Shiva, V., 1993. *Ecofeminism* (1st ed.), London: Zed Books.

Milkias, P., 2011. *Ethiopia*, Santa Barbara, CA: ABC-CLIO.

Millar, M., 2006. Popular theatre and the Guatemalan peace process. *Latin American Theatre Review*, 39(2), pp. 97–116.

Mittal, S., & Thursby, G. eds., 2004. *The Hindu world*, New York: Routledge.

Mlama, P. M., 1991. *Culture and development: The popular theatre approach in Africa*, Uppsala: Nordiska Afrikainstitutet.

Moges, T., 2010. Remarkable headway through capacity building training programs. *Media Communication For Social and Behavior Change*, Population Media Center Publications, pp. 48–55.

Mohan, D., 2004. Reimagining community: Scripting power and changing the subject through Jana Sanskriti's political theatre in rural North India. *Journal of Contemporary Ethnography*, 33(2), pp. 178–217.

Mohanty, C. T., Russo, A., & Torres, L. eds., 1991. *Third world women and the politics of feminism* (1st ed.), Bloomington: Indiana University Press.

Morán, P. R., 2004. *Escaping the poverty trap*, New York: Inter-American Development Bank.

MOTHER tour, 2011. *Mothers Acting Up*. Available at: http://www.mothersactingup.org/ mother-tour-2/ [Accessed December 21, 2012].

Mothers Acting Up, 2011. Mothers Acting Up: Mobilizing mothers to act on behalf of the world's children. Available at: http://www.mothersactingup.org/ [Accessed January 26, 2013].

Muhammed, Z., 2010. Zinet Muhammed interview.

Narayan, D., 1993. *Participatory evaluation: Tools for managing change in water and sanitation*, Washington, DC: The World Bank. Available at: http://www.chs.ubc.ca/archives/ files/Participatory%20Evaluation%20Tools%20for%20Managing%20Change%20 in%20Water%20and%20Sanitation.pdf.

Nariman, H., 1993. *Soap Operas for Social Change: Toward a methodology for entertainment-education television*, Westport, CT: Praeger.

National Center for Health Statistics, 1997. NCHS Pressroom—1997 Fact Sheet—Mothers education and birth rate. *Centers for Disease Control and Prevention*. Available at: http://www.cdc.gov/nchs/pressroom/97facts/edu2birt.htm [Accessed November 23, 2012].

National Geographic, 2013. India Facts, India Flag. *National Geographic*. Available at: http://travel.nationalgeographic.com/travel/countries/india-facts/ [Accessed February 23, 2013].

Nelson, D., 2011. Indian gender gap widens due to number of female foetus abortions. *Telegraph.co.uk*. Available at: http://www.telegraph.co.uk/news/worldnews/asia/india/ 8533467/Indian-gender-gap-widens-due-to-number-of-female-foetus-abortions.html [Accessed February 24, 2013].

Nike, 2013. NIKE, Inc.—Our work. Available at: http://nikeinc.com/pages/our-work [Accessed March 6, 2013].

Ning, T., Bajan, N., & Saloj, V., 2012. Interview with Starfish One by One staff.

NoVo Foundation, 2013. Available at: http://novofoundation.org/ [Accessed March 6, 2013].

Ogundipe-Leslie, M., 1994. *Re-creating ourselves: African women & critical transformations*, Trenton, NJ: Africa World Press.

Okagbu, O., 1998. Product or process: Theatre for development in Africa. In K. Salhi (ed.), *African theatre for development: Art for self-determination*, Exeter, England: Intellect, pp. 23–41.

Okollet, C., 2012. Rio+20 and women's lives: A cross-generational dialogue. A presentation on June 20, 2012 at the Ford Foundation Pavilion at Rio+20 in Rio de Janeiro, Brazil.

Olson, R., 2011. Population 7 billion: How your world will change. *National Geographic*, 219(1), pp. 32–69.

Osnes, B., 2001. *Acting: An international encyclopedia of traditional culture*, Santa Barbara, CA: ABC-CLIO.

Osnes, B., 2012a. Engaging women's voices through theatre for energy development. *Renewable Energy*, Available at: http://www.sciencedirect.com/science/article/pii/ S096014811200047X [Accessed August 17, 2012].

Osnes, B., 2012b. Voice strengthening and interactive theatre for women's productive income-generating activities in sustainable development. *Journal of Sustainable Development*, 5(6), pp. 49–56.

Osnes, B., & Forbes, J., 2011. Mothers Acting Up: Mobilizing mothers to act on behalf of the world's children. In A. O'Reilly (ed.), *The 21st century motherhood movement:*

Mothers speak out on why we need to change the world and how to do it, Toronto: Demeter Press, pp. 732–745.

Osnes, B., & Gammon, M., 2013. Striking the Match: A web-based performance to illuminate issues of Sustainability and ignite positive social change. *Sustainability*, 6, pp. 167–170.

O'Toole, J., 1976. *Theatre in education: New objectives for theatre, new techniques in education*, London: Hodder and Stoughton.

Oxfam, 2013. Oxfam International | Working together to find lasting solutions to poverty and injustice. Available at: http://www.oxfam.org/ [Accessed March 3, 2013].

Parpart, J. L., Connelly, P., & Barriteau, E., 2000. *Theoretical perspectives on gender and development*, Ottawa: International Development Research Centre. Available at: http://public.eblib.com/EBLPublic/PublicView.do?ptiID=295164 [Accessed October 31, 2012].

Patwardhan, A., 2013. Interview with Arun Patwardhan of ARTI.

Pausewang, S., Tronvoll, K., & Aalen, L., 2002. *Ethiopia since the Derg: A decade of democratic pretension and performance*, New York: Palgrave.

Peak to Peak, 2013. Peak to Peak Project | University of Colorado at Boulder. Available at: http://www.colorado.edu/AcademicAffairs/p2p.html [Accessed February 25, 2013].

Pearson, R., 2007. Reassessing paid work and women's empowerment: Lessons from the global economy. In A. Cornwall, E. Harrison, & A. Whitehead (eds.), *Feminisms in development: Contradictions, contestations and challenges*, New York: Zed Books, pp. 201–213.

People's Sustainability Treaties, 2012. Manifesto. *Peoples' Sustainability Treaties*. Available at: http://sustainabilitytreaties.org/pst-manifesto/ [Accessed October 24, 2012].

Pérez, E., 1991. Sexuality and discourse: Notes from a Chicano survivor. In C. Trujillo (ed.), *Chicana lesbians: The girls our mothers warned us about*, Berkeley: Third Woman Press, pp. 159–184.

Philanthropiece, 2013. Philanthropiece Foundation | Building Healthy and Sustainable Communities Through Community Development and Empowerment. Available at: http://philanthropiece.org/ [Accessed March 7, 2013].

Phillips, A., 2012. *A creator's guide to transmedia storytelling: How to captivate and engage audiences across multiple platforms*, New York: McGraw-Hill.

Plastow, J., 1996. *African theatre and politics. The evolution of theatre in Ethiopia, Tanzania and Zimbabwe. A comparative study*, Atlanta GA: Rodopi B. V. Editions.

Plastow, J., 1998. Uses and abuses of theatre for development: Political struggle and development theatre in the Ethiopia-Eritrea war. In K. Salhi (ed.), *African theatre for development art for self-determination*, Exeter, England: Intellect.

Plastow, J., 2004. Dance and transformation: the Adugna Community Dance Theatre, Ethiopia. In R. Boon & J. Plastow (eds.), *Theatre and empowerment: Community drama on the world stage*, New York: Cambridge University Press, pp. 125–154.

Plastow, J., 2013. Jane Plastow interview.

Plastow, J., & Boon, R., 1998. *Theatre matters: Performance and culture on the world stage*, New York: Cambridge University Press.

Poindexter, D., 2004. A history of entertainment-education, 1958–2000. In A. Singhal (ed.), *Entertainment-education and social change: History, research, and practice*, New York: Routledge, pp. 21–37.

Population Media Center, 2006. "Yeken Kignit": The story of the two antagonistic characters. *Media and Communication for Social Development*, Special Issue, pp. 15–16.

Population Media Center, 2009a. *Eradicating female genital mutilation in Ethiopia*, Addis Ababa, Ethiopia: Population Media Center.

Population Media Center, 2009b. Population Media Center. Yeken Kignit. Available at: http://www.populationmedia.org/where/ethiopia/yeken-kignit/ [Accessed January 20, 2013].

Population Media Center, 2010. *PMC-Ethiopia celebrates 10 years*, Population Media Center.

Population Media Center, 2012a. Ethiopia. Available at: http://www.populationmedia.org/where/ethiopia/ [Accessed January 10, 2013].

Population Media Center, 2012b. Where. Available at: http://www.populationmedia.org/where/ [Accessed January 9, 2013].

Population Media Center, 2013a. Ethiopia—Background. Available at: http://www.populationmedia.org/where/ethiopia/ethiopia-background/ [Accessed January 26, 2013].

Population Media Center, 2013b. Staff—Country Representatives. Available at: http://www.populationmedia.org/who/staff-country-reps/ [Accessed March 8, 2013].

Population Media Center, 2013c. Blog Archive—Population Media Center and Champlain College tackle gender based violence through video gaming. Available at: http://www.populationmedia.org/2013/01/08/population-media-center-and-champlain-college-tackle-gender-based-violence-through-video-gaming/ [Accessed January 23, 2013].

Population Reference Bureau, 2010. *Female genital mutilation/cutting: Data and trends*. Available at: http://www.prb.org/pdf10/fgm-wallchart2010.pdf.

Prendergast, M., & Saxton, J., 2009. *Applied theatre international case studies and challenges for practice*, Chicago: Intellect. Available at: http://public.eblib.com/EBLPublic/PublicView.do?ptiID = 475768 [Accessed July 26, 2012].

Prentki, T., & Etherton, M., 2006. Drama for change? Prove it! Impact assessment in applied theatre. *Research in Drama Education*, 11(2), pp. 139–155.

Prentki, T., & Preston, S., eds., 2008. *The applied theatre reader* (1st ed.), New York: Routledge.

Pretty, J., Guijt, I., Thompson, J., & I. Scoones, 1995. *Participatory learning and action*, London: International Institute for Environment and Development.

Proyecto Payaso, 2012. Home page. Available at: http://www.proyectopayaso.org/nuevaweb/index.php?q=en/node/77 [Accessed November 29, 2012].

Radulescu, D., 2007. Winnie in the attic: Towards a feminist awakening in Beckett's Happy Days. In A. E. Armstong & K. Juhl (eds.), *Radical acts: Theatre and feminist pedagogies of change*, San Francisco: Aunt Lute Books, pp. 27–44.

Rahnema, M., 2008. Participation. In T. Prentki & S. Preston (eds.), *The applied theatre reader*, New York: Routledge, pp. 141–147.

Ramanan, N., 2003. Actor by accident, director by choice | India Currents. *India Currents: The Complete Indian American Magazine.* Available at: http://www.indiacurrents.com/articles/2003/02/12/actor-by-accident-director-by-choice [Accessed December 19, 2012].

Ramaswamy, R., 2013. Centre for Community Dialogue and Change. Available at: https://sites.google.com/a/ccdc.in/web/ [Accessed February 24, 2013].

Ramesh, J., 2007. Self-help groups revolution: What next? *Economic & Political Weekly*, 42(36). Available at: http://www.jstor.org/discover/10.2307/40276360?uid=3739568&uid=2&uid=4&uid=3739256&sid=21101822020757.

Rangacharya, A., 1999. *Natyasastra* (revised), New Delhi: Munshiram.

Rashid, A., & Alim, A., 2005. *Building positive attitudes towards gender equity: A baseline survey of gender quality action learning programme*, Bangladesh: BRAC Research and Evaluation Division. Available at: research@brac.net.

Rehfuess, E., 2006. Fuel for life: Household energy and health. *World Health Organization.* Available at: http://apps.who.int/iris/handle/10665/43421 [Accessed January 3, 2013].

Rich, A., 1976. *Of woman born: Motherhood as experience and institution*, New York: Norton.

Rogers, E., & Singhal, A., 2003. Empowerment and communication: Lessons learned from organizing for social change. In P.J. Kalbfleisch (ed.), *Communication Yearbook 27*, London: Routledge, pp. 67–85.

Rohd, M., 1998. *Theatre for community conflict and dialogue: The hope is vital training manual*, Portsmouth, NH: Heinemann.

Rowe, N., 2007. *Playing the other dramatizing personal narratives in playback theatre*, London: Jessica Kingsley. Available at: http://public.eblib.com/EBLPublic/PublicView. do?ptiID = 334138 [Accessed October 9, 2012].

Rowlands, J., 1997. *Questioning empowerment: Working with women in Honduras*, Oxford, UK: Oxfam.

Ryerson, B., 2012. Population Media Center—President's Message. Available at: http://www. populationmedia.org/who/message-from-the-president/ [Accessed January 6, 2013].

Ryerson, W., 2012. William Ryerson interview about the Population Media Center.

Ryerson, W., & Negussie, T., 2004. Organizing a comprehensive national plan for entertainment-education in Ethiopia. In A. Singhal (ed.), *Entertainment-education and social change history, research, and practice*, Mahwah, NJ: Lawrence Erlbaum, pp. 177–190. Available at: http://search.ebscohost.com/login.aspx?direct=true&scope= site&db=nlebk&db=nlabk&AN=102225 [Accessed January 18, 2013].

Said, E.W., 1979. *Orientalism* (1st Vintage Books ed.), New York: Vintage.

Salem, R., Bernstein, J., Sullivan, T., & Lande R., 2008. *Population reports: Communication for better health*, Baltimore: John Hopkins Bloomberg School of Public Health.

Samba, E.N., 2005. *Women in theatre for development in Cameroon: Participation, contributions and limitations*, Bayreuth, Germany: [Bayreuth University].

Samuchit, 2012. Biomass fueled household energy devices. *Samuchit Enviro Tech Pvt. Ltd.* Available at: http://www.samuchit.com/index.php?option=com_content&view=article &id=1&Itemid=3 [Accessed January 4, 2013].

Sanford, V., 2004. *Buried secrets: Truth and human rights in Guatemala*, New York: Palgrave Macmillan.

Schechter, J., 2003. *Popular theatre: A sourcebook*, New York: Routledge.

Schwarzman, M., 2005. *Beginner's guide to community-based arts*, Oakland, CA: New Village Press.

Seham, A., 2007. Play fair: Feminist tools for teaching improv. In A.E. Armstong & K. Juhl, eds. *Radical acts: Theatre and feminist pedagogies of change*, San Francisco: Aunt Lute Books, pp. 135–151.

Sen, A., 2001. *Development as freedom*, New York: Knopf.

Shannon, C.E., & Weaver, W., 1998. *The mathematical theory of communication*, University of Illinois Press.

Shaughnessy, N., 2012. *Applying performance: Live art, socially engaged theatre and affective practice*, New York: Palgrave Macmillan.

Shillington, J., 2002. *Grappling with atrocity: Guatemalan theater in the 1990s*, Cranbury, NJ: Associated University Presses.

Shiva, V., 1989. *Staying alive: Women, ecology and development*, London: Zed Books.

Singhal, A., Cody, M., Rogers, E., & Sabido, M., eds., 2003. *Entertainment-education and social change: History, research, and practice*, New York: Routledge.

Singhal, A., & Rogers, E., 2004. The status of entertainment-education worldwide. In *Entertainment-education and social change: History, research, and practice*, Mahwah, NJ: Lawrence Erlbaum, pp. 3–20. Available at: http://search.ebscohost.com/login.aspx?

direct=true&scope=site&db=nlebk&db=nlabk&AN=102225 [Accessed January 18, 2013].

Singhal, A. M., & Rogers, E. M., 2003. *Combating AIDS: Communication strategies in action*, London: Sage.

Smith, D. M., 2006. *Just one planet: Poverty, justice and climate change*, Warwickshire, UK: Intermediate Technology.

Smyth, I., 2012. Interview with Dr. Ines Smyth at Oxford, UK, Oxfam.

Soul City, Edutainment in South Africa: A force for change in health. Available at: http://www.ncbi.nlm.nih.gov/pmc/artilces/PMC2733254/ [Accessed June 15, 2013].

Soul City, 2001. *Series 4: Impact evaluation—AIDS [Television Series]* , Parkerstown, South Africa: Soul City Institute for Health and Development Communication.

Spolin, V., 1999. *Improvisation for the theater 3E: A handbook of teaching and directing techniques* (3rd ed.), Evanston, IL: Northwestern University Press.

Starfish One by One, 2010. *Starfish One by One organizational overview 2010*, Starfish One by One. Available at: http://www.starfishonebyone.org/sf_overview2010.pdf.

Starfish One by One, 2012a. Our history. *Starfish One by One.* Available at: http://www.starfishonebyone.org/ourhistory.html [Accessed November 27, 2012].

Starfish One by One, 2012b. Our programs. *Starfish One by One.* Available at: http://www.starfishonebyone.org/ourprograms.html [Accessed November 27, 2012].

Starfish One by One, 2012c. What we do. *Starfish One by One.* Available at: http://www.starfishonebyone.org/whatwedo.html [Accessed November 27, 2012].

Starfish One by One, 2012d. Why girl's education. Available at: http://www.starfishonebyone.org/whygirls.html [Accessed December 10, 2012].

Starfish One by One, 2012e. Why girls? *Starfish One by One.* Available at: http://www.starfishonebyone.org/whygirls.html [Accessed November 27, 2012].

Sternberg, P., 2003. *Theatre for conflict resolution: In the classroom and beyond*, Portsmouth, NH: Heinemann.

Sumner, A., & Tribe, M. A., 2008. *International development studies: Theories and methods in research and practice*, Thousand Oaks, CA: Sage.

Taylor, P., 2006. Applied theatre/drama: An e-debate in 2004. *Research in Drama Education: The Journal of Applied Theatre and Performance*, 11(1), pp. 90–95.

Taylor, V., Whittier, N., & Pelak, C. F., 2007. The women's movement: Persistence through transformation. In V. Taylor, N. Whittier, & L. Rupp, eds., *Feminist frontiers*, New York: McGraw-Hill, pp. 503–518.

Tedlock, D., 2005. *Rabinal Achi: A Mayan drama of war and sacrifice*, New York: Oxford University Press.

Teffera, N., 2008. Hearing is believing: Creating radio serial dramas to help educate Ethiopian listeners about key health issues proves a stunning success. *Communication World*, 25(2), pp. 33–36.

The Girl Effect, 2013. Adolescent girls are the most powerful force for change on the planet. Available at: http://www.girleffect.org/ [Accessed March 6, 2013].

The Indian Express, 2011. Gender gap divides India from the rest—Indian Express. Available at: http://www.indianexpress.com/news/gender-gap-divides-india-from-the-rest/869804 [Accessed February 24, 2013].

Thiong'o, N., 1982. *I will marry when I want*, London: Exeter.

Thiong'o, N., 1986. *Decolonising the mind: The politics of language in African literature*, Portsmouth, NH: Heinemann.

Thyagarajan, M., 2002. *Popular theater, development and communication*, Chapel Hill, NC: University of North Carolina. University Center for International Studies.

Tolba, M. K., Abdel-Hadi, A., & Soliman, S., 2010. *Environment, health, and sustainable development*, Toronto: Hogrefe.

Torgovnick, M., 1991. *Gone primitive: Savage intellects, modern lives*, Chicago: University Of Chicago Press.

Truman, H., 1949. Harry S. Truman inaugural address. Available at: http://www.trumanlibrary.org/calendar/viewpapers.php?pid=1030 [Accessed July 23, 2012].

UN Women, 2012. *A world in balance requires gender equity, says UN Women.* Available at: http://www.unwomen.org/2012/06/a-world-in-balance-requires-gender-equality-says-un-women/.

UNESCO, 2012. *UNESCO Global Partnership for Girls and Women's Education.* Available at: http://www.unesco.org/eri/cp/factsheets_ed/ET_EDFactSheet.pdf.

UNFPA (United Nations Population Fund), 1995. *Report of the International Conference on Population and Development—ICPD—Programme of Action*, New York: UNFPA.

UNICEF & UNICEF, 2006. *The state of the world's children 2007: women and children: the double dividend of gender equality*, New York: United Nations Children's Fund.

United Nations Millennium Development Goals, 2000. Available at: http://www.un.org/millenniumgoals/ [Accessed September 2, 2012].

United Nations News Service, 2012. UN senior officials highlight Rio+20 achievements. *UN News Service Section.* Available at: http://www.un.org/apps/news/story.asp?NewsID = 42352 [Accessed July 12, 2012].

United Nations Department of Economic and Social Affairs, 2010. *Rethinking poverty: Report on the world social situation 2010*, New York: United Nations, Department of Economic and Social Affairs.

University of Essex Centre for Environment and Society, 1999. *Reducing food poverty with sustainable agriculture: A summary of new evidence.* Essex: University of Essex.

Usdin, S., 2009. Edutainment in South Africa: A force for change in health. *Bulletin of the World Health Organization*, 87(8), pp. 578–579.

Vallins, G., 1971. Drama and theatre in education. In J. R. Brown, ed. *Drama and theatre with Radio, film and television: An outline for students*, London: Routledge, pp. 161–184.

Waal, A. D., 1991. *Evil days: 30 years of war and famine in Ethiopia*, New York: Human Rights Watch.

Welbourn, A., 1995. *Stepping stones: A package for facilitators to help you run workshops within communities on HIV/AIDS, communication and relationship skills*, London: ActionAid.

Welbourn, A., 1997. Rehearsing for reality: Using role-play to transform attitudes and behaviour in the fight against HIV and sexual abuse of young women. POPLINE.org. Available at: http://www.popline.org/node/525825 [Accessed February 5, 2013].

Welbourn, A., 2002. Stepping Stones: shifting gender inequities to combat HIV. *Agenda*, 17(53), pp. 54–60.

Welbourn, A., 2008. *Stepping stones plus new exercises and sessions for use with the original "Stepping Stones" training manual*, Herts, England: TALC [distributor].

Welbourn, A., et al., 2008. *Stepping Stones Plus: New exercises and sessions for use with the original Stepping Stones training manual*, Oxford, UK: Strategies for Hope Trust.

West, C., & Zimmerman, D. H., 1987. Doing gender. *Gender & Society*, 1(2), pp. 125–151.

Wildcat, D. R., 2009. *Red alert! Saving the planet with indigenous knowledge*, Golden, CO: Fulcrum.

Wilkerson, M., 1991. Demographics and the academy. In S.-E. Case & J. Reinelt (eds.), *The performance of power: Theatrical discourse and politics*, Iowa City: University of Iowa Press, pp. 238–241.

Wilkinson, D., 2004. *Silence on the mountain: Stories of terror, betrayal, and forgetting in Guatemala*, Durham, NC: Duke University Press.

Wilson, N., 2012. Jamaica urged to reconsider abortion laws for cases of rape, incest. *Jamaica Observer.* Available at: http://www.jamaicaobserver.com/magazines/allwoman/Jamaica-urged-to-reconsider-abortion-laws-for-cases-of-rape—incest_12632445.

WINGS, 2013. Home page. Available at: http://www.wingsguate.org/ [Accessed March 6, 2013].

Winniefridah, M., 2011. Who is dependent, third or first world, women or men? Salient features of dependency and interdependency. *Journal of Sustainable Development in Africa*, 13(6), pp. 314–327.

World Commission, 1987. *Our common future*, New York: Oxford University Press.

World Renewable Energy Congress/Network, 2012. Home page. Available at: http://www.wrenuk.co.uk/ [Accessed December 19, 2012].

Wragg, U. K., 2012. Rio+20 and women's lives: A cross-generational dialogue, a presentation on June 20, 2012 at the Ford Foundation Pavilion at Rio+20 in Rio de Janeiro, Brazil.

Yasin, A., 2010. Literature for social development. *Media Communication for Social and Behavior Change*, pp. 24–35.

Index